THE DATA EXCHANGE

MOVING DATA BETWEEN 1–2–3®, dBASE®, AND OTHER POPULAR PROGRAMS

THE DATA EXCHANGE

MOVING DATA BETWEEN 1–2–3®, dBASE®, AND OTHER POPULAR PROGRAMS

Alfred Poor

Dow Jones-Irwin
Homewood, Illinois 60430

©RICHARD D. IRWIN, INC., 1990

Dow Jones-Irwin is a trademark of Dow Jones & Company, Inc.

Sponsoring editor: Susan Glinert Stevens, Ph.D.
Project editor: Ethel Shiell
Production manager: Diane Palmer
Jacket design: Michael S. Finkelman
Compositor: Weimer Typesetting Company, Inc.
Typeface: 11/13 Century Schoolbook
Printer: The Maple-Vail Book Manufacturing Group

Library of Congress Cataloging-in-Publication Data

Poor, Alfred E.
    The data exchange : moving data between 1–2–3, dBase, and other popular programs / by Alfred Poor.
        p.   cm.
    ISBN 1-55623-281-0
    1. Data base management.   I. Title.
QA76.9.D3P66   1989
005.74—dc20   89–23361
                                                          CIP

Printed in the United States of America
1 2 3 4 5 6 7 8 9 0 MP 6 5 4 3 2 1 0 9

This book is dedicated to the proposition that for every problem, no matter how complex and hopeless the situation may appear, there is at least one simple solution . . . and it is usually wrong.

LIST OF TRADEMARKS AND PRODUCTS

PUBLISHER OR MANUFACTURER, PRODUCT

Adobe Systems, Inc.: PostScript

Aldus Corporation: PageMaker

Alpha Software: Keyworks, Alpha/three

Apple Computer: Macintosh, MacPaint, Apple II

Ashton-Tate: MultiMate, dBASE II, dBASE III, dBASE IV

Autodesk, Inc.: AutoCAD

Borland International: SideKick, Paradox, Sprint

CompuServe Information Services: CompuServe

Computer Associates: SuperCalc4

Creative Synergy Corporation: Good Numbers

DAC Software, Inc.: Dac Easy, Graph + Mate

Data General Corporation: CEOwrite

Datastorm Technologies: Procomm Plus

Digital Equipment Corporation: DEC DX

Digital Research Inc.: GEM Draw, GEM Paint

Emulation Technologies, Inc.: Xchange

Fifth Generation Systems, Inc.: The Logical Connection

General Parametrics, Inc.: Video Show

Great Plains Software: Great Plains Accounting Series, Import Manager, Report Maker Plus

Hercules Computer Technology: Hercules Graphic Card

Hewlett-Packard Corporation: LaserJet Series II

Inset Systems, Inc.: Inset and Hijaa k

International Business Machines: PC, XT, AT, Personal Series 2, PS2, DisplayWrite, DisplayWriter, Personal Decision Series, Personal Editor II

Iomega Corporation: Bernoulli Box

Lifetree Software Inc.: Volkswriter

Lotus Development Corporation: 1–2–3, Symphony, PrintGraph, Jazz, Manuscript, Express

MARC Software, Inc.: WordMARC

MCI Mail: MCI Mail

Media Cybernetics: DR Halo

Mentor Graphics Corporation: Mentor Graphics

MicroPro International Corporation: WordStar

Microsoft: Microsoft BASIC, Microsoft WORD, Microsoft Windows, Windows Write, and Windows Paint, MultiPlan, Microsoft Mouse

MSC Technologies, Inc.: PC Paint

Osborne Computer: Osborne

Peachtree Software: Peachtree Complete, Peachtree Data Query II

Quicksoft: PC-Write

Samna Corporation: Samna Word

SBT Corporation: SBT

Software Arts: VisiCalc

Software Publishing Corporation: PFS:file, PFS:First Publisher

The Lasers Edge: VP/Tabs, VP/Base

The Source: The Source

Tools & Techniques Inc.: Data Junction

Traveling Software, Inc.: LapLink, DeskLink

VS Software: SLEd

Wang Laboratories, Inc.: Wang PC

WordPerfect Corporation: WordPerfect

Xerox: Ventura Publisher

XYQUEST Inc.: XyWrite

Z-Soft Corporation: PC Paintbrush

ACKNOWLEDGMENTS

If you could see them, you would find a sizable crowd of people standing behind the pages of this book. You would see the many programmers, publicists, and product managers who supported this project by providing copies of their programs, access to their knowledge and experience, and enthusiasm for my endeavor.

You would also see many friends and colleagues: PC Magazine staff and free-lancers, clients, and others who live the daily struggle with computer data. You would see Bruce Brown, who worked with me on a related project in a past life. You would see my nephew Shep, who helped with the BASIC programs in Chapter 11, and my brother David, who shared advice and encouragement.

You would see Susan Glinert, my Dow Jones-Irwin editor, who offered unprecedented support without hesitation at a rather critical and spectacular point in this book's development. You would see my agent, Carol Mann, who frees me to focus on what I do best without worrying about what I do badly because she handles them so well.

And most of all, you would see my family: Bebe, Anna, and Alex. A book of any size can produce an emotional roller-coaster ride for all who are close to it, even before it becomes a small stack of pages. This effort was especially turbulent at times. Through it all, my family has been generous with their love and support, and they have been gentle with help in keeping work and home in proper perspective. The pride and love I feel about this book is but a small reflection of the pride and love my family has given to me, gifts that I treasure above all else.

Alfred Poor

CONTENTS

ix

INTRODUCTION

This book contains a treasure of information. It unlocks the information stored on your personal computer (PC), and makes it available in ways that you have only dreamed were possible. In fact, this book may be almost as important to your productivity as your computer.

There are few tasks in the microcomputing world as frustrating as trying to move information from one program to another. As many people will tell you, if you haven't yet experienced it, it often appears faster to reenter the information rather than waste time and energy on complex conversion procedures.

Some writers refer to the *fritter factor,* which too often is responsible for lessening the productivity gains offered by computers. Nowhere is this more apparent than in data transfer. Too many products live in an egocentric universe, and they communicate with other programs only on their own rigid and limited terms.

This book is your key to unlock the apparent mysteries, to reveal the hidden pitfalls, and to uncover the undocumented tricks encountered when trying to move information between two programs.

This book is the direct result of real world experiences. As a computer user, I have frequently been stymied by data that was trapped in one application when it was needed in another application. As a consultant, I have lived through similar experiences with many clients. As a writer of software reviews for major national magazines, I have seen the best and worst of data exchange facilities among famous and not-so-famous programs on the market.

I hope you view this book as a personal assistant, an expert data-exchange consultant who sits on your shelf—waiting to hop down and speed you past whatever roadblocks you may encounter.

WHO CAN USE THIS BOOK

The primary goal of this book is to offer thorough information that any PC user can understand and use. You do not need an advanced degree in computer science to understand this material. You will not have to probe hexadecimal file dumps and master the DEBUG utility commands to benefit from this book.

If you use two or more programs on a PC, then you will eventually need this book. If you work with other people, if you must exchange information with them, and if you use different programs, then you need this book. If you are responsible for helping others work with their computers, then it is a safe bet that you have already encountered instances where you could use this book.

While novices will find the information accessible and useful, advanced and "power" users will also find a wealth of tips and tricks. The book does not cover the little details about binary header record fields in data files, but it goes in depth about technical matters.

HOW TO USE THIS BOOK

It may be helpful to scan the book's structure. It is designed as a working reference, so that you can dive in and get the information you need quickly—without having to wade through endless manuals, limited tutorials, or abstract theoretical discussions.

Almost every reader should read the first section. This is a basic survival course in data-file recognition. It lays the groundwork for the following sections, and it provides a common terminology for use throughout the other sections. The next chapters cover moving data in and out of specific programs. You will find coverage of Lotus® 1–2–3®, dBASE III Plus®, word-processing programs, desktop publishing, and accounting programs.

There are many instances where your needs will not be met by the facilities offered by standard programs. The next part demonstrates techniques that you can apply safely and effectively. There are various ways to use a simple text editor to perform major transformations on data files. Also included are some simple BASIC programs that you can run to use for some operations.

Not everyone wants to be a programmer, however. That is why there is a section devoted to products available from other sources that you can use to simplify and automate the data-exchange process. This section only lists the winners, although you will find that the definition of *winner* varies depending on who you are and what you need to accomplish.

Finally, the last part covers what to do when you must move data between computers and between programs. This is strictly survival-level coverage, since PC communication is a topic that can fill volumes. In this chapter, you will learn enough to solve most of the problems, and you will learn where to go for help when the easy answers do not work.

The Data Exchange is an old-world bazaar; you enter through a common gate that opens onto a courtyard surrounded by stalls and small shops. Use the gateway to orient yourself and learn the language (Part 1), then go straight to the shop that interests you most or simply browse among them all—depending on your needs and interests. In any case, enjoy the trip; you will find treasures waiting around each corner.

A NOTE TO ENGLISH TEACHERS:

I know the difference between a single datum and many data. Yet, the English language is a living, evolving creature. While I rant and rave about my usage peeves (such as the "verbification" of the language), I also acknowledge that some errors have become so common through usage that the "correct" approach now sounds stilted to the mind's ear. How many of you use a "floppy disc drive," for example?

As a result, I use *data is* . . . throughout this book. The primary goal is to give the reader unobstructed access to the information. If bending the rules of proper usage makes this book more readable, then I will gladly stray from the straight and narrow.

PART 1

DATA BASICS

Data Exchange makes it easy for you to jump in and quickly find information that will make data transfer tasks faster, easier, and safer. Feel free to read this book in almost any sequence you wish, except for the first two chapters. They contain general information that is of vital importance to novice and experienced users. Even if you think you may already know most of the content, take a few minutes to skim this section.

In the next pages, you will find strategic concepts that are guides in planning a data-transfer project. You will also learn about standard data-file formats, their essential structures, and how to identify them. These two chapters provide a common vocabulary and a set of concepts that are used throughout the book.

CHAPTER 1

THE IMPORTANCE OF DATA

If it weren't for data, you wouldn't be reading this book. Why is data important, and how should you and your organization view this important asset?

This chapter shows how to assess the importance of information stored in your computer and begins to look at ways to extend that value. You will also learn some basic principles to apply before starting any data-exchange project.

THE THREE VALUES OF DATA

When the IBM® PC first appeared on the market, it came with floppy disks that could hold a full 160 kilobytes. Demand soon led to increased capacities—first to 180K, then to 360K, then the AT with 1.2 megabyte floppies, and now the Personal Series 2 computers with 1.4 megabyte floppies that are about half the size of original PC disks.

More floppy space quickly became insufficient in the marketplace, however. Third-party companies flourished by providing hard disks for the early PCs (only to vanish with the XT's arrival). The original 10 megabyte XT drive was displaced by the 20 megabyte AT drive, which soon grew to 30 megabytes, and now you can buy hard disks for PCs and PS/2 computers that go far beyond 100 megabytes.

In fact, most computers now have at least 10 megabytes or more of on-line disk storage. Since 10 megabytes is the equivalent of 5,000 typewritten pages, or an entire case of paper, there is much information being stored on the hard disks of our computers. Why do we have all this information lying around? In most cases, the data is worth something.

Intrinsic Value

To start with, the data must have some intrinsic value. The information contained within the files typically has some strategic or operational value to the company or individual.

Strategic data helps management make decisions about products and marketing choices. It points the way toward one course of action or away from another action. Strategic decisions can have a major impact on a company's future.

Operational data is possibly more important, if only from a short-range perspective. Most workers would agree that payroll information is more important than long-range sales projections. The IRS has similar views about certain accounting records requirements. Also, there are other groups within and around an organization that tend to view Accounts Receivable and Accounts Payable with an almost proprietary interest.

Cost to Reenter

But, in considering the value of a certain bit of stored information, you must look beyond its direct value to the organization. What if you lose it? What does it cost to get it back?

The costs vary widely. If the information was of low value, perhaps you do not attempt to recover it. If it is important, and it is available elsewhere in a machine-readable form (such as a back-up disk), then perhaps recovery is not too expensive.

But what if it is 10 megabytes of typed information that only exists on printouts? Will anyone volunteer to key in 10 reams of information? If you have to pay them, the cost is significant.

What if the data does not exist in a tidy form anywhere else? What if the data was a result of creative effort? How can that be recovered? In such a case, the cost to recreate the data may be limitless.

Synergistic Value

There is another value to data, however; one that is more positive. That is the value of the data when viewed in other ways that account for different purposes with the same information.

For example, what if you can take the operational accounting data and manipulate it in ways that yield important strategic information? What if you can take sales data for different products or divisions during different periods and bring them into a spreadsheet for analysis? Or bring them into a graphics package to chart the information visually? Or bring them into a powerful statistics package to make complex projections?

What if you could take lists of names from an order-entry system and bring them into a database program to analyze for patterns? What if a client list could be easily merged with solicitation letters? What if a database of products could be quickly formatted for desktop publishing to create attractive and inexpensive catalog typesetting?

The list is endless. Imagination and need can combine to reveal new and powerful ways to use data already stored on your disks. Data-exchange techniques unlock this valuable potential.

THE IMPORTANCE OF BACK-UP PROCEDURES AND DISASTER RECOVERY PLANS

Before we look on the bright side, however, a brief harangue on a topic that everyone agrees on and that no one does much about: data backups.

If much of the data stored on your disks has value, then it is likely worth a small amount of effort to protect and preserve it. People routinely purchase insurance for their cars, homes, businesses, and lives. Yet, a few minutes a day can seem too much time to spend on ensuring the safety of information that is vital to an organization.

When was the last time your data was backed up? If you do not know, do not feel too bad because you are among a majority of users. There are plenty of reasonably priced alternatives to the poky DOS BACKUP command that make backing up massive amounts of data faster and easier. Weigh the costs of retyping those 10 reams of paper on your 10 megabyte hard disk against the cost of a tape-backup unit. Data backup can be a cost-effective investment.

Remember that back-up procedures lower the negative costs of data. It is cheaper to restore a lost or damaged file from some machine-readable form (like a disk or tape) than in any other form.

Incidentally, many people have discovered an unexpected benefit that comes with a Local Area Network (LAN). Since most (or all) of the data can be stored on the central shared-disk storage, it is possible to have a single procedure that regularly backs up every person's data files. In some cases, this increase in data security justifies the cost of purchasing a network.

One other point: there is more to backup than data and program files. Mainframe installations have long had "disaster recovery plans" that cover all sorts of unthinkable physical disasters. Your micro applications may not require such sophisticated plans, but there are two components you may need to consider.

Do you have back-up equipment? If your equipment is out of commission for a week or two, are there any applications that you would have to run, and if so, where? If you haven't considered this yet, and you do not have sufficient redundancy within your organization, remember that there are computer rental firms in most parts of the country that can supply all sorts of configurations on a short-term basis. Some, such as GE Rents, will ship anywhere in the country.

The other point is trickiest: is your personnel backed up? If one person is out ill, are there others on staff who could run needed applications regularly? (A related question is, "Are your spreadsheet, database, and word-processing files adequately documented so that other people can use them?") Personnel backup is sometimes the most expensive form of backup, but it is often overlooked until it is too late to recover gracefully.

POSSIBLE DATA-EXCHANGE APPROACHES

So you have data in one application, and you see how it could be useful in another application. How do you move it there?

There are many options open as you approach the task. Table 1–1 lists seven major alternatives.

The first is rekeying by hand. Data-transfer problems can turn into "black holes" that suck up all the time and personnel they can. There is nothing virtuous about automating the transfer process using sophisticated techniques when it then takes twice the resources compared to reentering by hand. So, if you have a mailing list of a few hundred names that need to be transferred, remember that a good typist could do the job in an hour or two, and at a cost significantly less than an hour of time spent by a technical wizard trying to get two programs to talk.

In many cases, however, transferring data from one program to another makes better economic sense. There are different options to consider when looking for the best approach. Consider the following alternatives.

The simplest method is to do it "by hand," using transfer utilities provided by one of the programs involved. This is simplest because you are likely working with a program that you already know. It is also the simplest because these facilities are typically menu-driven, and they lead you through different phases of the process. These facilities are often simple in another sense; they may be limited in terms of their capacities, speed, or accuracy. As shown in later chapters, there are some

TABLE 1–1
Data-Transfer Strategies

Rekey by hand
Perform transfer "manually"
Create "macro" or procedure for transfer
Use third-party program
Turn to resident expert
Hire outside consultant
Send to outside service

sneaky "gotchas" hiding in the most reasonable-looking packaged utilities.

Running the transfer by hand every time for repetitive tasks can be tiresome, especially if you must start from scratch whenever you make a mistake. For this reason, you may choose to make a macro or procedure file that can automate the process. Many word processors have macro capabilities built in, and database programs such as dBASE let you write complex procedures. This can soon cross the line into real programming, and so it may be out of easy reach for some users.

Third-party publishers have responded to some of these problems by offering canned solutions. There are programs designed to make it easier to move data from database to spreadsheet, from spreadsheet to word processor, and from word processor to word processor. These programs are often improvements over the utilities that come with the original programs in terms of speed, accuracy, and/or flexibility.

Another viable solution may be to turn to the resident PC guru who works near you. This may be someone with the formal title of "Information Center Staff," or may be some tortured soul who loves trying to make 1–2–3 macros do improbable tasks. (If your company is not big enough for this solution, or if you are the guru, consider joining a local computer users group—where you will find helpful people.) Ask around and see who has the most experience with either end of the programs you are using; peer support networks work surprisingly well.

If you can't find a resident expert, you may need to go outside. You have the choice of bringing in an outside consultant or sending the data out to a conversion service.

Finding a consultant can be tricky. You may know the saying "Those who can, do. Those who can't, teach. Those who can't teach, consult." There are some excellent consultants, but it takes effort to find them. The best advice is to ask around for referrals from people who have had similar problems.

Data conversion service bureaus are a little easier to choose since their national visibility simplifies checking their references. If you are in the market for such a service, check the back pages of *PC Week* and *InfoWorld* for the many conversion services that advertise there.

HOW TO SELECT A METHOD

With all these options, how can you choose? First, consider what you can afford. There are six measures of your budget listed in Table 1–2. Depending on your budget, some transfer techniques may be more attractive than others.

The most obvious limitation can be available dollars. If you have no money for the project, that cancels half your options since third-party programs and outside services are difficult to obtain for free.

Less obvious, however, is your time budget. This line item has two essential components. The first is a question of when the transfer must be completed. If your drop-dead deadline is near, then you may want to look at expert-help solutions first, rather than play "pioneer in the wild data frontier." Similarly, you may have no time for the project (most people get computers because they have too much to do). Again, this might steer you toward some expert help.

The next two budget items are on the supply side of the ledger, but are essential to consider. How much data needs to be transferred, and how often? If it is a small amount that must be moved over for a one-time shot, then it may not pay to try to automate it. Just key it back in by hand. If the one-time transfer involves a large file, or many small ones, then some electronic method or outside service will be more cost effective. If the process is regularly repeated, then you can afford to invest in developing a system of macros or programs that can automate the transfer for easy repetition.

The last two items, accuracy and security, are not immediately obvious to some people. Consider the nature of the data

TABLE 1–2
Budget Constraints

Dollar budget
Time budget
Size of data
Frequency of transfer
Level of accuracy required
Level of security required

to be transferred and how it will be used. For example, what level of accuracy do you need in the transfer? Textual information contains what is technically called *data redundancy,* which means that you can garble the individual letters in spots without losing meaning. Witness your ability to understand a report riddled with typos and misspellings.

Numeric data, on the other hand, requires a much more accurate transfer. Changing a "1" to a "9," or dropping a few 0's can significantly alter the message conveyed by a financial statement.

If accuracy is critical, then you want to consider an electronic means of transfer. Most significant errors in data files come in through the keyboard; they are transcription mistakes by the operator. When done correctly, electronic data exchange can be 100 percent accurate.

Security is another issue. Some data is relatively harmless, but other data can be worth millions to your organization and to others. If you are dealing with sensitive data, you cannot afford to expose it to more people than necessary. If your information is confidential, don't put it in the hands of other people. Learn how to do the transfers yourself. One way to do this is creating dummy data, and using a consultant to build a procedure that will work with the real data. Another way is to use this book and learn how to do it yourself.

There is no right answer for each individual data-exchange project. Use these different factors as starting points, then pick the approach that feels like it will give you the best results within your limitations. In this way, you consider alternatives and are least likely to fall into one of the black holes of data transfer.

SECRETS TO SUCCESSFUL DATA TRANSFER

No matter which approach you select, there are some general principles to apply that help improve chances for success.

The most important issue is timing. Do not leave a data-exchange project for the last minute (unless you do not need sleep and are immunized against ulcers). Just as with a new software program, don't try to learn how to perform a specific exchange while under deadline pressure. The best way to do it is to schedule a trial run well in advance of the required time, and experiment with data similar to the information that will be used in the real exchange.

For example, you may want to extract information from year-end accounting reports and bring it into a graphics program to prepare for a major presentation. Assume that the final reports won't be ready until the week before the meeting. Do not wait for the final data. Start weeks before the deadline, and use the files from the prior year's close if possible or use year-to-date figures if necessary. Try to duplicate conditions you will face when using the live data. When it is time for the real transfer, you will approach it with confidence—knowing how long you can expect it to take and how much work is required to get the final results.

The second factor is not so much a planning issue as it is a subjective matter. Try to put yourself in a problem-solving mindset in approaching a data-transfer project. View it as a challenge, as a puzzle to be solved. Expect that some steps may not proceed as expected, and that these surprises will be one more piece of the puzzle to solve. It is easier to wear this relaxed attitude if you are not facing a deadline, but it is even more important when there is time pressure. If you get frustrated or angry, it is unlikely that your attitude will help you solve the problems, so return to the project when you can give it a fresh look.

SUMMARY

Your data has value. It is worth your time and money to protect the investment and make it grow by expanding the information's usefulness. There are a number of approaches for planning a data-exchange project, and your choices should be guided by the project's nature and the resources available to make it happen. Above all, do not wait for the last minute to start, and keep an open, inquisitive attitude as you approach the task of exchanging data between programs.

CHAPTER 2

THE BASICS OF DATA FILES

Almost every PC program uses data that is stored in a file for the program's reference. Data files are not all alike. They take on many forms, and locked within them lie the arcane secrets of your favorite programs.

This chapter takes a nontechnical view of these important files; it explains how and why files are different, and how this information can be useful. We start with basic information about how data is stored, and we end with a field guide to different data-file formats so that you can readily identify them on a disk.

TEXT AND BINARY FILES

It has been said that the world is made up of two kinds of people—those who divide the world into two kinds of people, and those who don't. The situation is similar in the world of computer files. There are two large file classes: program files and data files.

The Difference between Data and Programs

A program file is a set of computer instructions stored in a file that can be read into the computer's memory and executed. In general, these programs come with file names that end with either the extension .EXE or .COM. A DOS file name has two components: a name of up to eight characters followed by a period and an optional extension of up to three characters.

A data file, on the other hand, contains information that will be used by a program as it runs. Examples are spreadsheets or word-processing documents.

Do not be too concerned about the fuzzy region that bridges these two groups. For example, there are dBASE "programs" that are more like data files to be used by dBASE than they are programs. Then, there are program overlay files that are not exactly data files but cannot do anything useful without their .EXE or .COM program files.

For now, if a file will do something when invoked from the DOS prompt, then it is a program. If not, it is probably some sort of data file.

A Brief Introduction to ASCII

There is a major split between data files as well. Data files are either text files or not. The category a file belongs in depends on what type of characters it contains.

It is easy to see the difference between these two groups of files. If you are adventurous, you may have encountered it. DOS includes a command called TYPE, which sends the contents of a file to the screen (or printer or other port through redirection). At the DOS prompt, type the word TYPE followed by a filename, and its contents will be displayed on the screen. This merely reads the file and cannot change it, so you cannot damage the file.

If you experiment, you will probably find that some files produce meaningful results on the screen, while others are less intelligible. For example, if you TYPE a batch file (a file that ends with a .BAT extension), you will see a list of DOS commands. On the other hand, if you TYPE a program file (one that ends in .EXE or .COM), you will probably see a screen full of garbage with strange symbols and little smiley faces.

The difference between the two results is explained in how information is stored in the two files. In general, programs are stored in a form that can be loaded directly into the computer's memory and executed as machine-level commands. This is often referred to as a *binary* format, although the codes are actually stored in hexadecimal (base 16) number format. How the program instructions are stored is of little interest at the moment.

The batch files, as well as many data-file formats, are stored as *text files,* which means that they are composed of standard text characters, or characters that can be displayed on the screen. To understand better what this means, we need to take a small detour to explain the text characters and their relationship to the ASCII code.

The Common Code

ASCII stands for the American Standard Code for Information Interchange. While the Interchange probably was meant to cover the exchange of data between two pieces of equipment, think of it as the translation link between people and computers.

Computers are digital beasts; their universe is composed of a series of on and off switches, and they count by throwing these switches in rapid succession. All information is represented by a precise combination of on's and off's, or a specific numeric value. This gives rise to the term *digital.*

Humans are analog creatures; we perceive shades of gray. We also deal in whole concepts that we communicate through words and pictures. For us to interact most comfortably with a computer, we need a numeric way to represent our letters so that the computer can understand and manipulate them.

As you write with your word-processing program, for example, you press lettered keys on a keyboard that cause similar letters to appear on the computer screen. That magic occurs because the keyboard sends a numeric signal to the computer, which processes it along with other numeric values (like where it thinks the cursor is located on the screen), and it then uses the result to cause a specific pattern of dots (again numerically defined) to appear in the right location on the screen.

Fortunately, computers and people generally agree about what values should represent what characters. In some worlds, like mainframe computers, the code that translates between computers and people is called EBCDIC. Almost all microcomputers and their peripherals, however, speak some dialect of ASCII. The reason I say *dialect* is due to a lack of agreement on the ASCII code, which is a result of the code's evolution.

The ASCII code was originally designed for telecommunications systems, such as teletype machines. A series of off and on signals were sent in batches that were decoded at the other end resulting in a certain letter printed on the page. If each off and on is a single bit, how many bits were required to send messages?

Since it is a binary code (made up of off and on signals), the number of possible combinations goes up as powers of 2. This means that a one-bit code can only define two characters, and a two-bit code can only describe four characters. Neither are sufficient to send the alphabet.

Once we get up to a five-bit code, we get 32 combinations, but that is not enough for an upper-case alphabet and the 10 numeric digits. Six bits yields 64 combinations, but that won't handle upper and lower case, plus digits, plus punctuation. So, we finally arrive at a seven-bit system, which gives 128 different possible codes.

As it turns out, 128 is more than enough for all the printable characters, including upper- and lower-case letters, 10 digits, and plenty of punctuation symbols. Don't forget that a space is a character as far as the computer is concerned, and it needs to have its own assigned code. Look at standard daisy-wheel printers to see how many characters this involves; typically, there are 92 or 96 characters on their print wheels, which leaves about 32 codes unused.

Since ASCII was originally designed for communication, it was decided that these extra codes could be reserved for special commands for the teletype machines. For example, it would be nice to signal the operator at the other end when a transmission was starting or ending, so one code was assigned to ring a bell on the teletype. This was assigned the value of 7, which explains why a CTRL-G character in a file will make your computer beep.

Other codes were used to start and stop the transmission flow, or to signal the arrival of lengthier commands. Many of these codes are still used in similar ways on your PC and peripherals. For example, ASCII 13 is a Carriage Return, which moves the cursor or printhead back to the start of a line; ASCII 10 is a Line Feed, which moves the cursor or printhead to the same column on the next line; and ASCII 12 is a Form Feed, which usually advances the paper to the next page in a printer, or it will clear the screen in some PC applications.

The advent of the microcomputer created new possibilities and problems, however. These machines were designed around eight-bit data elements. Instead of 128 possible codes, this gave computer designers 256 combinations. While the lower 128 have been relatively untouched, the upper 128 combinations have no standard assignments. This is the reason that if you send a PC screen with character line graphics to some printers, such as an older Epson or IBM dot matrix, you get capital italics instead of the lines and boxes shown on the screen.

Fortunately, most printer and computer manufacturers have standardized on the IBM PC character set for the higher 128 ASCII codes, but other sets still appear. For example, the Hewlett Packard LaserJet® Series II contains not only the PC set, but other symbol sets that can print foreign language characters.

Text files are files that contain only printable characters from the lower 128 ASCII codes. This includes all the letters, digits, and punctuation, but generally does not include the first 32 codes assigned for special commands. There are two major exceptions to this. The two nonprintable characters that appear routinely are the Carriage Return and Line Feed characters, and most often they appear together as a pair. You cannot "see" them when you TYPE a file to the screen, but you can see their effect wherever the data starts on a new line—as opposed to simply wrapping to the next line because the line is too long to fit on the screen.

Often, you will hear text files referred to as being in a straight ASCII format. This is a synonym for text file as used in this book.

THE TWO MOST COMMON TEXT DATA FILE FORMATS

Some text files have no particular structure, such as word processing files stored in ASCII format. The words are laid down in sequence, and lines end haphazardly.

Data files used by databases, spreadsheets, and similar programs are more structured. For the program to assign individual elements of information in their proper positions, the file must have a specific structure that organizes the data in a predictable format. Typically, information is organized into records that are analogous to a collection of 3 by 5 note cards. Just as each note card has the same blanks on it as the others for the various pieces of information, records contain a common set of fields that contain individual data elements. The relationship between records and fields is illustrated in Figure 2–1.

Such data files are built on a variety of structures, but two specific formats are the most common: fixed length and comma delimited.

Fixed-Length Record Files

The simplest is the fixed-length record format. Figure 2–2 illustrates a typical fixed-length format file that has been TYPED on a PC screen.

Even though the individual lines of information are longer than a single screen-width, you can still see a number of important patterns in this display. For example, you should immediately notice that the first name in each record starts at

FIGURE 2–1
Records and Fields

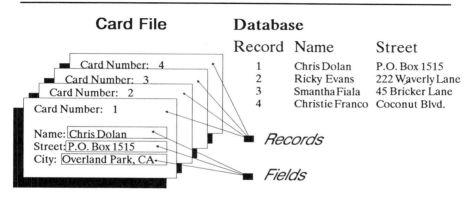

FIGURE 2–2
Fixed-Length Record File

```
Dolan      Christine 6867001P.O. Box# 1515            Overland Park      KS6621
0269-111-2222F 40000.0036019040925
Evans      Ricky      7169002222 Waverly Lane         San Rafael         CA9490
3904-111-2222F 45000.0036019040928
Fiala      Samantha  2825770#45 Bricker Lane          San Jose           CA9513
4904-111-5656F 70000.0036019041005
Franco     Christie  69630305555 Coconut Grove Blvd   Torrance           CA9050
5111-222-3333F144000.0010019050621
Gabriele   Louis      31762500998 Atlantic Blvd.      Teaneck            NJ0766
6125-478-6325T 12000.0024019050122
Gall       Justine    3225670#09 Old Wire Road        Norcross           GA3009
2987-236-5668F 25000.0036019040924
Giles      Cynthia    41270045555 East Coast Drive    Cambridge          MA0213
8709-455-6233F 30000.0036019041005
Greenberg Taylor      73315066969 Ocean Blvd, Apt 3A  Pacific Grove      CA9395
0123-456-7899T 12000.0024019050123
Haughton  Robert      91600051919 First Street East   Arlington          VA2220
9258-974-6623T 40000.0036019040925
Hertzig    Samantha  95760063333 Beach Blvd           New York           NY1002
8901-256-8954F 15000.0012019050527
Hinlicky  Courtney   40609705987 River Road, 4th Floor Montgomeryville   PA1893
6806-325-5625F 20000.0010019050614
Horch      Jennifer   35775043306 Knight Street        Bellevue           WA9800
```

the beginning of a new line. This is because there is a Carriage
Return and Line Feed combination at the end of each record.

Also notice that the data appears to line up in regular columns. Note how the city field always starts in the same relative
horizontal position for each record. This happens because the
same amount of space is assigned to each field.

You can see this best by looking at the first and last name
fields. There are varying amounts of space between the end of
the first name and the start of the last name. The data in the
first name field has been padded with spaces to fill it out to the
same length in each record. This padding has been added to
the data in all necessary fields to bring the data up to the defined field length.

Since all the fields have the same length from record to record, and all records comprise the same fields, then each record must have the same length. This is why the data lines up on the screen. This is also the source of the file-type name: fixed-length record format. This means that each record has a fixed length, or in other words, each record contains the same number of characters.

So a working definition of a *fixed-length record format* is that it contains only printable text characters, with all records containing the same number of characters, and the individual records are separated by a Carriage Return/Line Feed combination.

Fixed-length records are possibly the most common text-data file format around. Mainframe data that has been downloaded to a PC typically arrives in this format. Most database programs can produce output in this format. Quite a few programs use this format as the form for their working data files.

Fixed-length formats are also commonly used as an import format by many programs. Database programs can often separate the fields and place the data in the appropriate parts of a new or existing file. Many word processors can read fixed-length files directly for inclusion in a document. In short, fixed-length record files can play an important role in many data-exchange projects.

Comma-Delimited Files

The other common text format for data files is the comma-delimited format. A sample file is shown in Figure 2–3, using the same data as in the last section.

Notice immediately some important differences between this format and the fixed-length format. The records do not end in the same position and the information does not line up in neat columns. There are no extra spaces padding the fields. There are lots of commas and double quotes that were not in the first version. Some features, however, are the same. The order of fields and the positioning of the first-name field is the same.

From these observations, we can infer some rules about this format. Like the other format, each record ends with a

FIGURE 2–3
Comma-Delimited Text File Format

```
"Dolan","Christine","6867001","P.O. Box# 1515","Overland Park","KS","66210","269
-111-2222",F,40000.00,360,19040925
"Evans","Ricky","7169002","222 Waverly Lane","San Rafael","CA","94903","904-111-
2222",F,45000.00,360,19040928
"Fiala","Samantha","2825770","#45 Bricker Lane","San Jose","CA","95134","904-111
-5656",F,70000.00,360,19041005
"Franco","Christie","6963030","5555 Coconut Grove Blvd","Torrance","CA","90505",
"111-222-3333",F,144000.00,100,19050621
"Gabriele","Louis","3176250","9990 Atlantic Blvd.","Teaneck","NJ","87666","125-4
70-6325",T,12000.00,240,19050122
"Gall","Justine","3225670","#09 Old Wire Road","Norcross","GA","30092","987-236-
5668",F,25000.00,360,19040924
"Giles","Cynthia","4127004","5555 East Coast Drive","Cambridge","MA","02138","78
9-455-6233",F,30000.00,360,19041005
"Greenberg","Taylor","7331506","6969 Ocean Blvd, Apt 3A","Pacific Grove","CA","9
3950","123-456-7899",T,12000.00,240,19050123
"Haughton","Robert","9160005","1919 First Street East","Arlington","VA","22209",
"258-974-6623",T,40000.00,360,19040925
"Hertzig","Samantha","9576006","3333 Beach Blvd","New York","NY","10028","901-25
6-8954",F,15000.00,120,19050527
"Hinlicky","Courtney","4060970","5987 River Road, 4th Floor","Montgomeryville","
PA","18936","886-325-5625",F,20000.00,100,19050614
"Horch","Jennifer","3577504","3306 Knight Street","Bellevue","WA","98004","465-6
```

Carriage Return/Line Feed combination. Fields are separated by commas, and character (as opposed to numeric) information is enclosed with double quotes.

Not all comma-delimited files have quotes around the character data. Fortunately, it is rare to find one that doesn't have them since it can lead to unwanted or disastrous results. A program uses the commas to signal the end of one field and the start of another field.

If a program is only looking at the commas for its cues, you can get strange results. Notice in the 15th line from the top of Figure 2–3 (Taylor Greenberg's record) that the street address field includes an apartment number. For the record before this one, you can match fields with data accurately based on the commas with this result:

Last Name: Giles
First Name: Cynthia
ID Number: 4127004
Street: 5555 East Coast Drive
City: Cambridge
State: MA

On the next line, however, you end up with this result:

Last Name: Greenberg
First Name: Taylor
ID Number: 7331506
Street: 6969 Ocean Blvd
City: Apt 3A
State: Pacific Grove

Clearly, a Mr. Greenberg is probably not living in the city of Apt. 3A, or the state of Pacific Grove.

This is the reason for quotes around the character fields. (Since in BASIC programs variables that hold characters are called *string* variables, these fields are often referred to as *double-quoted strings*.) The program that is trying to interpret the quoted-string comma-delimited file can use the quotes as an extra guidepost. Whenever it encounters a quote, it assumes that everything that follows is part of the field data until it encounters the next quote. This solves the problem of embedded commas, like the one in the address.

Quoted-string fields can lead to similar problems, however, if your data file should contain any quotes in a field. Problems can best be avoided, however, by ensuring that if you have any quotes in the data fields of a file that they are single quotes (') rather than double quotes(").

In sum, this file format is so named because the field information is separated (or delimited) by commas. Each line ends in a Carriage Return/Line Feed combination, and is otherwise composed entirely of printable characters.

Microsoft® BASIC programs store their data files in this format, as do many other programs. WordStar® uses this format for its mail-merge files. Many database, spreadsheet, and graphics programs import comma-delimited files with a minimum amount of fuss.

As you will see in the later sections of this book, if you can get your data into one of the two basic text-file formats, you can move it into almost any program.

OTHER COMMON FORMATS

Most programs do not store their data in standard text-file formats. This may arise from considerations including speed of access, file compression, and the need to store unprintable information such as an attribute for bold print in a word-processing file.

Don't worry; there are numerous ways to identify the type of files you have. The two best ways are by looking at the file-name extension, by typing the file to the screen, or both.

Common File Extensions

For some files it doesn't matter what you name their data files or what extensions are used, such as WordPerfect®. Other files provide defaults, but you can override them if you wish, such as with Enable®. Other programs care passionately what extension you use on their data files; they will refuse to recognize the file if you use anything else.

Table 2–1 lists many common file extensions and their most common sources. Check the manuals for your application programs (typically in an appendix) for other file-name extensions used by that package. An extension is a strong indicator, but it is not foolproof. Nothing keeps you or someone else from using the DOS COPY or RENAME commands to give a file a new extension that is usually associated with a different format.

TABLE 2–1
Common File-Name Extensions

.BAK	Back-up copy, as created by WordStar or EDLIN
.BAS	MS-BASIC program, either in binary or text format
.BAT	DOS batch file
.COM	Executable program file
.DBF	dBASE database file format
.DCA	Document Content Architecture format, used by word processors— may be RFT or FFT, but most likely RFT
.DIF	Data Interchange Format, used by spreadsheets and database programs
.DOC	Document file, possibly MultiMate or Microsoft Word
.DXF	CAD file format: Drawing Interchange Format
.EPS	PostScript Encapsulated format—used for graphics
.EXE	Executable program file
.FFT	Final Format Text—a version of DCA format used with word-processing files
.GEM	GEM Draw graphics format
.IMG	GEM Paint bit-image graphic
.MAC	Macpaint bit-image
.MSP	Microsoft Windows Paint bit-image graphic
.NDX	Index file, typically dBASE
.OVL	Possible overlay file called by .EXE or .COM program
.PCX	PC Paintbrush graphics file format
.PIC	Lotus image format, as from 1–2–3 graph
.PIX	Screen-capture format used by Inset and Hijaak, or PC Paint format
.PLT	Plot file, which contains the commands to plot an image on a plotter typically using the HPGL command set
.PRG	Program file, typically a dBASE procedure file
.PRN	Text file format, possibly from Lotus 1–2–3 print-to-disk
.RFT	Revisable Format Text—a version of DCA format used with word-processing files
.SDF	System Data Format—dBASE's name for fixed-length records
.SEQ	Sequential file—another name for comma-delimited
.SLD	AutoCAS Slide Format
.TIF	TIFF graphics file
.TXT	Text-file format (possibly produced by dBASE)
.WK1	Lotus 1–2–3 Release 2 worksheet format
.WKS	Lotus 1–2–3 Version 1A worksheet format
.WR1	Symphony 1.1 worksheet format
.WRK	Symphony 1.0 worksheet format

A Field Guide to Data Files: How to Identify What You Have

There are times when you may not know a file's origin based on its extension. The next 10 screen shots illustrate the contents of files in some of the most common formats. Don't be turned off by the smiley faces and other garbage that appears in many of these screens.

Again, you can examine the contents of nearly any DOS file with ease. From the DOS prompt—"C>" or something similar—simply use the DOS TYPE command, like this:

```
TYPE filename
```

where filename is the name of the file you want to look at. The contents of the file will be displayed on the screen. If a line is longer than 80 characters, it will wrap and start on the next line. DOS doesn't know anything about word wrap; the line will break at the 80th character whether that is the start of a new word or not. And when you have more than 25 lines on the screen, the top lines scroll off and out of view to make room for the new lines that push up from the bottom of the screen.

The display may or may not make sense. You might get a nice, clear listing of readable text, or you might be assailed by a display-full of gibberish accompanied by disconcerting and incessant beeping. Regardless of the result, you do not need to worry about damaging your file; the TYPE command will read it but not alter it.

Figures 2–4 to 2–13 show the results of using this approach on some files in popular formats.

Figure 2–4 shows a dBASE III Plus file. The dBASE IV format is different, but it looks similar to the dBASE III Plus format. You can identify a number of important features from the screen shot.

First, you will see lines of data starting on the eighth line. The records run together; each does not start on a new line. You should spot a *barber-pole effect,* however, where the same data fields line up on a diagonal throughout the display. See how the cities line up on slanted lines running from the upper left to the lower right corners of the screen. This is a sign that the data is stored in fixed-length records—each has the same number of characters. This is one sign of a dBASE file.

Another sign is the garbage at the top of the file, which forms the file's header. You will find a number of nonprintable ASCII characters at the start of the header followed by the field names. The header contains the details about the database

FIGURE 2–4
dBASE File

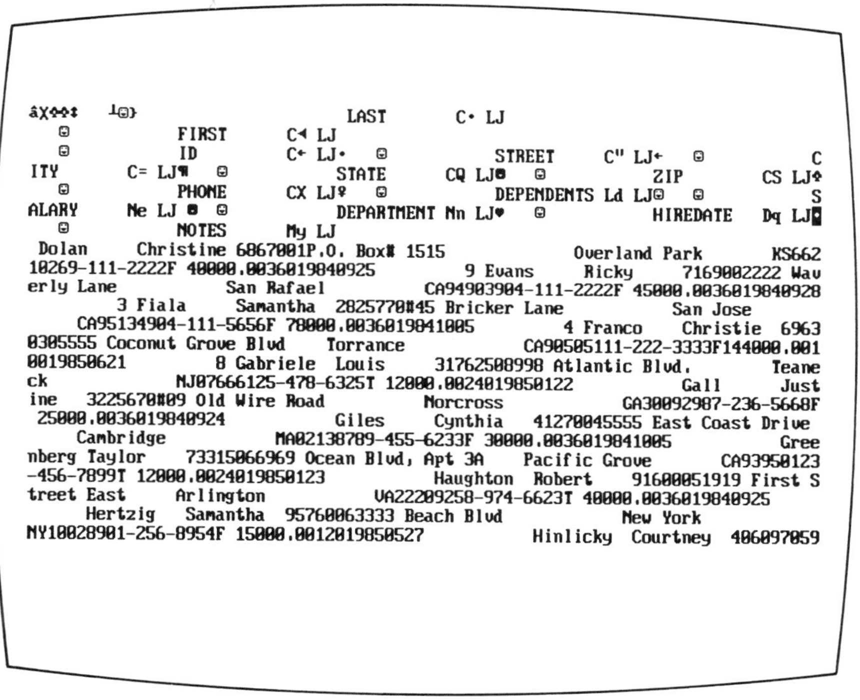

```
âX♦♦‡    ↓⊡}                      LAST      C∙ LJ
        ⊡        FIRST      C◄ LJ
        ⊡          ID       C✦ LJ∙   ⊡            STREET      C" LJ✦    ⊡              C
ITY     C= LJ¶   ⊡           STATE      CQ LJ⊟   ⊡              ZIP        CS LJ✦
        ⊡        PHONE       CX LJ⁇   ⊡         DEPENDENTS Ld LJ⊡   ⊡                 S
ALARY   Ne LJ ⬛ ⊡         DEPARTMENT Mn LJ♥   ⊡              HIREDATE    Dq LJ⬛
        ⊡        NOTES       My LJ
  Dolan    Christine 6867001P.O. Box# 1515            Overland Park           KS662
10269-111-2222F 40000.0036019040925       9 Evans    Ricky    7169002222 Wav
erly Lane           San Rafael              CA94903904-111-2222F 45000.0036019040928
        3 Fiala    Samantha  2825770#45 Bricker Lane          San Jose
     CA95134904-111-5656F 70000.0036019041005              4 Franco    Christie  6963
0305555 Coconut Grove Blvd    Torrance        CA90505111-222-3333F144000.001
0019050621         8 Gabriele  Louis    31762500998 Atlantic Blvd.        Teane
ck       NJ07666125-478-6325T 12000.0024019050122             Gall     Just
ine    3225670#09 Old Wire Road       Norcross            GA30092907-236-5668F
  25000.0036019040924          Giles    Cynthia  41270045555 East Coast Drive
    Cambridge        MA02138789-455-6233F 30000.0036019041005            Gree
nberg Taylor    73315066969 Ocean Blvd, Apt 3A   Pacific Grove       CA93950123
-456-7899T 12000.0024019050123          Haughton  Robert    91600051919 First S
treet East    Arlington    VA22209258-974-6623T 40000.0036019040925
    Hertzig    Samantha  95760063333 Beach Blvd         New York
NY10020901-256-8954F 15000.0012019050527          Hinlicky  Courtney  406097059
```

structure, including field names, lengths, and field types. This is also a good indicator of a dBASE file.

The next two screen shots (Figures 2–5 and 2–6) show Lotus 1–2–3 files for the same worksheets. The first is in .WKS format (Lotus 1–2–3 Release 1A) and the second is in .WK1 format (Lotus 1–2–3 Release 2.01).

As with the dBASE file, the .WKS file has a fair amount of header information at the start of the file. The .WK1 version has a shorter preamble.

The worksheet used to create this file is mostly composed of label cells. In both cases, the contents of these cells are identifiable in the screen shots. Note that cells containing numeric or formula data will not appear as clearly as this; expect to see many more garbage characters.

FIGURE 2–5
Lotus 1–2–3 .WKS File

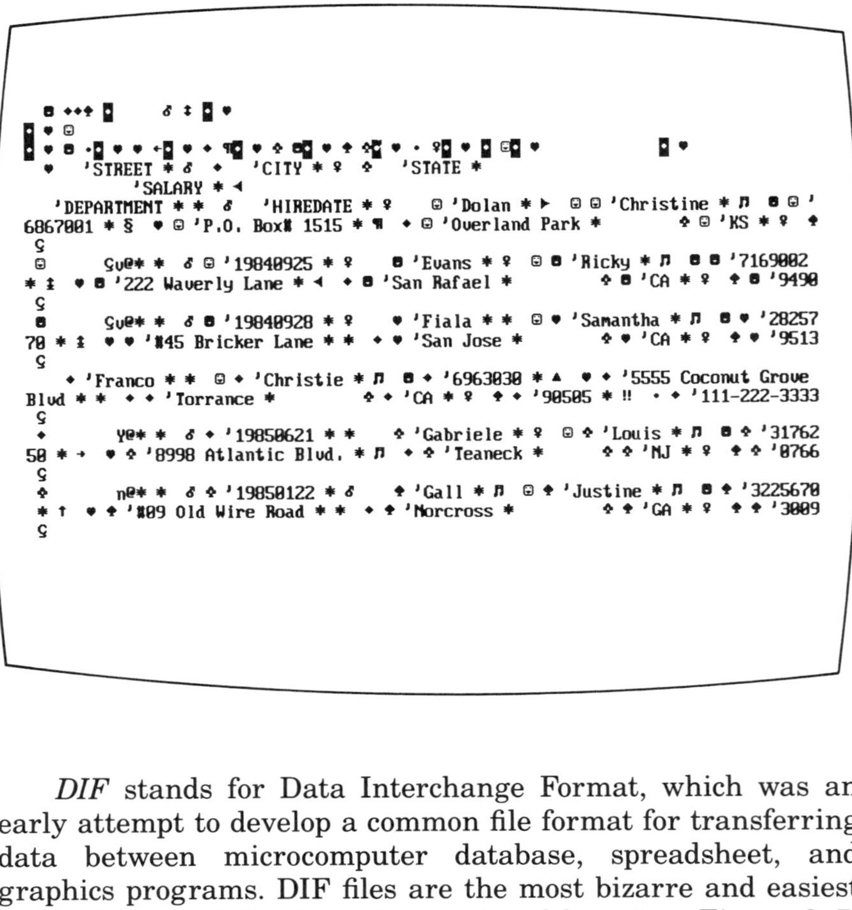

```
 ⊟ ◆◆◆ ▯    δ ‡ ▯ ♥
 ▯ ♥ ⊡
 ▯ ♥ ⊟ ·▯ ♥ ♥ ◆▯ ♥ ◆ ¶▯ ♥ ◇ ◆▯ ♥ ◆ ◇▯ ♥ · ◇▯ ♥ ▯ ⊟▯ ♥        ▯ ♥
    ♥  'STREET * δ  ◆  'CITY * ♀  ◇  'STATE *
        'SALARY * ◀
    'DEPARTMENT * *  δ   'HIREDATE * ♀    ⊟ 'Dolan * ▶   ⊟ ⊟ 'Christine * ♫  ⊟ ⊟ '
6867001 * §   ♥ ⊟ 'P.O. Box‖ 1515 * ¶   ◆ ⊟ 'Overland Park *          ◇ ⊟ 'KS * ♀  ◆
 ç
 ⊟        çu⊕* *  δ ⊟ '19840925 * ♀    ⊟ 'Evans * ♀  ⊟ ⊟ 'Ricky * ♫  ⊟ ⊟ '7169002
* ‡  ♥ ⊟ '222 Waverly Lane * ◀  ◆ ⊟ 'San Rafael *          ◇ ⊟ 'CA * ♀  ◆ ⊟ '9490
 ç
 ⊟        çu⊕* *  δ ⊟ '19840928 * ♀    ♥ 'Fiala * *   ⊟ ♥ 'Samantha * ♫  ⊟ ♥ '28257
70 * ‡  ♥ ♥ '‖45 Bricker Lane * *  ◆ ♥ 'San Jose *          ◇ ♥ 'CA * ♀  ◆ ♥ '9513
 ç
    ◆ 'Franco * *  ⊟ ◆ 'Christie * ♫  ⊟ ◆ '6963030 * ▲  ♥ ◆ '5555 Coconut Grove
Blvd * *  ◆ ◆ 'Torrance *          ◇ ◆ 'CA * ♀  ◆ ◆ '90505 * ‼  · ◆ '111-222-3333
 ç
 ◆        y⊕* *  δ ◆ '19850621 * *    ◆ 'Gabriele * ♀  ⊟ ◆ 'Louis * ♫  ⊟ ◆ '31762
50 * →  ♥ ◆ '8998 Atlantic Blvd. * ♫  ◆ ◆ 'Teaneck *          ◇ ◆ 'NJ * ♀  ◆ ◆ '8766
 ç
 ◆        n⊕* *  δ ◆ '19850122 * δ    ◆ 'Gall * ♫  ⊟ ◆ 'Justine * ♫  ⊟ ◆ '3225670
* ↑  ♥ ◆ '‖09 Old Wire Road * *  ◆ ◆ 'Norcross *          ◇ ◆ 'GA * ♀  ◆ ◆ '3009
 ç
```

DIF stands for Data Interchange Format, which was an early attempt to develop a common file format for transferring data between microcomputer database, spreadsheet, and graphics programs. DIF files are the most bizarre and easiest to identify of all the formats mentioned here (see Figure 2–7, page 32). There are a number of details to notice in the screen shot. First, the characters are printable ASCII characters (plus the Carriage Return/Line Feed combinations at the end of each line.)

Next, the first three words are: "TABLE," "TUPLES," and "VECTORS"—this is part of the DIF definition. These initial lines describe the numbers of rows and columns of data that are contained in the file. Note that the illustration shows the

FIGURE 2–6
Lotus 1–2–3 .WK1 File

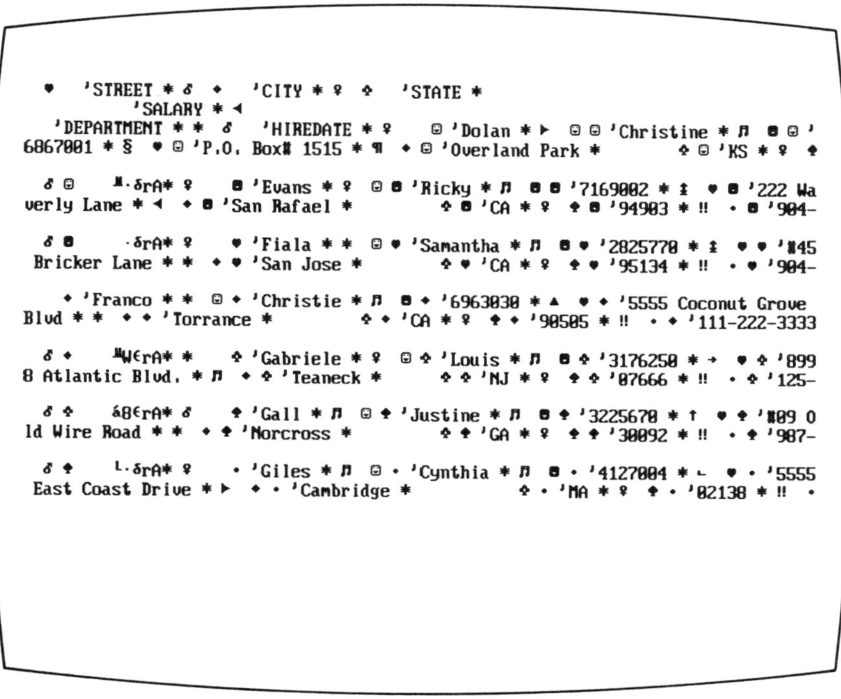

```
    ♦    'STREET * δ  ♦   'CITY * ♀  ♦   'STATE *
             'SALARY * ◄
       'DEPARTMENT * *  δ    'HIREDATE * ♀    ☺ 'Dolan * ► ☺☺ 'Christine * ♫ ☺☺ '
    6867001 * §  ♥ ☺ 'P.O. Box# 1515 * ¶  ♦ ☺ 'Overland Park *         ♦ ☺ 'KS * ♀  ♦

       δ ☺     ▮·δrA* ♀     ☺ 'Evans * ♀  ☺☺ 'Ricky * ♫ ☺☺ '7169002 * ‡  ♥ ☺ '222 Wa
    verly Lane * ◄  ♦ ☺ 'San Rafael *         ♦ ☺ 'CA * ♀  ♦ ☺ '94903 * !!  · ☺ '904-

       δ ☺     ·δrA* ♀     ♥ 'Fiala * *  ☺ ♥ 'Samantha * ♫  ☺ ♥ '2825770 * ‡  ♥ ♥ '▮45
    Bricker Lane * *  ♦ ♥ 'San Jose *         ♦ ♥ 'CA * ♀  ♦ ♥ '95134 * !!  · ♥ '904-

         ♦ 'Franco * *  ☺ ♦ 'Christie * ♫  ☺ ♦ '6963030 * ▲  ♦ ♦ '5555 Coconut Grove
    Blvd * *  ♦ ♦ 'Torrance *         ♦ ♦ 'CA * ♀  ♦ ♦ '90505 * !!  · ♦ '111-222-3333

       δ ♦    ▮W€rA* *    ♦ 'Gabriele * ♀  ☺ ♦ 'Louis * ♫  ☺ ♦ '3176250 * →  ♥ ♦ '899
    8 Atlantic Blvd. * ♫  ♦ ♦ 'Teaneck *         ♦ ♦ 'NJ * ♀  ♦ ♦ '07666 * !!  · ♦ '125-

       δ ♦    ▮8€rA* δ    ♦ 'Gall * ♫  ☺ ♦ 'Justine * ♫  ☺ ♦ '3225670 * ↑  ♥ ♦ '▮89 0
    ld Wire Road * *  ♦ ♦ 'Norcross *         ♦ ♦ 'GA * ♀  ♦ ♦ '30092 * !!  · ♦ '987-

       δ ♦    ▮·δrA* ♀    · 'Giles * ♫  ☺ · 'Cynthia * ♫  ☺ · '4127004 * └  ♥ · '5555
    East Coast Drive * ►  ♦ · 'Cambridge *         ♦ · 'MA * ♀  ♦ · '02138 * !!  ·
```

first lines of the file; in reality, these lines may scroll off the screen rapidly when the TYPE command is issued. Either stop the scroll with a Ctrl-S keystroke, or pipe the output to the DOS MORE command (as in TYPE filename | MORE), which will limit the display to one screen at a time.

Looking at the screen shot, you may also notice one more detail; there are a lot of extra characters associated with each element of data. This format is not particularly "dense" in its information storage, and as a result, DIF data files can be quite large. This, in turn, can lead to slower processing performance on import and export procedures. As a result, you may find it faster to use a denser format, such as comma-delimited or fixed-length records.

FIGURE 2–7
DIF File

```
TABLE
0,1
""
TUPLES
0,19
""
VECTORS
0,12
""
DATA
0,0
""
-1,0
BOT
1,0
"LAST"
1,0
"FIRST"
1,0
"ID"
1,0
"STREET"
1,0
```

Figure 2–8 shows a file from older versions of WordStar. (See Chapter 7 for an example of the version 5.5 file format that is similar but simpler.)

There is one characteristic trait of WordStar files. If you look at the ends of words in the paragraphs, in every case the last letter has been changed to a garbage character. If you look up the ASCII values of these characters in the ASCII table at the back of this book, you will make a curious discovery. These characters have a value that is exactly 128 greater than the letter they replaced. In other words, a lower-case a, which has an ASCII value of 97, becomes a β which has an ASCII value of 225.

FIGURE 2–8
WordStar File

```
.uj
.oj off

The following should be centered:

            Sample Text File for The Data Exchange
                 Wordsta2 Professiona▪ Version
.h1 Sample Word Processing Document
.h2 No Automatic System Date

This iS the sample texf fo2 the wor∑ processo2 portioє oᵖ the ı
bookⁱ⁄ The Date Exchangeᵉ The texf iS designe∑ tn tesf the ı
differenf standar∑ formattinᵀ an∑ texf attributᵉ featureS oᵖ the ı
differenf programS use∑ iє thiS sectionⁱ⁄ sn thaf the ı
effectivenesS oᵖ the differenf translatioє programS ma· bᵉ ı
objectivel· assessed.

Thesᵉ initia▪ paragraphS wil▪ sho= the effecf oᵖ multiplᵉ lineS ı
an∑ carriagᵉ returnsᵉ The ASCIₗ versioє oᵖ the filᵉ wil▪ comᵉ iє ı
twⁿ varieties▐ ᵖ carriagᵉ returє af the en∑ oᵖ eacᵍ lineⁱ⁄ an∑ ı
carriagᵉ returnS onl· betweeє paragraphs.

Thᵉ followinᵀ sectioє wil▪ tesf the effecf oᵖ taᴦ characterS oє ı
```

This strange modification of each word is part of how WordStar marks the breaks between words. This makes it possible to decide where to break lines for word wrap. You may also notice the "ı" character at the end of each line in the paragraphs. That is an ASCII 141, which is 128 more than the ASCII 13 code for Carriage Return. WordStar uses this character (plus a regular Line Feed character) to mark a *soft return,* which means it can be moved when the paragraph is reformatted. The program only uses the real Carriage Return/Line Feed combination to mark hard returns, such as at the end of a paragraph, which should not be changed by a reformat.

In spite of its strange appearance, you can read WordStar files fairly easily, as your mind will "strip the high bit" and fill in the correct last letter for each word. If you need to change one of these files to straight text, there are a number of utilities available, including a BASIC program included in Part 3 of this book.

Figure 2–9 is of the header section of a WordPerfect 5.0 file. It is filled with high-order ASCII characters, but you can make out the names of some printer fonts. Later on in the file (not shown in this shot), you can identify some of the text. WordPerfect uses Carriage Returns between lines of a paragraph, and Line Feeds at the end of paragraphs, which is different from straight ASCII formats.

FIGURE 2–9
WordPerfect File

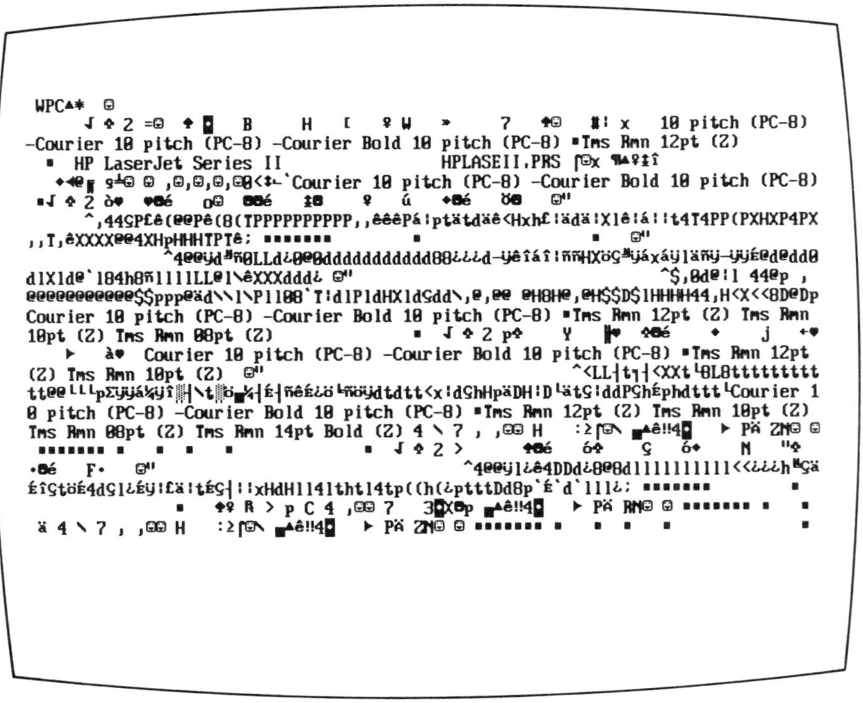

This can lead to trouble if you are not careful. If you call a text file into WordPerfect, such as a DOS batch file, it will appear to be correct on the screen. If you then save the file on the way out of WordPerfect, you will discover that your batch file no longer works. It will have been modified automatically by WordPerfect, and DOS will no longer be able to find the ends of the lines. As a result, bring batch files into WordPerfect and save them again using the Text In/Text Out options detailed in Chapter 7.

MultiMate® stores a fair amount of information in its word-processing document files in addition to the actual text. At the top of the screen in Figure 2–10 there is some header information at the start of the file. This is where the creation and last modification dates are stored, among other details.

FIGURE 2–10
MultiMate File

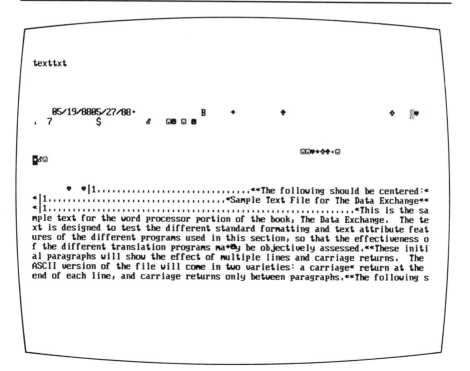

One of the key identifying features for a MultiMate file is the way that end-of-paragraphs are marked. In some word processors, this is achieved by using a Carriage Return, a Line Feed, or both. MultiMate uses neither of these characters, and instead uses the ASCII character: Û. You can see these at the start and end of some lines shown in the screen shot.

Like MultiMate, Microsoft Word® also stores header information in a document file. Among other details, the header contains details about the style sheet and printer driver associated with the file—as well as a modification date.

As shown in Figure 2–11, the text appears in a straightforward format; the characters are all legible and Carriage Return/Line Feed combinations mark the end of paragraphs. One side benefit of this fact is that you can use the DOS TYPE com-

FIGURE 2–11
MS Word File

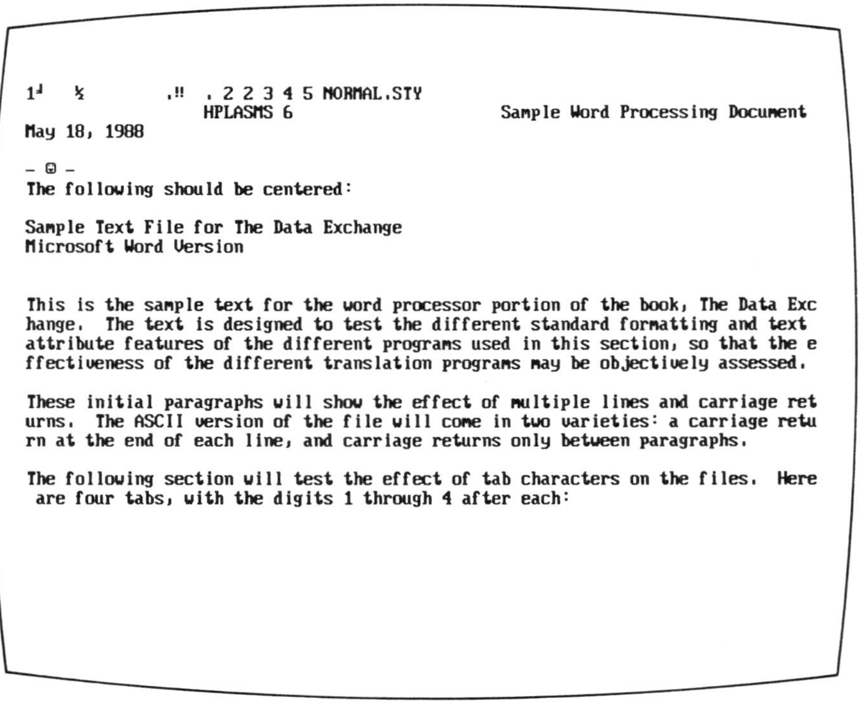

```
1ᴶ   ½        .ᴵᴵ  . 2 2 3 4 5 NORMAL.STY
              HPLASMS 6                      Sample Word Processing Document
May 18, 1988

- ☺ -
The following should be centered:

Sample Text File for The Data Exchange
Microsoft Word Version


This is the sample text for the word processor portion of the book, The Data Exc
hange.  The text is designed to test the different standard formatting and text
attribute features of the different programs used in this section, so that the e
ffectiveness of the different translation programs may be objectively assessed.

These initial paragraphs will show the effect of multiple lines and carriage ret
urns.  The ASCII version of the file will come in two varieties: a carriage retu
rn at the end of each line, and carriage returns only between paragraphs.

The following section will test the effect of tab characters on the files.  Here
  are four tabs, with the digits 1 through 4 after each:
```

mand to examine the contents of a Word document file without having to load the whole Word program. TYPE won't give you word wrap, but the file should be legible enough for easy deciphering.

In stark contrast with the legible contents of the Microsoft Word format, DisplayWrite® files appear as gibberish. Figure 2–12 illustrates the contents of a DisplayWrite document file, while Figure 2–13 shows the same file stored in DCA (Document Content Architecture) RFT (Revisable Format Text) format.

Neither of the two formats presents anything legible, but the second (DCA RFT) shows the presence of some data. The majority of the DCA file is stored in higher ASCII characters, however, and does not yield any hints about file contents.

FIGURE 2–12
DisplayWrite Document File

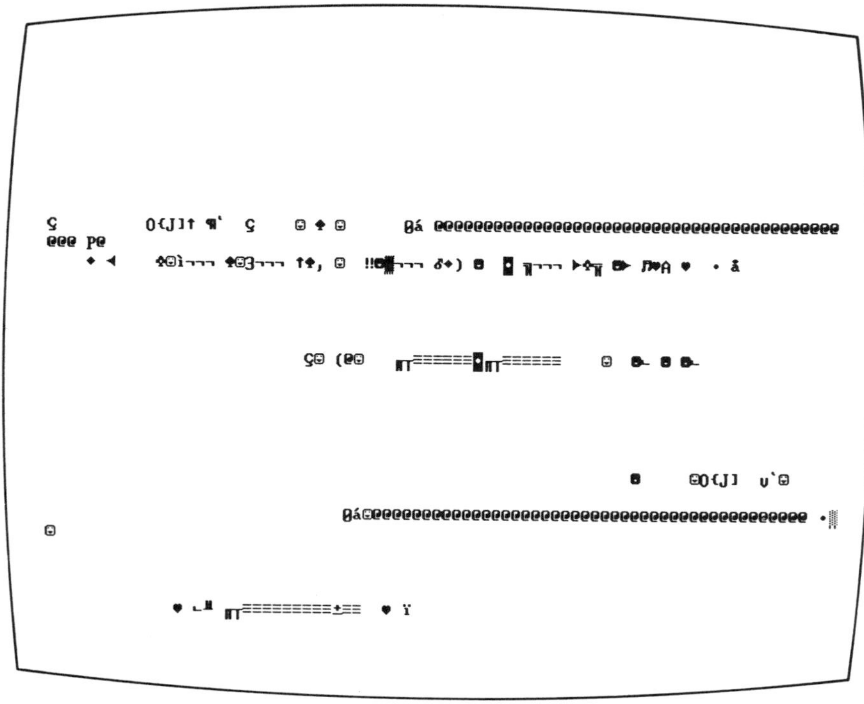

FIGURE 2–13
DisplayWrite DCA File

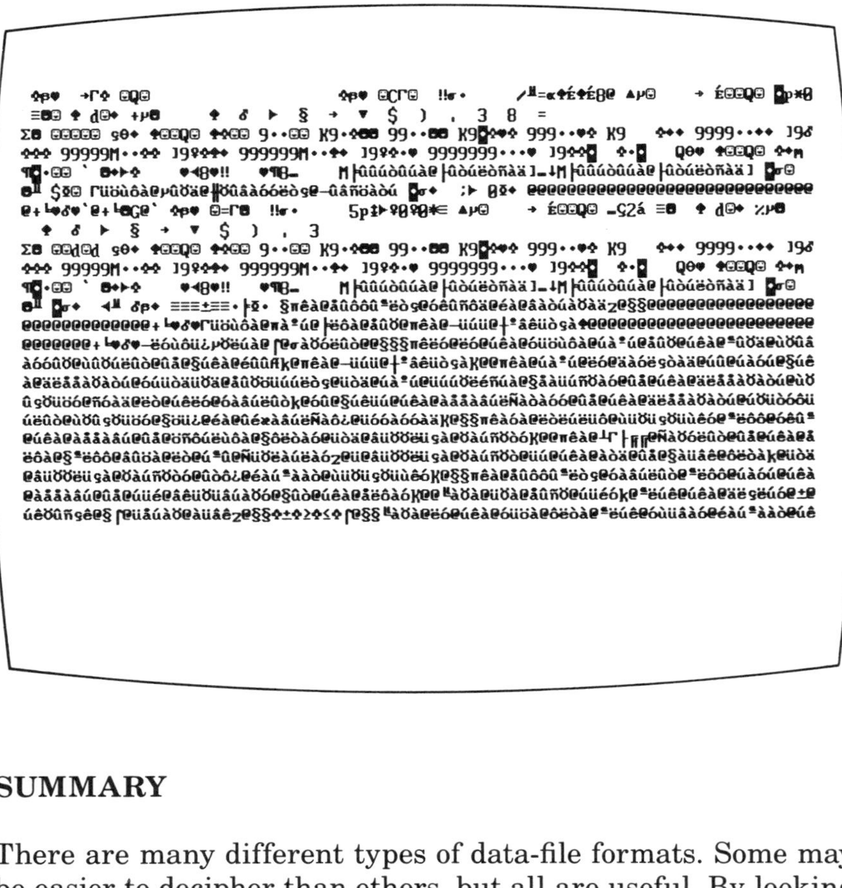

SUMMARY

There are many different types of data-file formats. Some may be easier to decipher than others, but all are useful. By looking at their contents and/or their file name extensions, you have a good chance of identifying their source, and you know how to make them work for you.

In Part 2, you will find ways to use these formats. You will see how to use these and other formats to move data in and out of 1–2–3, dBASE, and many other popular programs including word processors, accounting, and desktop publishing.

PART 2

WORKING WITH SPECIFIC PROGRAMS

"No program is an island; no data stands alone," to coin a phrase.

Many people only use one program for the majority of their work, and in most cases, the program is one of a select few. If the work is done with spreadsheets, then it is likely Lotus 1–2–3. If it is database work, chances are the program is dBASE III Plus. If it is word processing, odds are that most people use one of a small handful of products.

As long as you never need to cross the boundary of one package, you will have no problems with exchanging data. But for the remaining tasks, you can benefit from extracting data from the majority application.

In Part 2, there are seven chapters that cover the essential information about moving data into and out of a dozen programs. Do not feel the need to read every part of every chapter; there are few users who will come into contact with all 12 programs in a year. Instead, jump to the chapters that discuss the products you use frequently. There are pointers and pitfalls in each chapter that may solve problems you have encountered or give you ideas about new ways to use your data.

CHAPTER 3

MOVING DATA INTO LOTUS 1–2–3

Lotus 1–2–3 has various facilities that make it easier to bring in data from outside sources. Some of these techniques are clearly documented in the manuals and others are not. Some of them have serious limitations that are only briefly mentioned—if at all—in the manuals. Also, there are some alternative approaches that do not appear in the program documentation that can save time and energy.

In this chapter, you will learn some important facts about procedures in all these categories. Once you have mastered these techniques, you can bring in almost any kind of data file or understand why not.

Throughout this chapter, I have made the assumption that you are working with Lotus 1–2–3 Release 2.0 or 2.01. At significant points, I explain the important differences between these versions and Release 1A. As I write this book, Release 3.0 appears to be in a state of arrested development, destined perhaps to exist only in a state of limbo as a permanent beta test. If released, this new version is expected to offer significant changes to the program. Unfortunately, the program is not yet ready, so a discussion of its new features must await a future edition of this book.

THE TRANSLATE UTILITY

Lotus 1–2–3 has a front-end system menu system that comes up when you enter the LOTUS command. Few users bother with this opening menu, except perhaps to run the PrintGraph program, which is why many 1–2–3 users bypass it and start directly with the "123" command from the DOS prompt.

The Lotus Access menu has one important option that not everyone knows about, however. It is the translation program, which comes as TRANS.COM on the 1–2–3 Utility disk. TRANS uses a number of related programs depending on the source and destination of your file formats.

The Translate Menu

When you first call up the Lotus Access menu, you see a screen similar to the one in Figure 3–1. In this case, the cursor has been moved to highlight the Translate option—showing the ex-

FIGURE 3–1
Lotus 1–2–3 Release 2.01 Access Menu

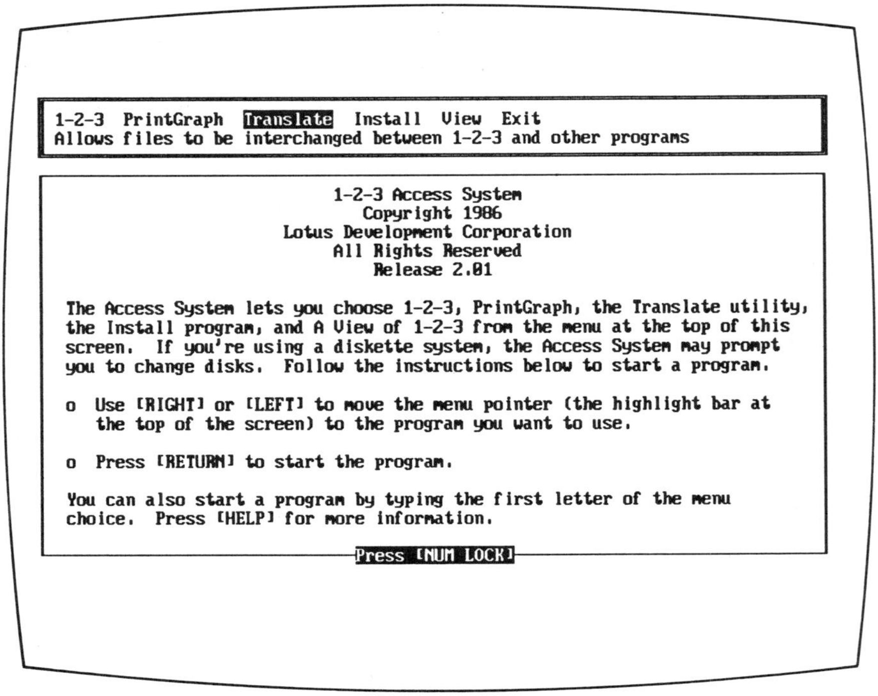

```
1-2-3  PrintGraph  Translate  Install  View  Exit
Allows files to be interchanged between 1-2-3 and other programs

                     1-2-3 Access System
                       Copyright 1986
                 Lotus Development Corporation
                     All Rights Reserved
                        Release 2.01

The Access System lets you choose 1-2-3, PrintGraph, the Translate utility,
the Install program, and A View of 1-2-3 from the menu at the top of this
screen.  If you're using a diskette system, the Access System may prompt
you to change disks.  Follow the instructions below to start a program.

o  Use [RIGHT] or [LEFT] to move the menu pointer (the highlight bar at
   the top of the screen) to the program you want to use.

o  Press [RETURN] to start the program.

You can also start a program by typing the first letter of the menu
choice.  Press [HELP] for more information.

                     Press [NUM LOCK]
```

planation "Allows files to be interchanged between 1–2–3 and other programs" on the line below.

Once you select the Translate option, you will see a screen that looks like Figure 3–2. Note that the Translate for Release 1A looks different. The differences between Release 2.x and Release 1A are covered at the end of this section.

The column at the left lists the supported source-file formats. Use the cursor keys to highlight the desired source, then press the Enter Key. Depending on your source selection, the screen will show different options in the second column, as shown in Figure 3–3. In this case, Release 1A was selected as the source format.

Just because a combination appears on the screen does not mean that it is supported by Translate. If you select Release

FIGURE 3–2
Lotus 1–2–3 Release 2.01 Translate Menu

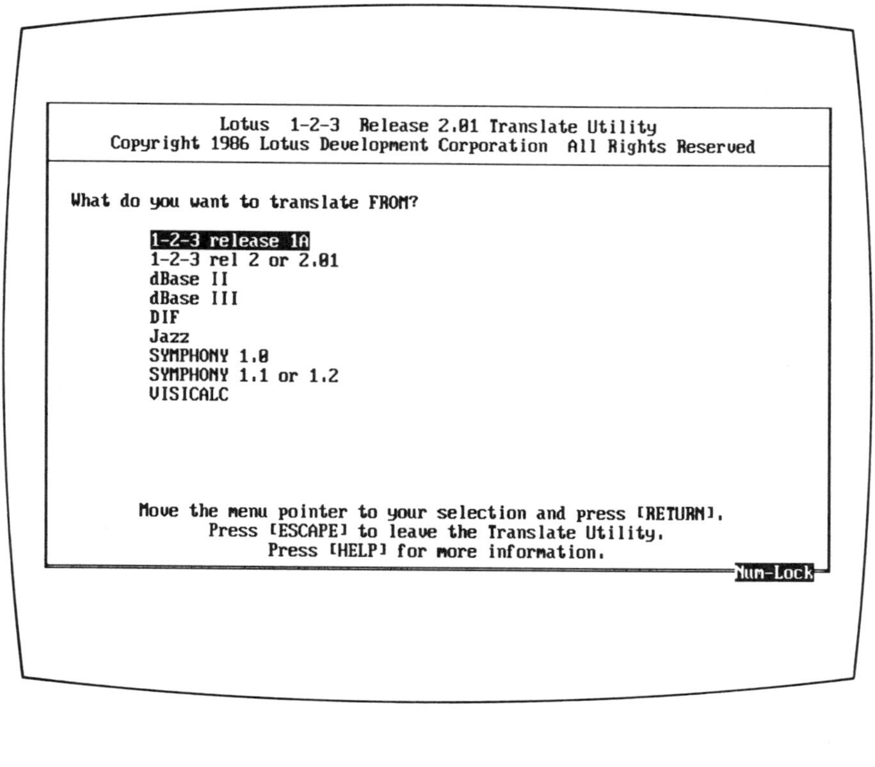

```
                Lotus  1-2-3  Release 2.01 Translate Utility
       Copyright 1986 Lotus Development Corporation  All Rights Reserved

What do you want to translate FROM?

        1-2-3 release 1A
        1-2-3 rel 2 or 2.01
        dBase II
        dBase III
        DIF
        Jazz
        SYMPHONY 1.0
        SYMPHONY 1.1 or 1.2
        VISICALC




        Move the menu pointer to your selection and press [RETURN].
            Press [ESCAPE] to leave the Translate Utility.
               Press [HELP] for more information.
                                                    Num-Lock
```

1A as the source, then Release 2.01 as the target format, you get the message shown in Figure 3–4.

Since Lotus 1–2–3 version 2.01 can read in Release 1A worksheets directly, there is no need to use the Translate program. Lotus designers deserve a commendation for including this combination of formats in the program and providing a handy reminder of the fact.

The same result holds true for other combinations. Here is a list of source and target formats that do not require any processing with the Translate Utility:

Source Format	Target Format
1–2–3 Release 1A	1–2–3 Release 2.01 Symphony 1.0 Symphony 1.1 or 1.2
1–2–3 Release 2.01	Symphony 1.1 or 1.2
Symphony 1.0	1–2–3 Release 2.01 Symphony 1.1 or 1.2
Symphony 1.1 or 1.2	1–2–3 Release 2.01

This still leaves a number of combinations that require some conversion, and in many cases, Translate can help. Note that there are some limitations in what the program can handle, however. Unfortunately, Translate is probably the worst-documented 1–2–3 facility; the reference manual gives it a single page.

On the plus side, the program is fairly self-explanatory. If you select an option that has limitations, it does its best to explain them. For example, Figure 3–5 (page 47) shows the message displayed when you try to convert a dBASE III file into Lotus 1–2–3 Release 2.01.

Note that there are three mentioned limitations; experience shows that there are other problems. To explore the detailed and hidden constraints more fully, let's turn to the conversion you will most likely use with Translate and see what lies in wait.

FIGURE 3–3
Translate Utility with Release 1A As Source Format

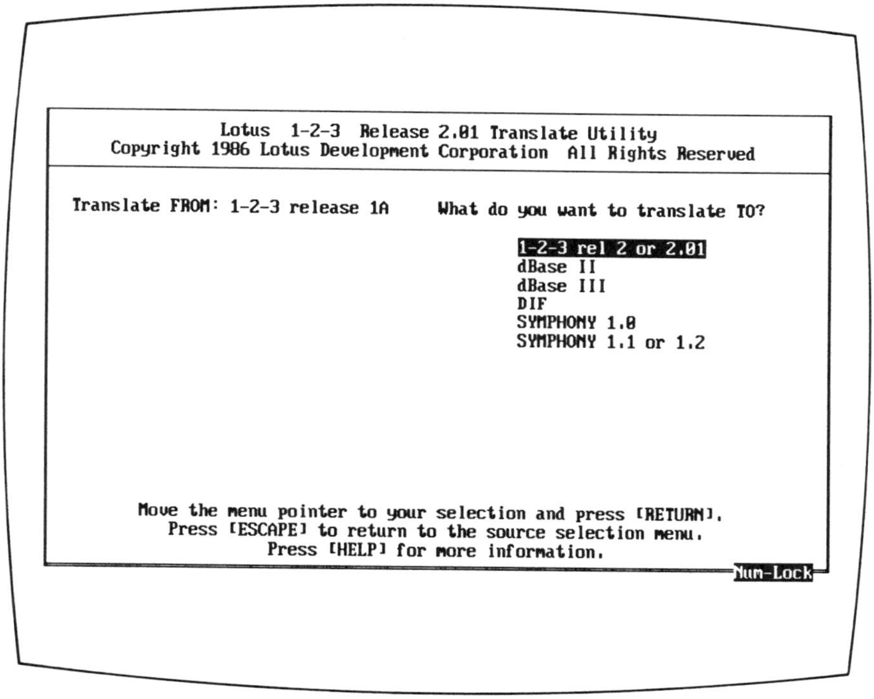

```
              Lotus  1-2-3  Release 2.01 Translate Utility
         Copyright 1986 Lotus Development Corporation  All Rights Reserved

  Translate FROM: 1-2-3 release 1A     What do you want to translate TO?

                                       1-2-3 rel 2 or 2.01
                                       dBase II
                                       dBase III
                                       DIF
                                       SYMPHONY 1.0
                                       SYMPHONY 1.1 or 1.2




          Move the menu pointer to your selection and press [RETURN].
            Press [ESCAPE] to return to the source selection menu.
                  Press [HELP] for more information.
                                                            Num-Lock
```

Translating dBASE III to Release 2.01

When you use Translate to convert a dBASE III file to a Release 2.01 worksheet, the program warns you of four limitations.

First, any records marked for deletion within the dBASE
file will not be translated. The dBASE III Memo fields also will
not get translated, in part since 1–2–3 has no corresponding
long text type of label, and besides, the dBASE memo fields are
stored in a file separate from the main .DBF database file.

Next, since 1–2–3 has a cell-width limitation of 240 characters, a dBASE file with a character field greater than 240

FIGURE 3–4
Translate Utility—Release 1A to 2.01

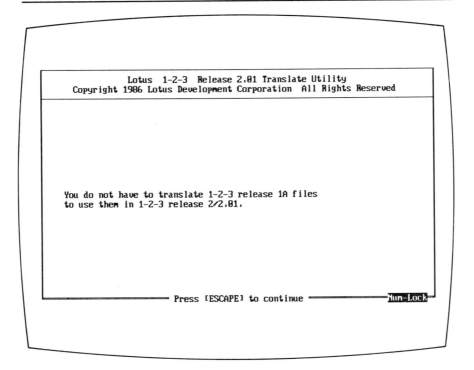

```
            Lotus  1-2-3  Release 2.01 Translate Utility
     Copyright 1986 Lotus Development Corporation  All Rights Reserved




You do not have to translate 1-2-3 release 1A files
to use them in 1-2-3 release 2/2.01.




                        Press [ESCAPE] to continue              Num-Lock
```

characters will be truncated. Since dBASE III permits character field lengths of 256, it is possible but unlikely that you will lose data from the extra 16 characters. Finally, Lotus 1–2–3 Release 2.01 only supports 8,191 rows per spreadsheet, so you can't bring in more than that number of records.

There are some other limitations hidden in those statements, however. For example, the 8,191-row limit is a theoretical maximum. The actual number of records that you can bring in from a dBASE file depends on a number of factors, including the number of characters per record and the amount of regular and expanded memory available in your computer. While you can convert 8,000 records, you will probably end up with a worksheet that will be too big to load.

FIGURE 3–5
Translate Utility—dBASE III to Release 2.01

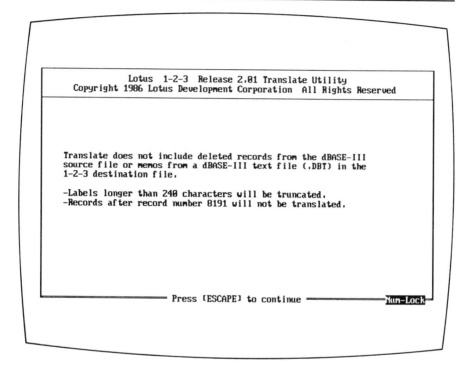

```
                    Lotus  1-2-3  Release 2.01 Translate Utility
          Copyright 1986 Lotus Development Corporation  All Rights Reserved



      Translate does not include deleted records from the dBASE-III
      source file or memos from a dBASE-III text file (.DBT) in the
      1-2-3 destination file.

      -Labels longer than 240 characters will be truncated.
      -Records after record number 8191 will not be translated.




                        Press [ESCAPE] to continue              Num-Lock
```

The Translate Utility handles the four main dBASE III field types without a problem. Character fields are brought in to the worksheet format as labels. Numeric fields are converted to values, with the appropriate format coding to display the same number of decimal points. dBASE date fields are brought in as 1–2–3 date cells, in the "DD–Mon–YY" format. Logical fields in dBASE are converted into the appropriate and corresponding 1–2–3 value: @TRUE or @FALSE. A Memo field results in a blank column on the 1–2–3 worksheet.

The column widths in the converted 1–2–3 worksheet are set to match the dBASE field-length definitions. The dBASE field names are used to fill the first row of the worksheet—

providing headings for the columns of data. Each record then appears on a separate row.

Here are screen images that demonstrate the conversion of a sample dBASE table into a Lotus 1–2–3 Release 2.01 worksheet. Figure 3–6 shows the structure of the source dBASE III table.

The screen in Figure 3–7 illustrates using the dBASE BROWSE command on the sample data file, showing some of the records in the database. The columnar display is similar to how data will appear in a 1–2–3 spreadsheet.

Figure 3–8 shows the Lotus Translate Utility at the point where the source and target file names have been selected. The

FIGURE 3–6
Sample dBASE III File Structure

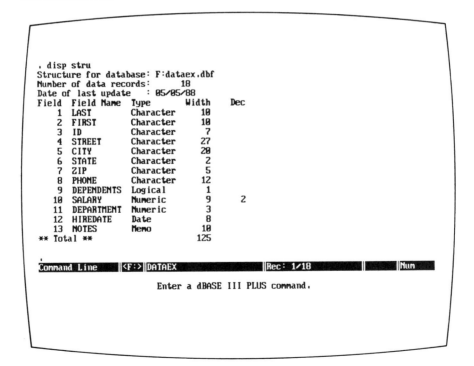

FIGURE 3–7
Sample dBASE III Data

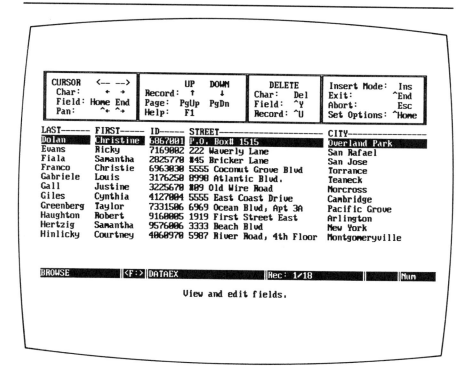

question at the center of the screen in the double box asks for confirmation before continuing.

The next step cannot be captured easily in an illustration. Once you tell Translate to proceed, the box in the middle of the screen is filled with a horizontal bar graph starting with a short bar that begins at the left side of the graph. This bar indicates the percentage of the dBASE III file that has been converted. The bar grows as the conversion proceeds, and when it hits 100 percent, the translation is complete. The program then lets you know of its success with a screen such as the one in Figure 3–9.

FIGURE 3–8
Translate Utility—dBASE III to Release 2.01

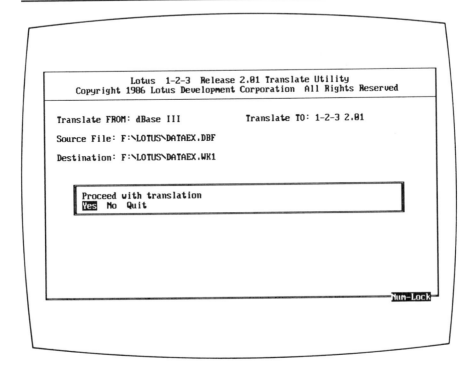

You can now exit Translate, call up 1–2–3, and retrieve the converted file in its new worksheet form. The original dBASE file remains unchanged in the process; only the new worksheet file is created. Figure 3–10 shows the worksheet created with Translate using our sample dBASE III file.

The spreadsheet looks much like the dBASE BROWSE display, as mentioned above. Also, the first row of the spreadsheet contains the dBASE field names as labels. Remember that while it can help by identifying the data in that column, it can throw off calculations or formulas that you may define over the entire range of converted data.

When you use Translate to bring in a dBASE file, you get all fields for all records. You can selectively import certain rec-

FIGURE 3-9
Translate Utility—Successful Translation

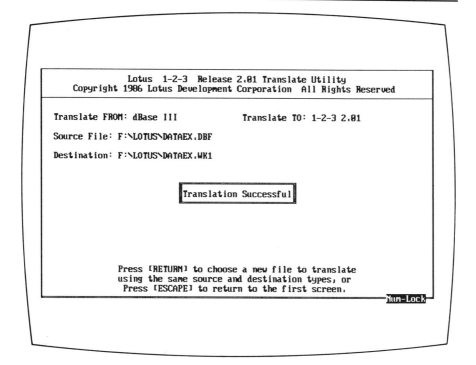

```
              Lotus  1-2-3  Release 2.01 Translate Utility
        Copyright 1986 Lotus Development Corporation  All Rights Reserved

  Translate FROM: dBase III          Translate TO: 1-2-3 2.01

  Source File: F:\LOTUS\DATAEX.DBF

  Destination: F:\LOTUS\DATAEX.WK1


                    ┌─────────────────────────┐
                    │ Translation Successful  │
                    └─────────────────────────┘



              Press [RETURN] to choose a new file to translate
              using the same source and destination types, or
              Press [ESCAPE] to return to the first screen.
                                                        Num-Lock
```

ords by marking the ones you don't want for deletion, since Translate will ignore the marked records. You will not lose those records from your database, however, since dBASE doesn't erase a deleted record until you issue the PACK command. As a result, you could select certain records for conversion by marking the others for deletion, perform the conversion, and then restore the deleted records to undeleted status.

There is no easy way, however, to limit the fields you import. You could bring in all the fields and then delete unwanted columns from the resulting spreadsheet—provided that the entire file will fit within the 1–2–3 memory limitations. You could

FIGURE 3–10
Worksheet Created with Translate from dBASE III File

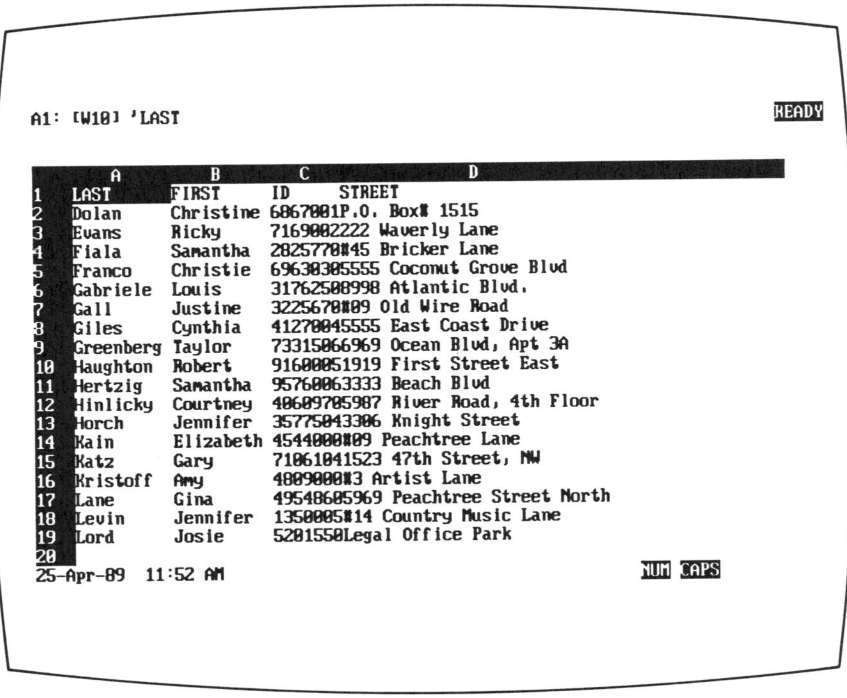

```
A1: [W10] 'LAST                                              READY

         A        B        C              D
 1  LAST      FIRST    ID       STREET
 2  Dolan     Christine 6867001P.O. Box# 1515
 3  Evans     Ricky    7169002222 Waverly Lane
 4  Fiala     Samantha 2825770#45 Bricker Lane
 5  Franco    Christie 69630305555 Coconut Grove Blvd
 6  Gabriele  Louis    31762500990 Atlantic Blvd.
 7  Gall      Justine  3225670#09 Old Wire Road
 8  Giles     Cynthia  41270045555 East Coast Drive
 9  Greenberg Taylor   73315066969 Ocean Blvd, Apt 3A
10  Haughton  Robert   91600051919 First Street East
11  Hertzig   Samantha 95760063333 Beach Blvd
12  Hinlicky  Courtney 40609705987 River Road, 4th Floor
13  Horch     Jennifer 35775043306 Knight Street
14  Kain      Elizabeth 4544000#09 Peachtree Lane
15  Katz      Gary     71061041523 47th Street, NW
16  Kristoff  Amy      4809000#3 Artist Lane
17  Lane      Gina     49548605969 Peachtree Street North
18  Levin     Jennifer 1350005#14 Country Music Lane
19  Lord      Josie    5201550Legal Office Park
20
25-Apr-89  11:52 AM                                   NUM CAPS
```

also copy your dBASE file, then modify the structure of the copy by deleting the unwanted fields.

A third problem is that Translate creates a new and separate spreadsheet each time. If you are trying to bring data into an existing spreadsheet, Translate requires that you make the import worksheet first, then use the /FILE COMBINE command in 1–2–3. This command requires that you either bring in the entire other worksheet or create a named range within the other file first before combining the two files. This is not a taxing process, but in some cases it is easier to bring the data straight into the existing worksheet.

None of these options will work suitably in all situations, and there will be times that you may need to leave Translate behind and take more direct control of the import process. The full discussion of these options occurs later in the section on the /FILE IMPORT NUMBERS and /FILE IMPORT TEXT commands, but for now, remember that there are sometimes better ways to bring dBASE data into a 1–2–3 spreadsheet.

Importing Other Formats

There are some important limitations and quirks to consider in using the other import formats.

DIF stands for Data Interchange Format, and it was developed by Software Arts, the company that created VisiCalc®. Originally, it was conceived as the data-exchange format for microcomputers and first incorporated in VisiCalc.

The DIF format is unusual; it breaks information into individual cells and then lists the cell's location and contents on separate lines. There are also section headers that refer to arcane features such as "tuples." The end result is that the file format is clearly defined but carries so much overhead information that it can create significantly larger files.

There is another, more significant feature about the DIF format. In its original design, it was aimed to be as flexible as possible. That meant that it was capable of inverting the original data. One use of this feature was that you could convert a spreadsheet into DIF format by columns but then read the data back in by rows. The result is that the rows and columns were swapped in going from one spreadsheet to the other spreadsheet.

This transposition was also needed in moving data from one program to another program—such as from a worksheet to a graphics program. You might have a time series of data arranged horizontally on the worksheet, but the graphics program needed the time variables arranged vertically. A DIF conversion could move the data over and rearrange it on the way.

Over time, many developers have ignored that DIF formats may be created either by columns or by rows. As a result, many graphics programs may not be able to accurately use a DIF file of your creation if it is arranged in a way different from what it expects. Many spreadsheet programs, including 1–2–3, now have internal means to transpose sections of a worksheet, which swaps the rows and columns.

Fortunately, however, Lotus has remained true to the concept, and Translate correctly implements the DIF conversion. If you select the option to go from DIF to 1–2–3 Release 2.x, you see the message shown in Figure 3–11.

Lotus 1–2–3 gives you the choice of making the conversion either by row or by column. Remember this concept if you ever find an application that cannot use a DIF file in the orientation you have on hand. You can use 1–2–3 as a bridge to success. Bring the file into a 1–2–3 spreadsheet using Translate, then transpose the set of data on the worksheet, then convert back

FIGURE 3–11
1–2–3 Translate: DIF to 1–2–3

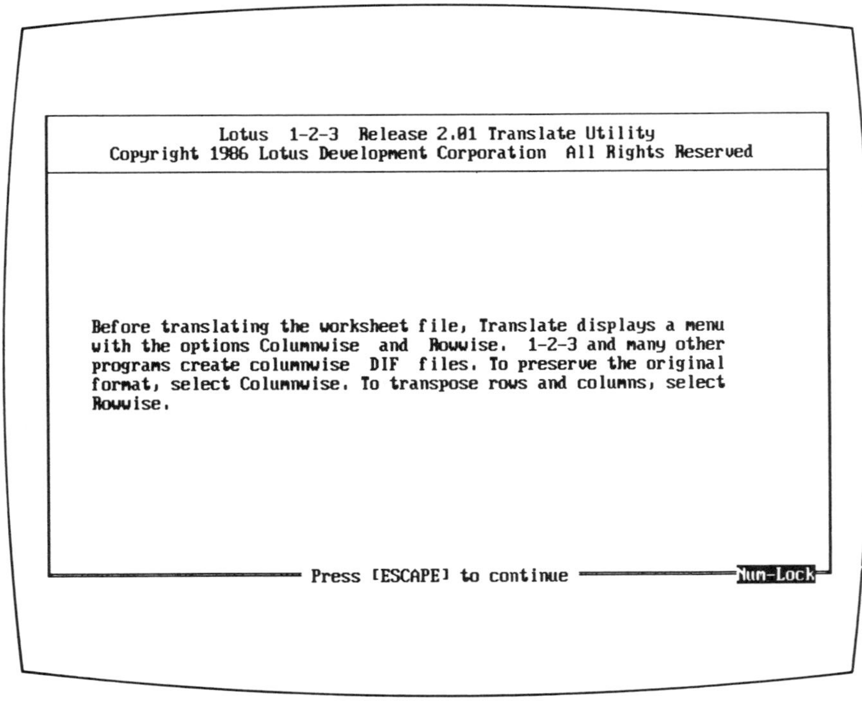

Lotus 1-2-3 Release 2.01 Translate Utility
Copyright 1986 Lotus Development Corporation All Rights Reserved

Before translating the worksheet file, Translate displays a menu with the options Columnwise and Rowwise. 1-2-3 and many other programs create columnwise DIF files. To preserve the original format, select Columnwise. To transpose rows and columns, select Rowwise.

Press [ESCAPE] to continue ———— Num-Lock

to DIF again. The other application should then be able to use the DIF file. On a related issue, there are some limitations that you may encounter when bringing in a VisiCalc file. Figure 3–12 shows the warning message displayed when you choose this option within Translate.

Since VisiCalc worksheets support some functions that do not have a direct equivalent in 1–2–3, Translate will display a message and enter the cell contents as a label instead of as a formula.

Lotus 1–2–3 Release 2.01 also supports conversions with JAZZ files. JAZZ® is an integrated program for the Macintosh® from Lotus. Figure 3–13 shows the Translate message that appears with this option.

FIGURE 3–12
1–2–3 Translate: VisiCalc to 1–2–3

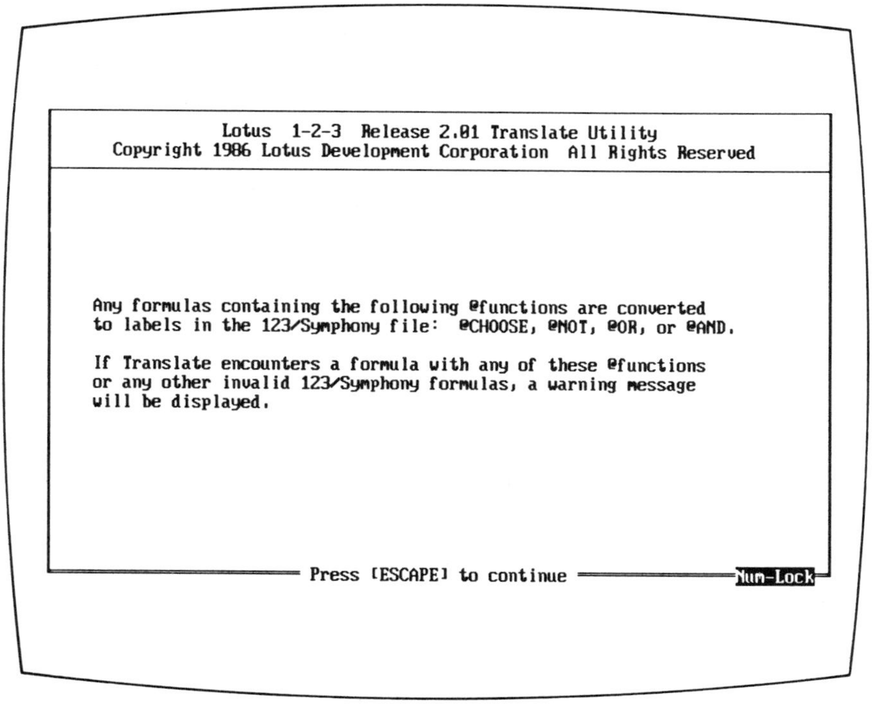

Lotus 1-2-3 Release 2.01 Translate Utility
Copyright 1986 Lotus Development Corporation All Rights Reserved

Any formulas containing the following @functions are converted to labels in the 123/Symphony file: @CHOOSE, @NOT, @OR, or @AND.

If Translate encounters a formula with any of these @functions or any other invalid 123/Symphony formulas, a warning message will be displayed.

Press [ESCAPE] to continue   Num-Lock

FIGURE 3–13
1–2–3 Translate: JAZZ to 1–2–3

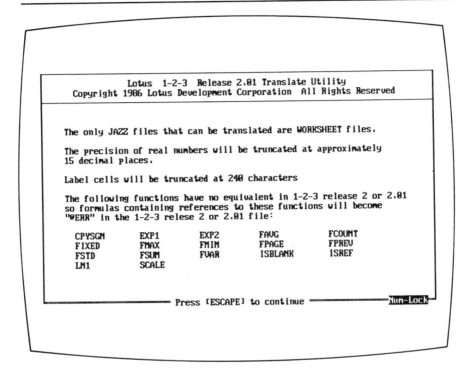

In addition to these functional differences, remember that since JAZZ is a Macintosh program, you first have to find a way to move the file from a Mac disk to a PC. There are alternative methods used to accomplish this task ranging from conversion services to communication-based file transfers. First, put the file on a disk that your PC can read before giving Translate the task of converting it to a 1–2–3 file.

Lotus 1–2–3 Version 1A Translate

Version 1A also has a Translate utility, which you can select from the same sort of Lotus Access menu system as found in version 2.x of 1–2–3. The main differences between the two versions are found in the formats covered and in the spreadsheet limitations of the program.

First, there are only three formats supported: VisiCalc, DIF, and dBASE II DBF files. These were the major players when 1–2–3 first appeared; Symphony®, dBASE III, and others were not yet on the market. There are some serious limitations in terms of what files can be converted. While dBASE II and dBASE III both use the same extension for their database files, DBF, they do not share the same format.

Version 1A also has some inherent limitations, as well. Its spreadsheets are limited to 2,048 rows, so you are limited to fewer records than with later versions of 1–2–3. Version 2.x of 1–2–3 uses a *sparse matrix* memory management, which makes more efficient use of memory when loading a spreadsheet. As a result, you may have a worksheet that fits in version 2.x but runs out of memory with 1A.

Memory management can work against the later versions, however. The newer releases of 1–2–3 are about 73K larger than 1A, and if your spreadsheet is a solid block of cells (no large, empty sections), then the memory-management feature gives no advantage. Most database conversions result in a dense packing of cells on a worksheet. As a result, you may find that a database file (provided it has less than 2,048 records) might not load successfully into a 2.x version of 1–2–3, but it will fit in version 1A. Another trick to remember is that successive versions of DOS have grown significantly larger; if you boot your system with an older version of DOS, you may be able to load a larger spreadsheet since you will have more available memory.

THE /FILE IMPORT OPTIONS

Fortunately, 1–2–3 in all its versions does not leave you stranded with the limitations of the Translate utilities. There are some options that allow you to bring data directly into a worksheet while you work with it.

The two command sequences are /FILE IMPORT TEXT, and /FILE IMPORT NUMBERS. Both work with ASCII text files but in different ways. In spite of their names, each can be used to import both values and labels. The following sections describe how they work and when to use them.

/File Import Numbers

If you want to bring in values directly to your worksheet, then use /FILE IMPORT NUMBERS. The basic rules for this command are simple. If the characters encountered are digits, they are entered as values. If a quote is encountered, then everything following it until the next quote is entered as a label. If the characters encountered are anything else, they are ignored.

/FILE IMPORT NUMBERS also "parses" the information so that it can determine where the contents of one cell end and the next cell starts. It makes this separation based on one of two criteria. If it encounters a comma, it assumes that is the mark for the end of the last cell's contents. In the same way, a space will trigger the start of a new cell. Commas and spaces within quotes do not start a new cell; instead they are treated as part of the label.

The ASCII text file is read by 1–2–3 line by line and is separated by the above rules into separate cells. Each Carriage Return marks the start of a new row. The lines in the ASCII file need not be similar; you could have a label in the first line, followed by many lines of mixed labels and values, and the cells would be formatted appropriately.

If you studied the first section of this book, or are familiar with different file formats, you may have already identified a standard ASCII format that is especially suited for this type of import. The quoted-string, comma-delimited format is perfect for bringing data into a 1–2–3 worksheet. The commas that separate the fields signal the start of each new cell. The quotes around the string-field contents cause this information to be entered into the spreadsheet as a label. As a result, you can make a clean and easy import.

Figure 3–14 shows the contents of a comma-delimited text file that was created using the same dBASE file used earlier in this chapter. This example demonstrates some of the strengths and weaknesses of this technique.

FIGURE 3–14
Comma-Delimited ASCII File from a dBASE File

```
"Dolan","Christine","6867001","P.O. Box# 1515","Overland Park","KS","66210","269
-111-2222",F,40000.00,360,19040925
"Evans","Ricky","7169002","222 Waverly Lane","San Rafael","CA","94903","904-111-
2222",F,45000.00,360,19040928
"fiala","Samantha","2025770","#45 Bricker Lane","San Jose","CA","95134","904-111
-5656",F,78000.00,360,19041005
"Franco","Christie","6963030","5555 Coconut Grove Blvd","Torrance","CA","90505",
"111-222-3333",F,144000.00,100,19050621
"Gabriele","Louis","3176250","8998 Atlantic Blvd.","Teaneck","NJ","07666","125-4
78-6325",T,12000.00,240,19050122
"Gall","Justine","3225670","#09 Old Wire Road","Norcross","GA","30092","987-236-
5668",F,25000.00,360,19040924
"Giles","Cynthia","4127004","5555 East Coast Drive","Cambridge","MA","02138","78
9-455-6233",F,30000.00,360,19041005
"Greenberg","Taylor","7331506","6969 Ocean Blvd, Apt 3A","Pacific Grove","CA","9
3950","123-456-7899",T,12000.00,240,19050123
"Haughton","Robert","9160005","1919 First Street East","Arlington","VA","22209",
"250-974-6623",T,40000.00,360,19040925
"Hertzig","Samantha","9576006","3333 Beach Blvd","New York","NY","10028","901-25
6-8954",F,15000.00,120,19050527
"Hinlicky","Courtney","4060970","5907 River Road, 4th Floor","Montgomeryville","
PA","18936","886-325-5625",F,20000.00,100,19050614
"Horch","Jennifer","3577504","3306 Knight Street","Bellevue","WA","90004","465-6
```

The original dBASE file had character, date, numeric, logical, and memo fields. The delimited file was created using the dBASE COPY command, and you may notice some peculiar features about the results. You can't see the memo field contents; they are not converted. The other point is that the fourth to last field is either a *T* or an *F*. Unlike the other character fields, this one has no quotes around it. This is because the contents came from a dBASE logical field. The details about dBASE fields and export conversions are covered in a later chapter, but the points about this file's fields are important to remember before going further.

In Figure 3–15, there is an empty worksheet ready to receive the data from our data file. I have already typed in a

FIGURE 3–15
1–2–3 Worksheet Waiting for Delimited File: /File Import

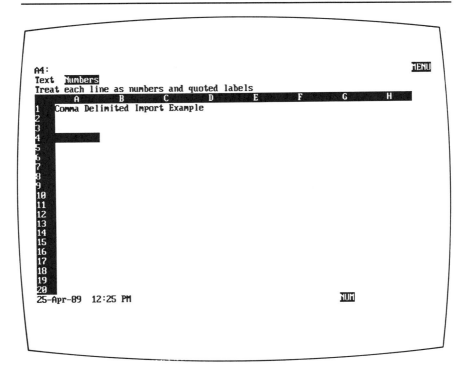

heading label, "Comma Delimited Import Example," so that we can keep track of what we get. You can see by the upper-left-hand corner of the screen that the cursor is sitting in an empty cell, A4.

Note across the top of the screen that I have already issued the /FILE IMPORT command and have moved the cursor to highlight the NUMBERS option. The next screen, Figure 3–16, shows the results of selecting the NUMBERS option. 1–2–3 asks you for the file name to use for the import and displays any available files in the default directory with the PRN extension.

Here is a tip that not many people know. The manual states that "you may need to rename the incoming file because all print files must have the .PRN extension." This isn't true.

FIGURE 3–16
1–2–3 /File Import Numbers: File Selection

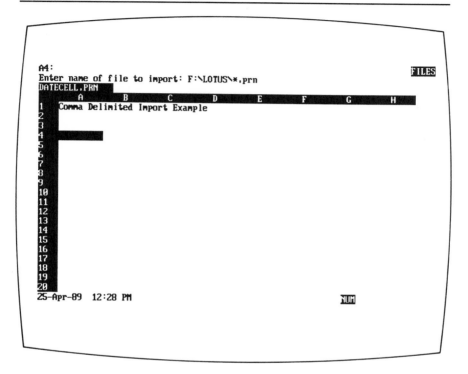

Only the .PRN files are displayed on the file selection line, but that doesn't stop you from typing in your own file name.

Here's the proof. In Figure 3–17, I have overwritten the default values shown in the last screen simply by typing away. Not only have I specified a file that does not end in .PRN, but it isn't even in the default directory.

Press the Enter Key after you finish entering or selecting the appropriate file, and 1–2–3 will start to convert the delimited file. The first information goes into the cell where you left the cursor when the command was issued. Subsequent information will be loaded into the cells to the right until a Carriage Return is encountered; then, the next information will be placed in the cell one row below the starting point.

FIGURE 3–17
/File Import Numbers: Entering a File Name

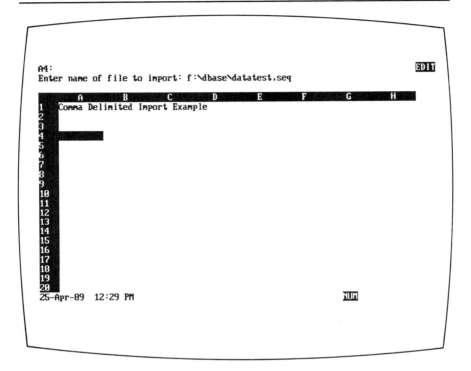

The screen in Figure 3–18 shows the results of this command. The cursor is still on cell A4.

Cell A4 has been filled with a label that contains the last name Dolan. This corresponds to the first data element in our delimited file, and since the information was in quotes, it was brought in as a label. The third column, *C*, contains the employee number, which was also surrounded by quotes. As a result, you can see that this data has been set flush left in the cells of that column, an indication that it was treated as a label rather than as a value by 1–2–3.

Columns *D* and *E* may appear a bit confusing at first, since the information runs together. These two columns contain the street and city fields of the address. Since 1–2–3 worksheets

FIGURE 3-18
/File Import Numbers: After Sequential File Is Imported

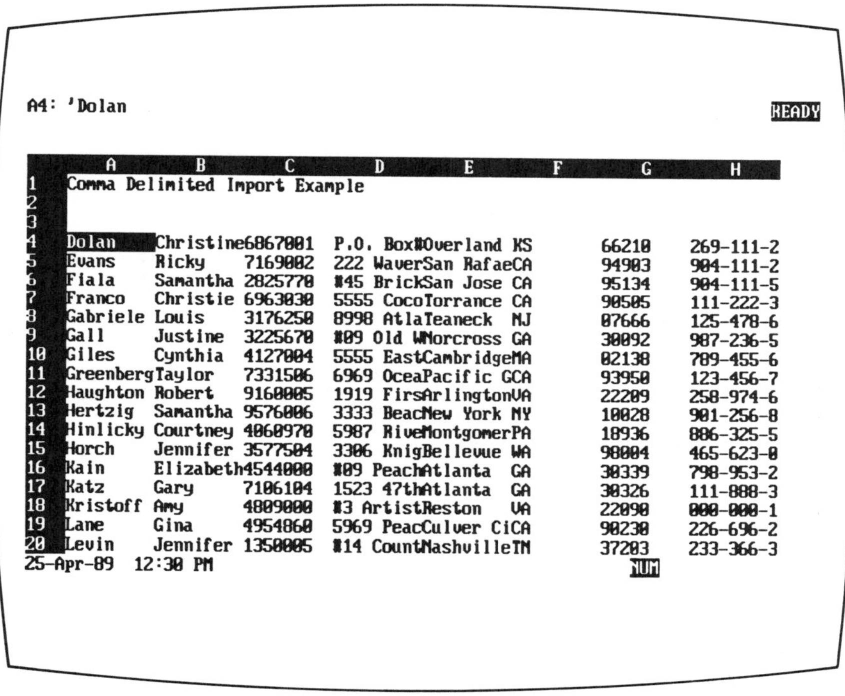

```
A4: 'Dolan                                                          READY

         A        B        C         D        E       F      G          H
 1  Comma Delimited Import Example
 2
 3
 4  Dolan     Christine6867001    P.O. Box#Overland KS       66210    269-111-2
 5  Evans     Ricky    7169002    222 WaverSan RafaeCA       94903    904-111-2
 6  Fiala     Samantha 2825770    #45 BrickSan Jose CA       95134    904-111-5
 7  Franco    Christie 6963030    5555 CocoTorrance CA       90505    111-222-3
 8  Gabriele  Louis    3176250    8998 AtlaTeaneck  NJ       07666    125-478-6
 9  Gall      Justine  3225670    #09 Old WNorcross GA       30092    987-236-5
10  Giles     Cynthia  4127004    5555 EastCambridgeMA       02138    789-455-6
11  GreenbergTaylor    7331506    6969 OceaPacific GCA       93950    123-456-7
12  Haughton  Robert   9160005    1919 FirsArlingtonVA       22209    258-974-6
13  Hertzig   Samantha 9576006    3333 BeacNew York NY       10028    901-256-8
14  Hinlicky  Courtney 4060970    5987 RiveMontgomerPA       18936    886-325-5
15  Horch     Jennifer 3577504    3306 KnigBellevue WA       98004    465-623-0
16  Kain      Elizabeth4544000    #09 PeachAtlanta  GA       30339    798-953-2
17  Katz      Gary     7106104    1523 47thAtlanta  GA       30326    111-888-3
18  Kristoff  Amy      4809000    #3 ArtistReston   VA       22090    000-000-1
19  Lane      Gina     4954060    5969 PeacCulver CiCA       90230    226-696-2
20  Levin     Jennifer 1350005    #14 CountNashvilleTN       37203    233-366-3
25-Apr-89   12:30 PM                                                   NUM
```

default to a column width of nine characters, only the first nine characters of these fields are displayed. The rest of the information has been safely imported, however, as demonstrated by adjusting the column widths shown in Figure 3-19.

The next screen, Figure 3-20, shows the last fields in the worksheet. Starting from the right, notice the numeric value that represents the date in column *K;* prior to that is the department code, salary, and in column *H,* the label that contains the phone number.

Compare this data with the information contained in the delimited file. It may be helpful to look at the original dBASE file structure displayed in Figure 3-6.

FIGURE 3–19
/File Import Numbers: Adjusted Column Widths to Show Address Data

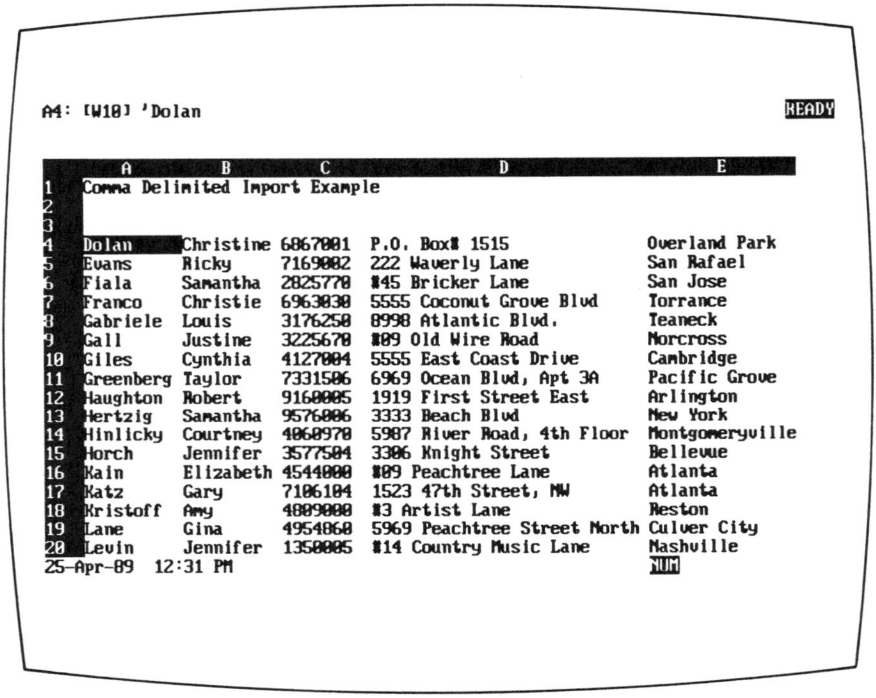

Something is missing. There was a field called DEPENDENTS between the phone number and salary fields, yet this does not appear in the imported worksheet. What happened to it?

Look closely at the delimited file illustration. This field's data consists of either a *T* or a *F,* and there are no quotes around them. According to the 1–2–3 /FILE IMPORT NUMBER rules, if the data is not a number or enclosed in quotes, it is ignored. That's what happened to the *T*s and *F*s; they were ignored.

This loss occurred because the original dBASE field was a Logical field, and when exported into a delimited format, dBASE did not put quotes around the information. If you need this information in your worksheet, you have some options.

FIGURE 3–20
/File Import Numbers: Through *K* Column

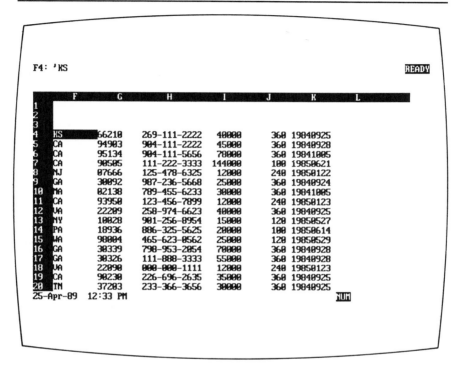

One option is to define the original dBASE as a one-place Character field, and enter *T*s or *F*s (or *Y*s, *N*s, or something else). You would then have put the information into 1–2–3, where you could evaluate the contents of the cell, and recreate the logical true or false contents. This is not a perfect solution, since you must ensure that only the appropriate letters are put in the original dBASE data file and design the structure correctly the first time.

There is another solution, however. You can create a simple dBASE program to solve this and other problems. This is covered in Chapter 6, which is devoted to getting information out of dBASE.

There is another problem with these results. The date is a single large number, but it has no relation to how Lotus maintains dates. To use this number, split it up and evaluate it in terms that 1–2–3 can handle as a date.

The process is a little complex, since you must first convert the contents to a label, break that string into its three component parts, evaluate these pieces as values again, and then use 1–2–3 date functions to reconstruct a date value in Lotus terms.

Rather than explain the process in detail, here is the formula that performs the manipulation. To do this, insert a new column adjacent to the imported date column. In the first row of data, insert the following formula in the new column; this example assumes that Row 4 is the first row of data, the date information is contained in Column *K*, and we are at work in Column *L:*

```
@DATE(@VALUE(@MID(@STRING(K4,0),2,2)),@VALUE(@MID((@STRING(K4,0)
,4,2)),@VALUE(@RIGHT(@STRING(K4,0)2)))
```

This formula is too long to fit on a single line in this book, so remember that the entire formula belongs in Cell L4. Format the cell for the 1–2–3 date format that you prefer, and the correct date should appear in that cell. Now, /COPY the formula and format to the rest of the cells in the column.

The bottom line on delimited-file format imports is that they are quick, easy, and painless. Aside from small matters like adjusting column widths or converting the date information as demonstrated above, there is little that needs to happen to your final worksheet. The key to success is ensuring that there are quotes around the string data in your delimited file— or else the data will be ignored by 1–2–3 and not appear in your worksheet.

/File Import Text with Data Parse

You may not be fortunate enough to have a quoted-string, comma-delimited data file to work with. As mentioned in Part 1, many data files appear in a fixed-length format.

Have no fear; 1–2–3 can handle this as well, although it may seem at times that you will never get the desired result.

This bit of magic is only available in version 2.0 and above. At the end of this section are tips about dealing with fixed-length files for version 1A, but for now, remember that you can't do everything shown here with that version.

We will begin with the same dBASE file, except this time we will export it in the SDF format. As mentioned in Part 1, SDF stands for Standard Data Format and is dBASE's term for a fixed-length format. Figure 3–21 shows the contents of the file we will use. It is in fixed-length format; all the fields line up from row to row, in spite of the fact that each record spans more than one line.

As in the last section, we will use the /FILE IMPORT command, but this time we will select the TEXT option. Figure 3–22 shows the empty worksheet ready for the import to begin.

FIGURE 3–21
/File Import Text; Sample Fixed-Length Record File

```
Dolan      Christine 6867001P.O. Box# 1515              Overland Park      KS6621
0269-111-2222F 40000.0036019040925
Evans      Ricky     7169002222 Waverly Lane            San Rafael         CA9490
3904-111-2222F 45000.0036019040928
Fiala      Samantha  2025770#45 Bricker Lane            San Jose           CA9513
4904-111-5656F 78000.0036019041005
Franco     Christie  69630305555 Coconut Grove Blvd     Torrance           CA9050
5111-222-3333F144000.0010019050621
Gabriele   Louis     31762500998 Atlantic Blvd.         Teaneck            NJ0766
6125-478-6325T 12000.0024019050122
Gall       Justine   3225670#09 Old Wire Road           Norcross           GA3009
2987-236-5668F 25000.0036019040924
Giles      Cynthia   41270045555 East Coast Drive       Cambridge          MA0213
8789-455-6233F 30000.0036019041005
Greenberg Taylor     73315066969 Ocean Blvd, Apt 3A     Pacific Grove      CA9395
0123-456-7899T 12000.0024019050123
Haughton   Robert    91600051919 First Street East      Arlington          VA2220
9258-974-6623T 40000.0036019040925
Hertzig    Samantha  95760063333 Beach Blvd             New York           NY1002
8901-256-8954F 15000.0012019050527
Hinlicky   Courtney  40609705987 River Road, 4th Floor Montgomeryville     PA1893
6886-325-5625F 20000.0010019050614
Horch      Jennifer  35775043306 Knight Street          Bellevue           WA9000
```

FIGURE 3–22
/File Import Text; Worksheet Ready for Import

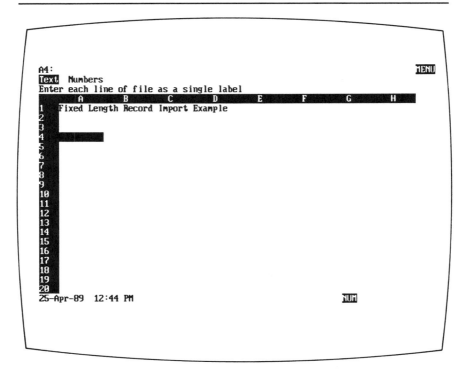

As before, we can override the default .PRN extension that 1–2–3 expects for text files, as demonstrated in Figure 3–23.

Press the Enter Key at this point and you are rewarded with the following results (Figure 3–24):

It all looks wonderful. You can see all the data neatly spaced across the worksheet and everything appears to be fine. All is not well, however.

First, you may notice a problem if you try to make sense out of the columns and the data. Column *A* has the last name, *B* has the first name, *C* has the employee number, *D* has the street address, and so do *E* and *F*. The city information starts to appear somewhere around Column *G*. What goes on here?

FIGURE 3-23
/File Import Text; Entering Import File Name

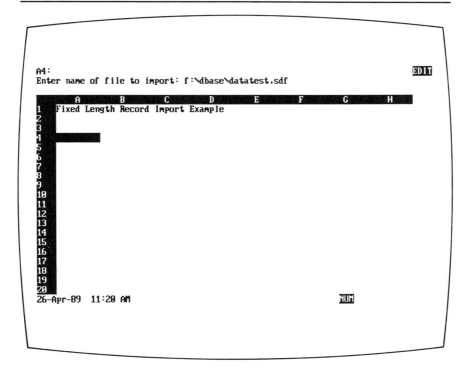

If you look at the upper-left-hand corner of the screen, you will see additional evidence of something amiss. The cursor is on Cell A4, as expected, and the contents are treated as a label, as expected. Look at the contents of the label, however, and you will see what is wrong.

The entire set of data for the first record has been dumped into Cell A4 as a label. Were we to move the cursor over a column to examine Cell B4, we would find that it is empty.

What a mess! How can we split up this information into the appropriate columns? We could /COPY the contents of Column *A* into Columns *B* through *K* and then edit each cell's contents by hand to delete the extraneous data, but that would

FIGURE 3–24
/File Import Text; after Import of Fixed-Length Record Data

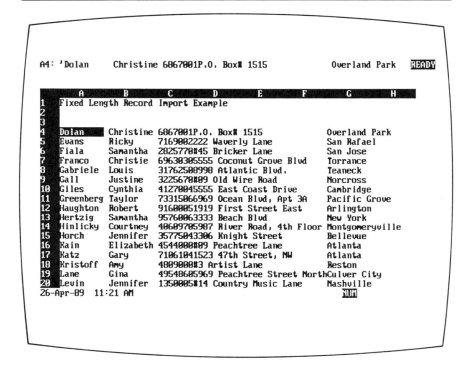

take forever. It would probably be faster to type in all the information from scratch.

If we were working with 1–2–3 version 1A, we would be out of luck. Fortunately, this is one of the 2.x versions, and we have a powerful command at our disposal: /DATA PARSE.

/DATA PARSE involves a number of steps, but it performs a useful service. It allows us to break up the label contents of a cell into multiple columns of properly formatted data. Labels are labels, values are values, and so forth.

Start by placing the cursor on the first cell in the column that contains the data you want to split. Figure 3–25 shows this sample worksheet after selecting the /DATA PARSE command.

FIGURE 3–25
/Data Parse; the Parse Menu

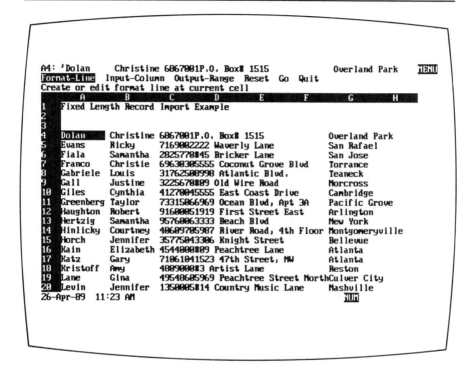

Note that the first option is marked FORMAT-LINE. The first step of the process is to create a template that 1–2–3 can use to break up the data. This is done in two steps; first we will let 1–2–3 make its best guess about how to do it, and then we will edit its choices to match our needs.

After the template is created, we need to mark the range of cells to be treated and the range where we want the results placed. If that is all done correctly, 1–2–3 will handle the data in a snap, splitting it into columns.

Figure 3–26 shows the results of selecting the FORMAT-LINE option. There are two choices: CREATE and EDIT.

When we select CREATE, 1–2–3 goes and looks at the first row of data and attempts to determine where each field starts

FIGURE 3–26
/Data Parse Format-Line; Create and Edit Options

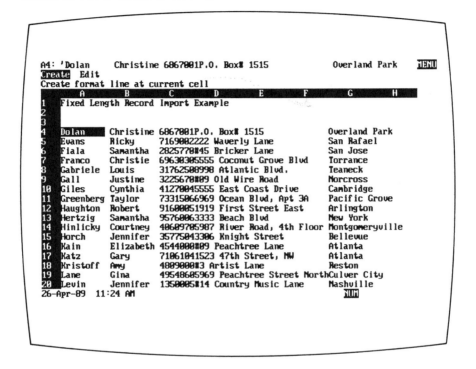

and stops. It then inserts a temporary line in the worksheet and enters a template called the FORMAT LINE that governs how the line will be parsed into the component columns.

In Figure 3–27, you can see the guesses that 1–2–3 made with the sample file.

Notice the results. The L symbols mark the points where the program thinks a label field starts. The $>$ symbols show the continuation of the field. A V symbol indicates the start of a value field, and an $*$ indicates that there is blank space below. The blank space can be used by the prior block if needed. 1–2–3 can also use two other symbols: T and D, which represent time and date blocks respectively.

FIGURE 3–27
/Data Parse Format-Line; Results of Create Option

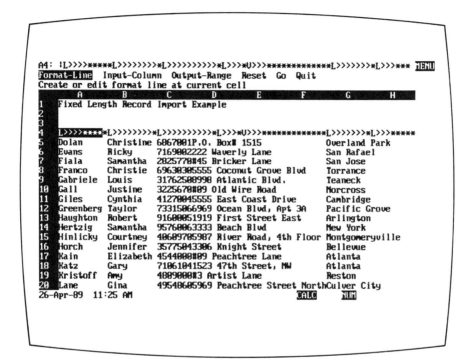

Looking at Figure 3–27, Lotus has guessed well but imperfectly. For example, the last and first name fields have been handled appropriately, but there are problems in the address field.

For example, the "P.O." and "Box" data are not supposed to be separate fields. The "1515" box number is also part of the address field; it's not a separate numeric value. The zip code must be a label, not a value. We need to make some changes to 1–2–3's guesses. For this operation, we select the FORMAT-LINE EDIT option, as shown in Figure 3–28:

The FORMAT-LINE EDIT option behaves differently from any other edit procedure in 1–2–3. Instead of working on the sec-

FIGURE 3–28
/Data Parse Format-Line; Results of Edit Option

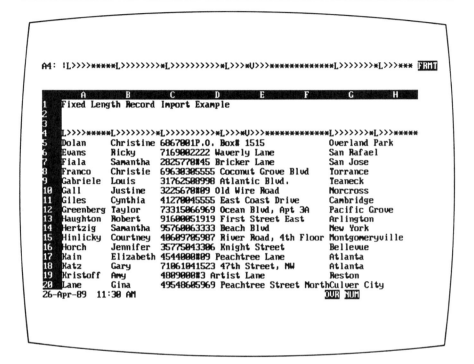

ond line of the screen, you work right on the spreadsheet. Furthermore, when you reach the right edge of the screen, the worksheet scrolls so that you can see the rest of the line and the columns of data below.

As you edit the Format Line, there is another symbol at your disposal. The S character in the Format Line signals that the data below should be skipped or, in other words, dropped during the parsing process. This is handy, since you can easily edit out extraneous fields from your import file at this step.

Figure 3–29 shows the results of our changes, with the modified Format Line reflecting the true structure of the data file. While they cannot be seen in this screen, additional changes were made to the rest of this line.

FIGURE 3–29
/Data Parse Format-Line; the Edited Line

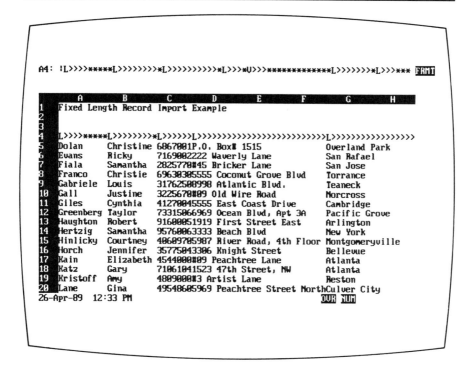

The next step is to show 1–2–3 which cells to change. For this task, define the column of cells as shown in Figure 3–30.

Be sure of two details in this step. First, start the column definition with the Format Line. Then, include all the cells in the column you want to parse. Do not include more than one column. This should not be a problem, since the /FILE IMPORT TEXT places all the data in one column, but be careful that you stick to that column.

All that remains is selecting a place for your new cells to go. Figure 3–31 illustrates how you can point to the upper left-hand corner of the range you wish to fill.

In this example, the output range is placed just below the last row brought in by /FILE IMPORT TEXT. Note for future ref-

FIGURE 3–30
/Data Parse Input-Column; the *A* Column Is Selected

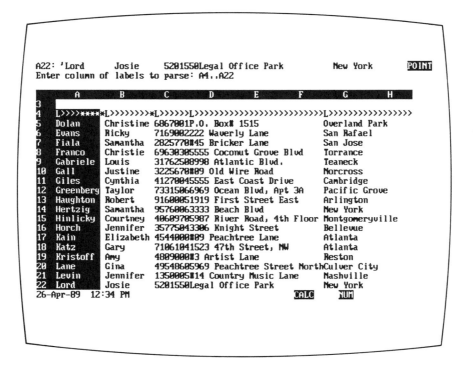

erence, however, that nothing says that you must put it in this position. In fact, you can specify the output range right over the input range, and it will still work. The advantage of such an approach is that it uses as little worksheet real estate as possible, and it reuses the rows taken up by the imported data. On the other hand, if you make a mistake, you will have overwritten the source data, and you will have to clear the range and repeat the import to try again. The final results of our parsing efforts are shown in Figure 3–32.

The end result is like the /FILE IMPORT NUMBERS example of the last section. The main difference is that we had to work harder to get to this point.

FIGURE 3–31
/Data Parse Output-Range

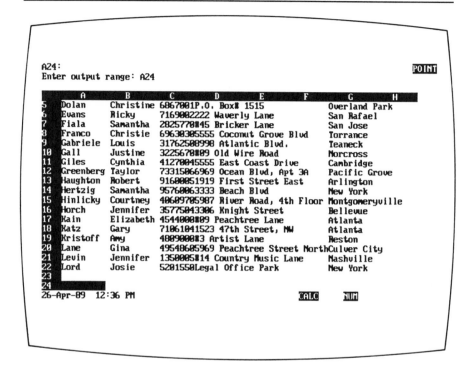

There are some significant similarities and differences between the two approaches. In the /FILE IMPORT NUMBERS, numeric strings such as employee number and zip code came in as labels without our intervention. On the other hand, 1–2–3 took these fields as values in the /DATA PARSE procedure, and we had to manually edit the Format Line to correct this mistaken impression.

The /FILE IMPORT NUMBERS approach dropped the logical DEPENDENTS field data since it was not in quotes, but through the Format Line, we were able to save the data and enter it as a label in its own column.

FIGURE 3–32
/Data Parse; Final Import Results

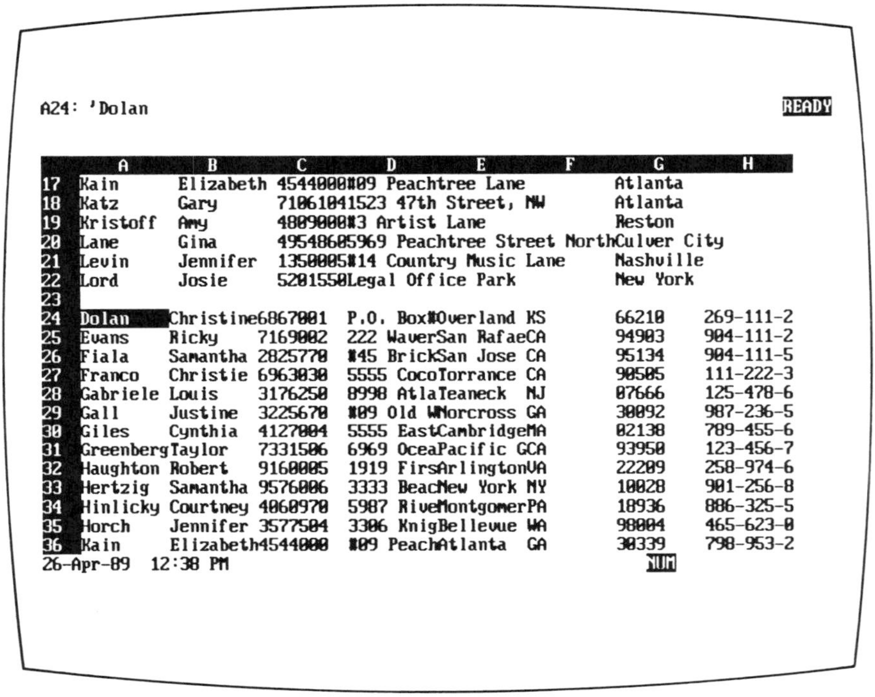

```
A24: 'Dolan                                                    READY

      A        B        C        D        E        F      G        H
17 Kain     Elizabeth 4544000#09 Peachtree Lane         Atlanta
18 Katz     Gary      71061041523 47th Street, NW       Atlanta
19 Kristoff Amy       4809000#3 Artist Lane             Reston
20 Lane     Gina      49548605969 Peachtree Street NorthCulver City
21 Levin    Jennifer  1350005#14 Country Music Lane     Nashville
22 Lord     Josie     5201558Legal Office Park          New York
23
24 Dolan    Christine6867001  P.O. Box#Overland KS      66210   269-111-2
25 Evans    Ricky     7169002  222 WaverSan RafaeCA     94903   904-111-2
26 Fiala    Samantha  2825770  #45 BrickSan Jose CA     95134   904-111-5
27 Franco   Christie  6963030  5555 CocoTorrance CA     90505   111-222-3
28 Gabriele Louis     3176250  8990 AtlaTeaneck  NJ     07666   125-478-6
29 Gall     Justine   3225670  #09 Old WNorcross GA     30092   987-236-5
30 Giles    Cynthia   4127004  5555 EastCambridgeMA     02138   709-455-6
31 GreenbergTaylor    7331506  6969 OceaPacific GCA     93950   123-456-7
32 Haughton Robert    9160005  1919 FirsArlingtonVA     22209   258-974-6
33 Hertzig  Samantha  9576006  3333 BeacNew York NY     10028   901-256-8
34 Hinlicky Courtney  4060970  5907 RiveMontgomerPA     18936   886-325-5
35 Horch    Jennifer  3577504  3306 KnigBellevue WA     98004   465-623-0
36 Kain     Elizabeth4544000   #09 PeachAtlanta  GA     30339   798-953-2
26-Apr-89  12:38 PM                                      NUM
```

Neither approach left us with a date field that 1–2–3 could use, but we have a formula that performs the conversion for us, as demonstrated at the end of the /FILE IMPORT NUMBERS section. We can use the same approach by bringing in the same data as a value with the Format Line in /DATA PARSE, and then using the same formula as before on the results.

/FILE IMPORT WITH 1–2–3 VERSION 1A

Again, the /FILE IMPORT NUMBERS works the same for version 1A. This version of 1–2–3 has no /DATA PARSE option, however, to go along with /FILE IMPORT TEXT.

There are a number of ways around this limitation. One way is to create your original data file in a structure that works with /FILE IMPORT NUMBERS. Remember that /FILE IMPORT NUMBERS can parse on either commas or spaces as delimiters.

If you do not have this option available, then you will need to turn to a separate utility for help. In Part 3, you will find a sample BASIC program that you can modify to transform most fixed-length record files into comma-delimited files. If you do not want to have to confront program code directly, you can find public-domain and commercial programs that can do the conversion for you. Some examples are described in Part 4.

SUMMARY

Between the conversion and /FILE IMPORT options, you have a number of powerful ways to bring outside data into your spreadsheets. Once converted or imported, you can proceed to massage and analyze the data using all the power of 1–2–3.

The key to a successful import is understanding how best to organize your information before you bring it in, a task best addressed when you are looking at how to bring it out of the source application. For example, you may find it more useful to export a dBASE file as a comma-delimited file rather than use the Lotus Translate facility. Also, consider how you bring data out of 1–2–3 spreadsheets for use in other programs, which is covered in Chapter 4.

CHAPTER 4

___

MOVING DATA OUT
OF LOTUS 1–2–3

___

It is likely that more people start with 1–2–3 that any other program that runs on PCs and compatibles. It has repeatedly proven valuable in thousands of businesses. Like its forebear, VisiCalc, it is a program that costs less than a few hundred dollars, but its use may justify spending thousands for a computer on which to use it.

There is a common trap for anyone who encounters a miracle product; you risk becoming a wild-eyed fanatic who sees how the product can be applied to any problem that ever plagued a business or organization. Your pet program becomes a magic bullet that can whittle the largest tasks down to size.

Lotus 1–2–3 devotees are no more immune to this delusion than any other group of users. Witness the templates you may have seen over the years—that format mail-merge letters, that maintain full-function accounting systems, or that even play blackjack.

There comes a time, however, when even the most dyed-in-the-wool Lotus lover has to admit that perhaps 1–2–3 is not the optimum program to maintain certain types of information or to produce certain kinds of output. How many people are truly satisfied with PrintGraph, for example?

This chapter shows how to get information out of 1–2–3 and make it available to other programs. Some methods harbor hidden pitfalls, and there are some simple tricks for beating the system nearly every time.

TRANSLATE REVISITED

The most obvious method for moving data out of 1–2–3 is to use the same Translate utility discussed in the last chapter.

As with bringing data into 1–2–3, there are some circumstances where no translation is required. If you are starting with a Lotus 1–2–3 Release 2.x version, you need not do anything to the file to use it with Symphony 1.1 or 1.2, since these programs can read the 1–2–3 files directly.

Moving to Older Versions

If you try to move worksheet data to older versions of Lotus programs, namely 1–2–3 Release 1A or Symphony 1.0, use the Translate utility.

Translate offers copious advice about the limitations of its capabilities in this area. In general, problems arise from the restrictions inherent in older programs. Both Symphony and 1–2–3, in the original versions, did not manage memory the same way that the new products do; it is possible for a version 2.x worksheet to fail to load when translated for use with Release 1A.

There are other limitations. Release 1A only supports worksheets that extend up to cell address IV2048, while 2.x can work with addresses far outside that range. The Translate screen warns that "formulas that refer to cells [beyond that lower right limit] will cause unpredictable answers."

Version 2.x also contains new formulas that were not found in Release 1A. If the Translate utility finds one of them, it fills the cell with a warning message, and you must then refer to the source worksheet to see what was lost.

The advantage of using Translate for this task is that both data and formulas are moved safely across—if you are clear of the above limitations. There are other methods to move data out of one version's worksheet and into another, but this is the only one that preserves the underlying formulas.

By the way, it might appear that there is a second method to convert a worksheet from 2.x to Release 1A—one that does not require Translate. When you use the /FILE SAVE command, version 2.x assumes that you want to save the file in .WK1 (version 2.x) format. However, you can enter a file name with the .WKS extension instead. Unfortunately, the file will not be saved in 1A format. The only way to get from a 2.x worksheet to a 1A worksheet is to leave 1–2–3 and start up the separate Translate utility.

Moving to dBASE

Translate also handles conversions between 1–2–3 files and dBASE. The restrictions are severe here, however. To start, you must use a file that is strictly a 1–2–3 database. This means that there can be no formulas: only cells containing labels or explicit values.

Each column in the range must have a label in the first row, and the contents of each label must begin with a letter. The second row must have data in every cell (or at least a format definition). Each row from then on may contain some empty cells, but the data for each field must appear in its column.

The columns must be wide enough to display the widest contents of the cells in that column. If not, the data will be truncated. This might not always be a hindrance, since there are times when you want to trim off a field to only the first few characters.

If you are creating a dBASE II file, you are limited to 32 columns of data. dBASE III can have as many as 128 fields per database, so you may use as many columns (*A* through *EX,* for example), which is more than most spreadsheets contain. The first-row labels must match the dBASE field name limitations—such as no spaces allowed.

Fortunately, you are not limited to bringing in whole spreadsheets with this Translate option. As shown in Figure 4–1, you have a choice of converting either an entire worksheet or just a named range.

Note that the conditions listed above apply in either case, and that the range must be named—you cannot simply define a range with cell limits.

FIGURE 4–1
1–2–3 Translate: 1–2–3 to dBASE Range Option

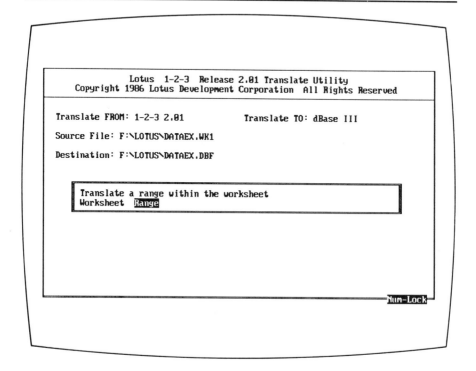

In total, Translate does not offer much flexibility for data conversion into dBASE formats. If you want to read data into certain fields, or don't want to name columns with the dBASE field names, or don't want to create a new and separate dBASE table with every conversion, then you might want a different approach.

1–2–3 to DIF via Translate

The Translate utility also will create a DIF file from a worksheet. There are a few limitations with this approach.

First, the conversion is applied to an entire worksheet; there is no range option—as with dBASE conversions. According to the Translate prompt, you must use a worksheet that has been /FILE SAVED, not just /FILE EXTRACTED, to work correctly with the Translate to DIF feature.

The other limitation is no choice about a row-wise or column-wise DIF table. 1–2–3 only creates the column-wise variety. This means that if the target program needs the data in a row-wise orientation, you must either transpose your cell data before converting it or you must rely on the receiving program to reverse the order.

Given the large storage and processing overhead required for DIF files, it may be better to use another data-exchange technique if there is an option available.

TIPS AND TRICKS FOR TEXT FILES FROM 1–2–3

As described in Part 1, the two most common data-exchange formats are standard text-file formats: fixed-length record, and quoted-string comma-delimited. If you shake your head in wonder because Lotus seems to have ignored these entirely, you will be comforted knowing that thousands of others are also amazed.

But you don't need to let the 1–2–3 programmers leave you out in left field; there are some easy steps to follow for creating text files from worksheets, without the aid of some slick conversion utility that might tie your hands with unnecessary restrictions.

Fixed-Length Record Format

Let's start with the easy one. A fixed-length record file from a 1–2–3 spreadsheet is perhaps the easiest trick not in the book.

Think about what a fixed-length file looks like. Look back at the example in Part 1. You may see a striking resemblance between this file format and the typical row and column format of spreadsheet printed reports.

That's the clue. If only we had an electronic way to clip that information out of the body of a spreadsheet printout and stick it in a file, we would be all set. And, of course, that's what we'll do. You can use the 1–2–3 /PRINT DISK option to send a report to a disk file instead of your printer. There are other restrictions and preparations involved, but none are terribly taxing.

The main limitation is that you may not export files that have records longer than 240 characters. The main reason for this limitation is that it is the longest line length supported by 1–2–3 version 2.x between its minimum left margin and maximum right margin.

The second problem is that you really do not want to include any rows that contain data in a format other than what you want in the final file. Ideally, the data should be consistent, with the same sort of information stored in each cell of a column and the rows representing the individual records.

Don't worry if you have subheadings sprinkled throughout your spreadsheet; these are easy to clean up with text-file editor. The techniques for editing text files are covered in Part 3, but all you need to do for extraneous lines such as subheads is to delete them. (Even the dreaded EDLIN will work for that task.)

Aside from these two considerations, there are no other restrictions. You can adjust column width to suit the destination program's requirements for field length. You can set a column's width to zero to hide it so that its data does not appear in the data file. If necessary, cell contents will be truncated to fit.

Here is a small problem: if a cell that contains a label is too narrow for its contents, and the adjacent cell is empty, the label will spill into the empty cell. This extra portion of the label will then appear in the next field in the data file, possibly creating problems when you perform the data import at the other end. To avoid this, make certain that all blank cells are filled with a label containing a single space. This will prevent any spillage without adding extraneous data to any fields. To make this technique work, however, you need a number of careful preparations. The first item to fix is ensuring that there are no global printer setup strings defined for 1–2–3. Figure 4–2 shows the screen displayed after issuing the command: /WORKSHEET GLOBAL DEFAULT PRINTER SETUP.

FIGURE 4–2
1–2–3—/Worksheet Global Default Printer Setup

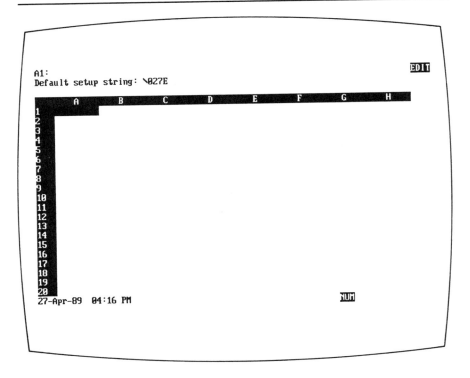

You may find different characters displayed here, depending on how your program is installed. The setup characters are used to send a printer command, such as to shift into condensed print, or to use letter-quality print, or to change to number of lines per inch. Erase all characters from this line so that these commands do not become part of the data file. You can erase them later from the file if they get in there, but it is easier to prevent them in the first place. If your copy of 1–2–3 does not have a printer setup string defined, don't be alarmed; most don't have it.

Also, don't worry about writing down the characters you erase if you find a setup string stored in the default settings. As long as you do not UPDATE the default settings (/GLOBAL

DEFAULT UPDATE is on the same menu as /GLOBAL DEFAULT PRINTER) after you change them, they will be restored to the original values next time you reload 1–2–3.

The other changes happen after you go into the /PRINT command option. Before you can get to the settings, however, you must make an important choice on the way in. Figure 4–3 shows the options offered after selecting /Print from the main menu.

Most people never choose anything from this menu except PRINTER. The FILE option is identical in its operation with one exception; it sends its stream of information not to a printer but to a disk file. 1–2–3 creates a text file with the same name as the worksheet except that it has a .PRN extension.

FIGURE 4–3
/Print

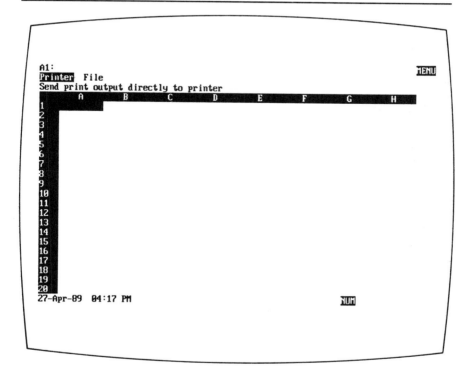

Even without getting into data-exchange issues, this option can be useful. Say you have a worksheet that you need for a presentation, and you have printed it on a dot-matrix printer until you have all the edits correct. You want to print it on someone else's printer, but they are too busy or don't have 1–2–3 on their machine.

Print your file to a floppy disk instead of to the printer. For discussion's sake, let's assume you called the file PRESENT.PRN on the floppy disk. Then, take the disk to the other person's machine, and at the DOS prompt, simply type:

```
COPY A:PRESENT.PRN LPT1
```

and press the Enter Key. Your report is on the second machine's printer quickly and easily without loading 1–2–3.

FIGURE 4–4
/Print File Menu, with Options Highlighted

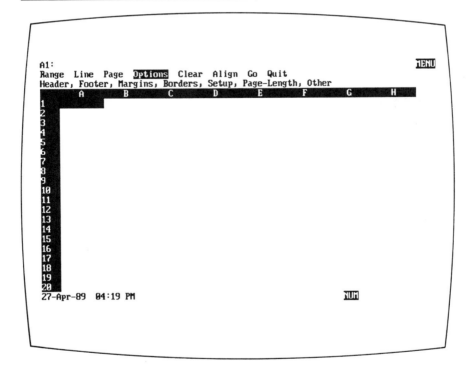

This works because in the first step, you rerouted the print stream to a disk file instead of the printer. It was captured there until you took it to another computer and then simply copied it to the attached printer. In other words, the floppy disk acted like a bucket to hold the letters and numbers so you could carry them from one computer and printer to another.

We use the same feature to create our fixed-length record file, but we need to ensure that we only get data in the file. After you select /PRINT FILE, choose the Options menu from the main Print menu as illustrated in Figure 4–4.

There are three areas that need to be addressed under the Options menu: Margins, Setup, and Other.

Figure 4–5 shows the Margins menu. Select this and change the left margin to zero. This will eliminate any extra

FIGURE 4–5
/Print File Options Margins

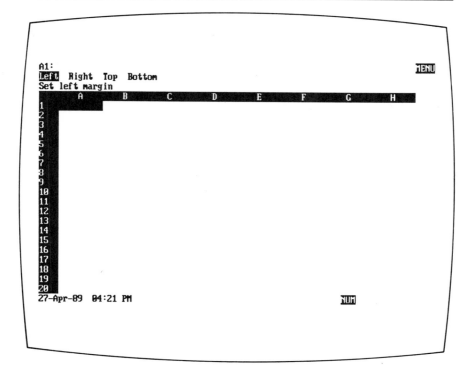

blank spaces from the first data field that would appear if there was left margin in the print settings.

Set the right margin as wide as the number of characters in each fixed-length record. Remember that this is the number of characters, not the number of fields or columns. Also remember that the maximum is 240.

Next, check that there is no printer setup string, which would appear under the SETUP command on the Options menu. (See Figure 4–6.)

The same instructions follow here as for the global default setup string. The only difference is that this setup string gets saved with the worksheet. If there is a string here, it will be lost if you subsequently save the worksheet under the same

FIGURE 4–6
/Print File Options Setup

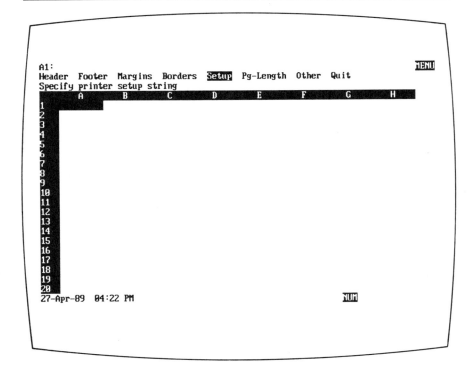

name. If you find a setup string here and are not comfortable recreating it on your own, either copy it down and reenter it later, or ensure that you do not save the worksheet after you remove the setup codes.

There is one other type of printer control command that you need to watch out for, but it isn't used all that often. In the 2.x versions of 1–2–3, you can embed printer commands using the double-bar (‖) prefix in a cell. For example, the cell contents ‖\027 embeds an Escape character at that point. Ensure that there are no cells of this sort within your print range, or later you will have to omit the extra characters before your data file works properly.

The third and final preparation is to issue the /PRINT FILE OPTIONS OTHER UNFORMATTED command, shown in Figure 4–7.

FIGURE 4–7
/Print File Options Other Unformatted

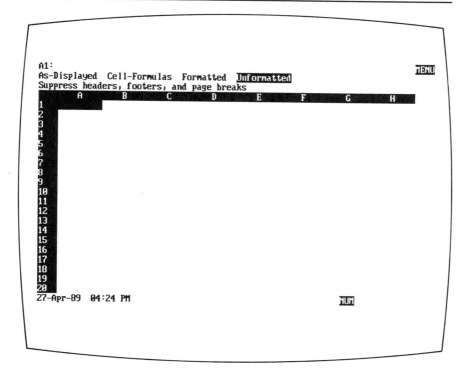

This causes the spreadsheet to be printed without headers, footers, page breaks, or top and bottom margins. It eliminates all extraneous rows from the printed report, so that you only get the rows of data you have specified from the spreadsheet.

Now we have set the margins appropriately, eliminated any setup strings, and selected unformatted output. The remaining steps are the typical ones used to create any 1–2–3 report. Specify the range to print, which are the rows that contain the data for the fixed-length data file, and then tell the program to Go.

You can use the 1–2–3 /DATA SORT command to group the rows. Then, use the print range to select a portion of the total rows available in your spreadsheet.

When the dust settles and the disk-access light goes off, you will have a perfect fixed-length record format file on your disk—ready to be poured into some deserving program's files.

Comma-Delimited Files from 1–2–3

It's more work to get a comma-delimited file out of a spreadsheet, but it can be done. The first step is to put in the commas. One easy way to do this is to insert columns between the data columns, fill them with a label that contains a single comma, and adjust their widths down to a single character.

Putting quotes around the label fields is more difficult, but perhaps the best method is to write a small macro that edits each cell in a column. It goes to the beginning of the label, inserts quotes, jumps to the end of the label, inserts quotes again, then advances to the next cell. It may take some time to add all these quotes, but it can be done. Ensure that the extra characters do not cause the contents of a cell to spill beyond the column width. If one of the characters lost is a quote, there will be dire results when you get to the import step.

The other problem with this method is that it can leave lots of spaces between field contents and commas. Some programs are more tolerant of extra spaces than others. If you have a program that objects, use the search and replace feature of any text editor to strip away the extra spaces. See Part 3 for more details.

Figure 4–8 shows a sample worksheet that is set up to create a comma-delimited file.

The results are displayed in Figure 4–9. They were produced by using the DOS TYPE command:

The file has a fixed-length structure, but it has the appropriate comma delimiters and quoted strings. As mentioned above, some programs will put up with the extra spaces better than others, but at worst, you will need to do only a little editing to put this file in perfect shape.

FIGURE 4–8
1–2–3 Sample Spreadsheet to Create a Delimited File

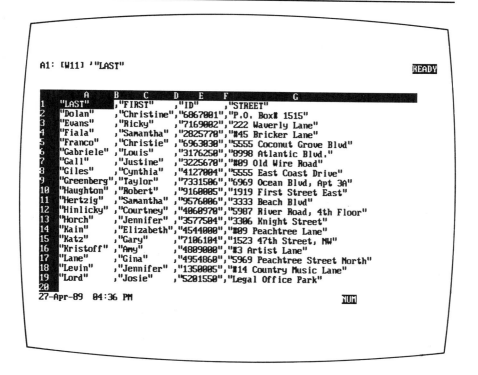

FIGURE 4–9
1–2–3 Exported Comma-Delimited File

```
"LAST"      ,"FIRST"    ,"ID"      ,"STREET"
"Dolan"     ,"Christine","6867001","P.O. Box# 1515"
"Evans"     ,"Ricky"    ,"7169002","222 Waverly Lane"
"Fiala"     ,"Samantha" ,"2825770","#45 Bricker Lane"
"Franco"    ,"Christie" ,"6963030","5555 Coconut Grove Blvd"
"Gabriele"  ,"Louis"    ,"3176250","8998 Atlantic Blvd."
"Gall"      ,"Justine"  ,"3225670","#09 Old Wire Road"
"Giles"     ,"Cynthia"  ,"4127004","5555 East Coast Drive"
"Greenberg" ,"Taylor"   ,"7331506","6969 Ocean Blvd, Apt 3A"
"Haughton"  ,"Robert"   ,"9160005","1919 First Street East"
"Hertzig"   ,"Samantha" ,"9576006","3333 Beach Blvd"
"Hinlicky"  ,"Courtney" ,"4060970","5987 River Road, 4th Floor"
"Horch"     ,"Jennifer" ,"3577504","3306 Knight Street"
"Kain"      ,"Elizabeth","4544000","#09 Peachtree Lane"
"Katz"      ,"Gary"     ,"7106104","1523 47th Street, NW"
"Kristoff"  ,"Amy"      ,"4809000","#3 Artist Lane"
"Lane"      ,"Gina"     ,"4954860","5969 Peachtree Street North"
"Levin"     ,"Jennifer" ,"1350005","#14 Country Music Lane"
"Lord"      ,"Josie"    ,"5201550","Legal Office Park"
```

Other Choices

If you don't want these complications to produce the comma-delimited format or the fixed-length record format, do not despair. Part 4 of this book covers some remarkable programs that solve these problems easily and gracefully.

SUMMARY

Lotus 1–2–3 leaves much to be desired in its ability to move data out to other programs, but there is sufficient flexibility in the print-to-disk feature that you can work around many of the limitations. The other most popular MS-DOS® productivity program is dBASE. It has its strengths and weaknesses in data exchange; they are covered in the next two chapters.

CHAPTER 5

MOVING DATA INTO
dBASE III AND IV

It's time for a short standardized test in the form of a simple analogy question. Spreadsheets are to Lotus 1–2–3 as database files are to:

a. a file cabinet
b. the public-domain file-card program that someone gave you
c. the shoe box of receipts on top of your bureau
d. dBASE

The correct answer is *d;* anyone with a different answer is invited to enroll in Computer and Society 151: "Popular PC Programs of the Late 1980s."

dBASE is neither the fastest nor the most powerful, nor the easiest database management product on the market today. But, it is one of the most widely used programs in any category. As a result, when talking about moving data into a database program, chances are excellent that dBASE is involved.

This chapter explores the capabilities and problems of moving data into dBASE, and the next one looks at moving data out of dBASE. There are not many commands involved, but there are some significant limitations and work-arounds that you need to know.

Many of you may not have upgraded to dBASE IV, since dBASE III probably still meets your needs. dBASE IV offers a superset of dBASE III's capabilities, so you can do anything in dBASE IV that is done in dBASE III. There are some things that dBASE IV can do that dBASE III can't, however. So, for the next two chapters, the focus is on dBASE III with information on the extra capabilities of dBASE IV.

While these chapters focus on dBASE, don't skip them just because you use a different program, such as RBase, KMan2, or Paradox. While the commands may be different, the general principles apply to other database management products.

THE dBASE IMPORT COMMAND

Starting with its earliest dBASE II incarnations back in the dark ages of the CP/M operating system, dBASE has been a leader. One major characteristic of leaders is that they do not have to follow. As a result, Ashton-Tate has been comfortable letting other producers worry about products that read and write dBASE data files, rather than build conversion programs into dBASE to read other formats that automatically create .DBF files.

There is one concession made in dBASE III: the IMPORT command. This command allows you to read in a PFS:file database and directly create a dBASE file as a result.

This feature makes sense, since PFS:file has been one of the most popular beginner databases. The beginner status is bestowed because it is easy to use but lacks power. It can only manage single files, which is the digital equivalent of a box of 3 by 5 index cards. Most people quickly outgrow the limitations of these programs.

Figure 5–1 shows how to execute the IMPORT command from the dBASE ASSIST mode. It makes the entire process quick and easy:

You can also execute the command from the dot-prompt mode using this syntax:

```
IMPORT FROM filename TYPE PFS
```

where "filename" is the name of a PFS:file data file.

FIGURE 5–1
dBASE ASSIST Mode: Import

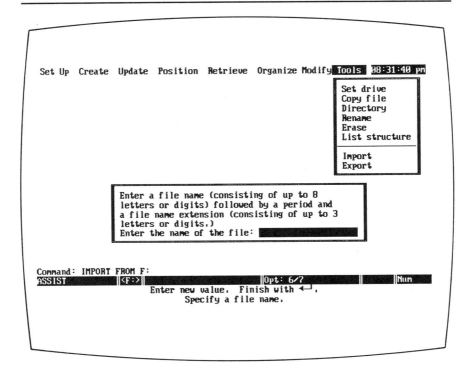

The usefulness of this feature is limited, however. In my tests, the resulting dBASE table is not too valuable. The field names were lost, and they were replaced with FIELD01 through FIELD12. The length of each field appeared to vary randomly, ranging from a low of 69 characters to a high of 254 characters for the 12th field. Most fields were defined as between 70 and 75 characters long.

These long fields may lead you to an interesting conclusion. Yes, the test-data file contained numeric, date, and logical fields and simple character fields. The IMPORT command, however, created a dBASE file where all the fields were defined as characters.

The end result is that the IMPORT facility can get the information into a dBASE file, but you will need to redefine the fields and massage the file to achieve a workable database.

dBASE IV offers four more options for import, three of which relate to other Ashton-Tate products. Figure 5–2 shows an equivalent screen in dBASE IV listing all five options.

There are some important details about using the dBASE IV import feature. Use the following file-name extensions: .wk1 for 1–2–3, .fw2 for Framework II, .rpd for RapidFile, and .db2 for dBASE II. This last extension requires renaming of the dBASE II file before you import it; dBASE IV uses the same .dbf extension, and it objects if you import from a filename

FIGURE 5–2
dBASE IV Import Options

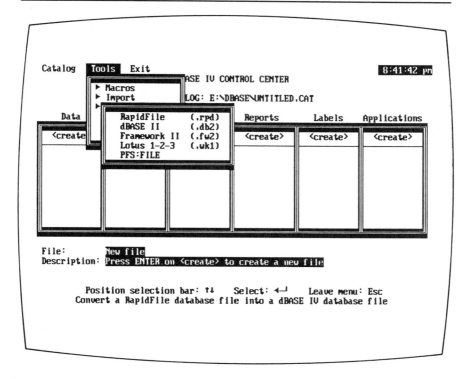

Catalog **Tools** Exit   8:41:42 pm

▸ Macros   ASE IV CONTROL CENTER
▸ Import   LOG: E:\DBASE\UNTITLED.CAT

Data   RapidFile   (.rpd)   Reports   Labels   Applications
            dBASE II   (.db2)
<create   Framework II (.fw2)   <create>   <create> <create>
            Lotus 1-2-3 (.wk1)
            PFS:FILE

File: New file
Description: Press ENTER on <create> to create a new file

Position selection bar: ↑↓   Select: ←┘   Leave menu: Esc
Convert a RapidFile database file into a dBASE IV database file

with that extension. In all cases, dBASE will create a new table with the same file name as the import file—but with the .DBF extension. Also note that dBASE IV can convert dBASE III files without any translation command on the fly. You also can issue the IMPORT command from the dBASE dot prompt just as in dBASE III.

IMPORTING FILES INTO dBASE WITH APPEND

For dBASE III, the dBASE APPEND command works better than IMPORT. The major difference is that dBASE will not create

FIGURE 5–3
Test .WKS Spreadsheet under Lotus, Left Portion

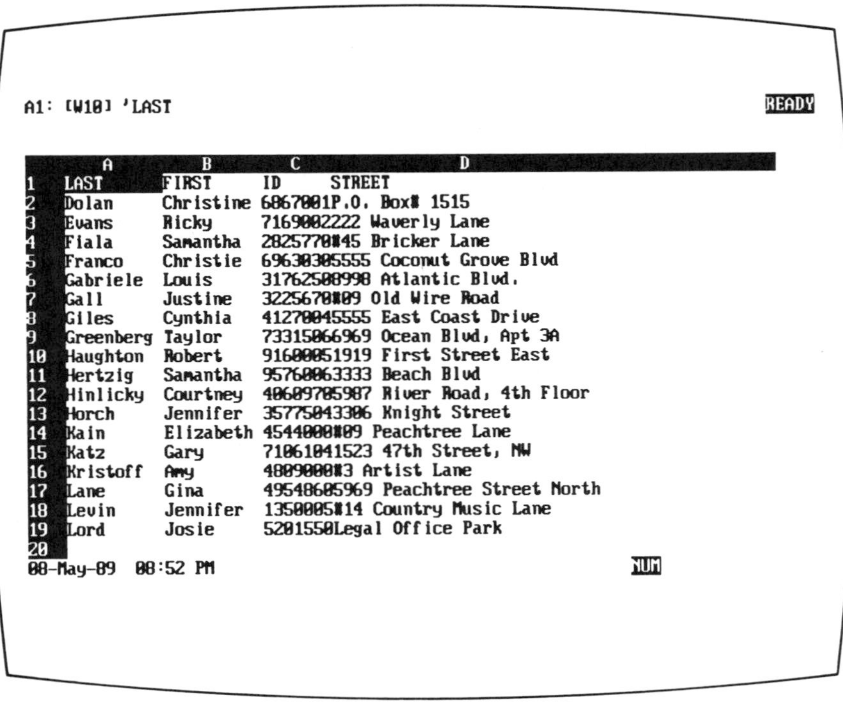

```
A1: [W10] 'LAST                                                    READY

         A          B          C        D
    1   LAST      FIRST      ID      STREET
    2   Dolan     Christine  6867001P.O. Box# 1515
    3   Evans     Ricky      7169002222 Waverly Lane
    4   Fiala     Samantha   2825770#45 Bricker Lane
    5   Franco    Christie   6963030555 Coconut Grove Blvd
    6   Gabriele  Louis      3176250099 Atlantic Blvd.
    7   Gall      Justine    3225670#09 Old Wire Road
    8   Giles     Cynthia    4127004555 East Coast Drive
    9   Greenberg Taylor     7331506696 Ocean Blvd, Apt 3A
   10   Haughton  Robert     9160005191 First Street East
   11   Hertzig   Samantha   9576006333 Beach Blvd
   12   Hinlicky  Courtney   4060970598 River Road, 4th Floor
   13   Horch     Jennifer   3577504330 Knight Street
   14   Kain      Elizabeth  4544000#09 Peachtree Lane
   15   Katz      Gary       7106104152 47th Street, NW
   16   Kristoff  Amy        4009000#3 Artist Lane
   17   Lane      Gina       4954060596 Peachtree Street North
   18   Levin     Jennifer   1350005#14 Country Music Lane
   19   Lord      Josie      5201550Legal Office Park
   20
08-May-89  08:52 PM                                              NUM
```

the file structure as it does under IMPORT. You must have a structure created in advance, and this structure must precisely match the data file you are trying to read.

This restriction can lead to difficulties, but they can be overcome. The final section of this chapter covers some of the most common problems and the techniques used to work around the pitfalls.

For the moment, however, let's turn to the APPEND command and see how it works with various data-exchange file formats. In general, the command works in a similar way with a variety of options. The command syntax is:

```
APPEND FROM filename TYPE filetype
```

FIGURE 5–4
Test .WKS Spreadsheet under Lotus, Right Portion

```
I2: [W1] 'F                                                          READY

        E               F  G     H          I     J     K    L              M
1  CITY                 STZIP  PHONE              DSALARY    DEPAH IREDATE
2  Overland Park        KS66210269-111-2222F      40000   360  19040925
3  San Rafael           CA94903904-111-2222F      45000   360  19040928
4  San Jose             CA95134904-111-5656F      78000   360  19041005
5  Torrance             CA90505111-222-3333F     144000   100  19050621
6  Teaneck              NJ07666125-478-6325T      12000   240  19050122
7  Norcross             GA30092987-236-5668F      25000   360  19040924
8  Cambridge            MA02138789-455-6233F      30000   360  19041005
9  Pacific Grove        CA93950123-456-7899T      12000   240  19050123
10 Arlington            VA22209258-974-6623T      40000   360  19040925
11 New York             NY10028901-256-8954F      15000   120  19050527
12 Montgomeryville      PA18936886-325-5625F      20000   100  19050614
13 Bellevue             WA98004465-623-0562F      25000   120  19050529
14 Atlanta              GA30339790-953-2054F      70000   360  19040928
15 Atlanta              GA30326111-888-3333F      55000   360  19040928
16 Reston               VA22090000-000-1111T      12000   240  19050123
17 Culver City          CA90230226-696-2635F      35000   360  19040925
18 Nashville            TN37203233-366-3656F      30000   360  19040925
19 New York             NY10011745-632-5665T      20000   360  19040925
20
08-May-89   08:53 PM                                                NUM
```

Remember that this command works only when you are reading the data into an existing .DBF format that exactly matches the data-file format.

Append Type WKS

dBASE III can read data directly from a Lotus 1–2–3 Release 1A .WKS file—provided that the data is arranged in rows and columns. Each record must appear in its own row with the spreadsheet columns holding the field information. These requirements are similar to the Lotus Translate utility.

Unlike the Lotus Translate utility, you need not have the field names in the first row nor do you need data in every cell

FIGURE 5–5
Sample .DBF Structure

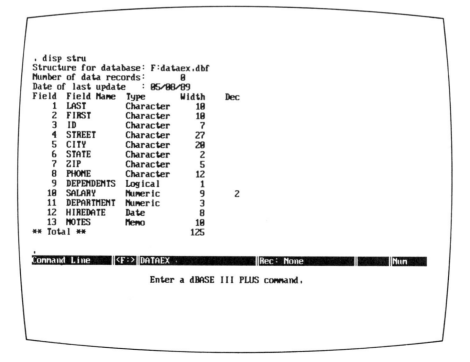

```
. disp stru
Structure for database: F:dataex.dbf
Number of data records:        8
Date of last update   : 05/08/89
Field  Field Name  Type       Width    Dec
    1  LAST        Character     10
    2  FIRST       Character     10
    3  ID          Character      7
    4  STREET      Character     27
    5  CITY        Character     28
    6  STATE       Character      2
    7  ZIP         Character      5
    8  PHONE       Character     12
    9  DEPENDENTS  Logical        1
   10  SALARY      Numeric        9      2
   11  DEPARTMENT  Numeric        3
   12  HIREDATE    Date           8
   13  NOTES       Memo          10
** Total **                    125
```

```
Command Line     <F:> DATAEX          Rec: None          Num
```

Enter a dBASE III PLUS command.

of the first record. You need some data, however, in the first row and column of your spreadsheet. The Lotus Translate utility offers some advantages over dBASE APPEND, including its ability to create the .DBF structure and to work with both Release 1A and 2.x spreadsheets.

The next two screens (Figures 5–3 and 5–4) show the test worksheet as it is displayed on the screen in 1–2–3.

Note the cells in Column *I* contain the label values of *T* or *F*. The aim is to import them into a dBASE Logic field. Note how the dates are formatted in Column *L*. This is not a standard 1–2–3 format, but it is in the value format dBASE needs to correctly import a date from a .WKS file: YYYYMMDD, where YYYY is a four-digit year, MM is a two-digit month, and DD is a

FIGURE 5–6
APPEND Command and Completed Message

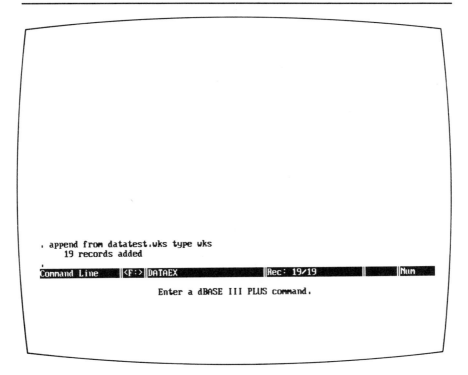

```
. append from datatest.wks type wks
    19 records added
```
Command Line |<F:>|DATAEX |Rec: 19/19 | |Num

Enter a dBASE III PLUS command.

two-digit day value. All other fields are formatted as labels or values as expected.

Under dBASE, you must create a structure to accept the data. The structure of the sample database is shown in Figure 5–5.

The fields are in the same sequence as the columns in the worksheet. Note that the last field is a memo field; there is no corresponding element in the worksheet, but the APPEND process works well anyway. Also, there are no records in the sample .DBF file at this point. APPEND may be used to add records to a file whether or not it already has records in it; in this case, an empty table helps keep it simple.

FIGURE 5–7
BROWSE View of APPENDed .WKS Worksheet, Left Portion

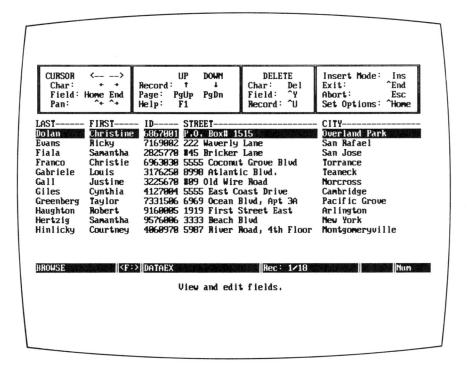

Figure 5–6 shows the APPEND command as it was issued, as well as the final results after the command was completed. The count of records appended is updated on the screen, so you can watch the command's process as it reads through the spreadsheet.

The next two screens (Figures 5–7 and 5–8) show the results of the APPEND process as viewed with the dBASE BROWSE command, which displays the records similarly to the original spreadsheet.

In these two screens, the data is brought in perfectly from the worksheet. If you can format date fields appropriately, the APPEND TYPE WKS is a useful tool. Remember that it only works

FIGURE 5–8
BROWSE View of APPENDed .WKS Worksheet, Right Portion

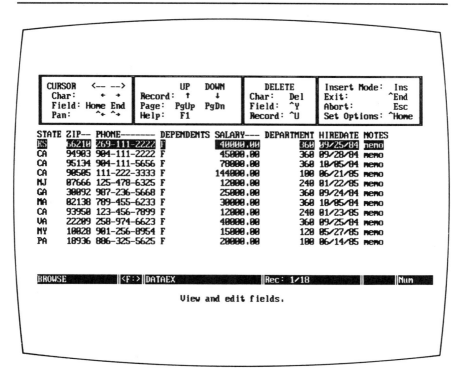

for Release 1A .wks files. If you have version 2.x .wk1 files, you must use another route, such as the Lotus Translate utility. If you need to move data from a worksheet that does not match the structure of your target database, there are some intermediate steps you must use, but they are covered in the later parts of this chapter.

APPEND TYPE DIF

dBASE also supports the exchange of DIF format files, although with less flexibility than most programs.

The main drawback is that dBASE doesn't recognize DIF's evolution, and it does not give a choice of either row-wise or

FIGURE 5–9
Sample DIF File

```
TABLE
8,1
""
TUPLES
8,19
""
VECTORS
8,12
""
DATA
8,8
""
-1,8
BOT
1,8
"LAST"
1,8
"FIRST"
1,8
"ID"
1,8
"STREET"
1,8
```

column-wise DIF files. It only produces (and reads) DIF files as columnar files. If you need to flop your data, you will have to do it at the sending program's end.

Figure 5–9 shows an excerpt of the data file used in this example. It is based on the same data as the last section.

Given the multiple-row-per-cell DIF format, you can see only a few of the first data elements in this screen, but it is enough to recognize the data from earlier screens. The APPEND command syntax and results are nearly identical to the last example:

```
APPEND FROM filename TYPE DIF
```

Press the Enter Key, and dBASE will again count the appended records until the full DIF file is read. The results are the same. The two BROWSE screens shown in the last section look exactly the same as the ones produced with this DIF file data.

A key here, again, is that you need to put your dates into the proper YYYYMMDD format for dBASE to accept them. The DIF format can handle logical values correctly, but you may not have a sending program that is capable of creating this correctly, so do not count too heavily on filling logical fields on the first pass with this method.

APPEND TYPE SYLK

In addition to the .WKS and .DIF formats, dBASE also will read data in a SYLK format. As described in Part 1, this format originally was used as a data-transfer format with Multi-Plan. While not as popular as other formats, it is still supported by many programs.

The APPEND command works the same as in prior cases. Figure 5–10 shows the contents of a SYLK file that carries a sample file.

Using the same .DBF structure as in prior examples, we can issue the command:

```
APPEND FROM filename TYPE SYLK
```

FIGURE 5–10
SYLK Format Sample-Data File

```
ID:PDB3
F:DG0G10
B:Y19;X12
C:Y1;X1;K"LAST"
C:X2;K"FIRST"
C:X3;K"ID"
C:X4;K"STREET"
C:X5;K"CITY"
C:X6;K"STATE"
C:X7;K"ZIP"
C:X8;K"PHONE"
C:X9;K"DEPENDENTS"
C:X10;K"SALARY"
C:X11;K"DEPARTMENT"
C:X12;K"HIREDATE"
C:Y2;X1;K"Dolan       "
C:X2;K"Christine "
C:X3;K"6867001"
C:X4;K"P.O. Box# 1515          "
C:X5;K"Overland Park     "
C:X6;K"KS"
C:X7;K"66210"
C:X8;K"269-111-2222"
```

where "filename" is the name of the SYLK file. The import results are identical. Note that the date must be in the YYYYMMDD format. Also note that logical fields are imported correctly.

APPEND TYPE SDF

These first four examples (IMPORT and three APPEND options) are handy only as long as you have a program that can create the appropriately formatted file. While dozens of programs support these formats, most users would be hard-pressed to create such a file from scratch. While there are documents that explain the details of .DIF or .WKS structures, they are too cumbersome and technical to create by hand.

Other programs are unable to create a file that matches one of these four "canned" structures. Fortunately, dBASE includes two other APPEND options that make it simple to bring in data from anywhere. These two options are TYPE SDF and DELIMITED; you can place data from almost any program in a dBASE table with these two options.

As described in Part 1, SDF is the dBASE term for "System Data Format," and it describes what we might otherwise call a fixed-length record text-file format. Each record is on its own row, ending with a Carriage Return. Each record has the same number of characters. Each field starts in the same relative location in the record.

Figure 5–11 shows our sample data file in SDF format. Note that because the lines are longer than the 80-column display screen, the lines have wrapped. You can still see the repetitive pattern of the fields as they begin in the same relative location.

There is no distinction between the numeric and character data elements in the file. dBASE determines what kind of data they are by comparing the import file to the data structure of the target .DBF table. The date field is in the YYYYMMDD format required by dBASE.

Again, this data is brought into the same sample database structure. Note how the sequence of data fields and their lengths in the SDF file correspond to the dBASE file structure definition.

The syntax in this case is:

```
APPEND FROM filename TYPE SDF
```

where filename is the name of the SDF data file. Again, the results are the same.

There are advantages to using this SDF format with APPEND. You can create the data file in a number of ways ranging from entering the data in a word processor that can create a pure ASCII file to printing a report to disk from a program and editing the resulting file into the fixed-length record for-

FIGURE 5–11
Sample File in SDF Format

```
Dolan    Christine 6867001P.O. Box# 1515           Overland Park    KS6621
0269-111-2222F 40000.0036019040925
Evans    Ricky      7169002222 Waverly Lane         San Rafael       CA9490
3904-111-2222F 45000.0036019040928
Fiala    Samantha  2825770#45 Bricker Lane          San Jose         CA9513
4904-111-5656F 70000.0036019041005
Franco   Christie  69630305555 Coconut Grove Blvd   Torrance         CA9050
5111-222-3333F144000.0010019050621
Gabriele Louis     31762500990 Atlantic Blvd.       Teaneck          NJ0766
6125-470-6325T 12000.0024019050122
Gall     Justine   3225670#09 Old Wire Road         Norcross         GA3009
2987-236-5668F 25000.0036019040924
Giles    Cynthia   41270045555 East Coast Drive     Cambridge        MA0213
8709-455-6233F 30000.0036019041005
Greenberg Taylor    73315066969 Ocean Blvd, Apt 3A   Pacific Grove    CA9395
0123-456-7899T 12000.0024019050123
Haughton Robert    91600051919 First Street East    Arlington        VA2220
9258-974-6623T 40000.0036019040925
Hertzig  Samantha  95760063333 Beach Blvd           New York         NY1002
8901-256-8954F 15000.0012019050527
Hinlicky Courtney  40609705987 River Road, 4th Floor Montgomeryville  PA1893
6886-325-5625F 20000.0010019050614
Horch    Jennifer  35775043306 Knight Street        Bellevue         WA9000
```

mat. Through these techniques, you can create procedures that permit you to enter data off-line and then batch load them into dBASE.

Also note that mainframe data, when captured on a PC, often arrives in fixed-length format. As a result, this APPEND technique may be the most efficient manner for bringing the data into a database.

APPEND FROM DELIMITED

The DELIMITED option of APPEND is one of the more powerful and flexible features of dBASE.

Used in its default settings, this command will read a data file that is in a comma-delimited text-file format. Character fields may or may not be surrounded by quotes and still be read successfully. Remember that you must not have any embedded commas or double quotes in the data, as explained in Part 1, or you will have scrambled data.

Figure 5–12 shows the sample data in a comma-delimited format. Note that the character fields are quoted, and that the fields match the structure of the target dBASE table.

Again, note the YYYYMMDD date format, and the fact that there are no quotes around the *T* and *F* values in the logic field position.

FIGURE 5–12
Sample File in Comma-Delimited Format

```
"Dolan","Christine","6867001","P.O. Box# 1515","Overland Park","KS","66210","269
-111-2222",F,40000.00,360,19840925
"Evans","Ricky","7169002","222 Waverly Lane","San Rafael","CA","94903","904-111-
2222",F,45000.00,360,19840928
"Fiala","Samantha","2825770","#45 Bricker Lane","San Jose","CA","95134","904-111
-5656",F,78000.00,360,19841005
"Franco","Christie","6963030","5555 Coconut Grove Blvd","Torrance","CA","90505",
"111-222-3333",F,144000.00,100,19850621
"Gabriele","Louis","3176250","8990 Atlantic Blvd.","Teaneck","NJ","07666","125-4
78-6325",T,12000.00,240,19850122
"Gall","Justine","3225670","#09 Old Wire Road","Norcross","GA","30092","987-236-
5668",F,25000.00,360,19840924
"Giles","Cynthia","4127004","5555 East Coast Drive","Cambridge","MA","02138","78
9-455-6233",F,30000.00,360,19841005
"Greenberg","Taylor","7331506","6969 Ocean Blvd, Apt 3A","Pacific Grove","CA","9
3950","123-456-7899",T,12000.00,240,19850123
"Haughton","Robert","9160005","1919 First Street East","Arlington","VA","22209",
"258-974-6623",T,40000.00,360,19840925
"Hertzig","Samantha","9576006","3333 Beach Blvd","New York","NY","10020","901-25
6-8954",F,15000.00,120,19850527
"Hinlicky","Courtney","4060970","5987 River Road, 4th Floor","Montgomeryville","
PA","18936","886-325-5625",F,20000.00,100,19850614
"Horch","Jennifer","3577504","3306 Knight Street","Bellevue","WA","98004","465-6
```

This time, the command is slightly different:

APPEND FROM filename DELIMITED

After issuing the command, dBASE will work as in the other examples—counting the records it finds and adding them to the table.

APPEND FROM DELIMITED has another option, however. It permits you to specify a different character to surround string fields instead of the typical double-quote character. Figure 5–13 shows the same data file with the backslash as a delimiter.

FIGURE 5–13
Data File in Backslash-Delimited Format

```
\Dolan\,\Christine\,\6867001\,\P.O. Box# 1515\,\Overland Park\,\KS\,\66210\,\269
-111-2222\,F,40000.00,360,19840925
\Evans\,\Ricky\,\7169002\,\222 Waverly Lane\,\San Rafael\,\CA\,\94903\,\904-111-
2222\,F,45000.00,360,19840928
\Fiala\,\Samantha\,\2825770\,\#45 Bricker Lane\,\San Jose\,\CA\,\95134\,\904-111
-5656\,F,78000.00,360,19841005
\Franco\,\Christie\,\6963030\,\5555 Coconut Grove Blvd\,\Torrance\,\CA\,\90505\,
\111-222-3333\,F,144000.00,100,19850621
\Gabriele\,\Louis\,\3176250\,\8998 Atlantic Blvd.\,\Teaneck\,\NJ\,\07666\,\125-4
78-6325\,T,12000.00,240,19850122
\Gall\,\Justine\,\3225670\,\#09 Old Wire Road\,\Norcross\,\GA\,\30092\,\987-236-
5668\,F,25000.00,360,19840924
\Giles\,\Cynthia\,\4127004\,\5555 East Coast Drive\,\Cambridge\,\MA\,\02138\,\78
9-455-6233\,F,30000.00,360,19841005
\Greenberg\,\Taylor\,\7331506\,\6969 Ocean Blvd, Apt 3A\,\Pacific Grove\,\CA\,\9
3950\,\123-456-7899\,T,12000.00,240,19850123
\Haughton\,\Robert\,\9160005\,\1919 First Street East\,\Arlington\,\VA\,\22209\,
\258-974-6623\,T,40000.00,360,19840925
\Hertzig\,\Samantha\,\9576006\,\3333 Beach Blvd\,\New York\,\NY\,\10028\,\901-25
6-8954\,F,15000.00,120,19850527
\Hinlicky\,\Courtney\,\4060970\,\5987 River Road, 4th Floor\,\Montgomeryville\,\
PA\,\18936\,\806-325-5625\,F,20000.00,100,19850614
\Horch\,\Jennifer\,\3577504\,\3306 Knight Street\,\Bellevue\,\WA\,\98004\,\465-6
```

In this case, tell dBASE what the field delimiting character is, and it will do the rest. Here, our command is:

```
APPEND FROM filename DELIMITED \
```

and the data file will be read into the table.

Additional dBASE IV APPEND FROM Options

In addition to the above options, dBASE IV can use some other file formats as a source for the APPEND command. It can also bring data into an existing table from dBASE II, Framework II, and RapidFile data files. As with the dBASE III options, the target table structure must match the source file.

WHAT TO DO WHEN THESE DON'T WORK

As mentioned in the last section, you must have a dBASE table in the correct structure waiting to receive your data before the APPEND techniques will work. What to do if you have a database that has different fields than the information you are trying to bring in from a separate data file? Are you stuck?

No—provided that your data file is in one of the formats already discussed in this chapter. The situation is not too grim, although you may have a few steps before the final destination.

There are two cases. One possibility is that your target database has more fields than are represented by your import file, but every element of information in the data file has a place to go in the table. The other possibility is that you have data-file fields that do not have a place to go in the dBASE table structure.

These two problems are closely related, and they are handled similarly. Let's assume that we start with the database structure shown in Figure 5–14, and that we will bring in the same sample data file as in the other examples in this chapter. This table is called FINAL1.DBF in this example:

FIGURE 5–14
FINAL1.DBF dBASE Structure

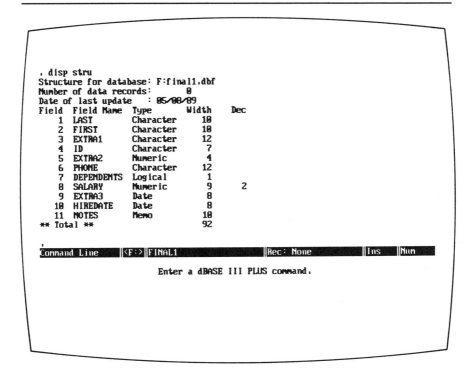

```
. disp stru
Structure for database: F:final1.dbf
Number of data records:       0
Date of last update   : 05/08/89
Field  Field Name  Type       Width    Dec
    1  LAST        Character      10
    2  FIRST       Character      10
    3  EXTRA1      Character      12
    4  ID          Character       7
    5  EXTRA2      Numeric         4
    6  PHONE       Character      12
    7  DEPENDENTS  Logical         1
    8  SALARY      Numeric         9      2
    9  EXTRA3      Date            8
   10  HIREDATE    Date            8
   11  NOTES       Memo           10
** Total **                      92
```

```
Command Line      <F:> FINAL1                    Rec: None          Ins    Num
```

Enter a dBASE III PLUS command.

Note that the target table in the illustration does not have all the same fields as the sample data file, and it also has some extra fields. For emphasis, they are named EXTRA1, EXTRA2, and EXTRA3.

If we tried to APPEND from the data file directly into this table, we would not succeed. You can only APPEND from a data file when the destination dBASE table has the same structure.

We need to divide the process into two steps. First, create a temporary table structure identical to earlier examples, as shown in Figure 5–15. This is referred to as FIRST.DBF.

The APPEND from the data file works with this combination, yet, there is one other essential point. The field names in

FIGURE 5–15
FIRST.DBF Example dBASE Table Structure

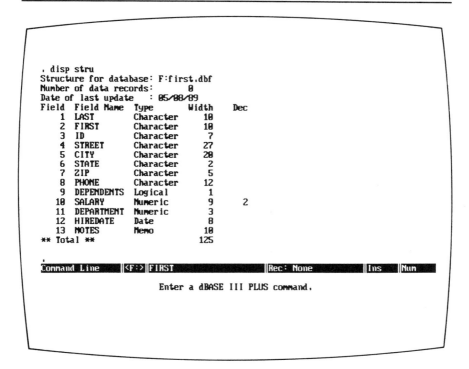

```
. disp stru
Structure for database: F:first.dbf
Number of data records:       0
Date of last update   : 05/08/89
Field  Field Name  Type       Width    Dec
    1  LAST        Character     10
    2  FIRST       Character     10
    3  ID          Character      7
    4  STREET      Character     27
    5  CITY        Character     20
    6  STATE       Character      2
    7  ZIP         Character      5
    8  PHONE       Character     12
    9  DEPENDENTS  Logical        1
   10  SALARY      Numeric        9       2
   11  DEPARTMENT  Numeric        3
   12  HIREDATE    Date           8
   13  NOTES       Memo          10
** Total **                    125
```

Command Line |<F:>|FIRST |Rec: None |Ins |Num

Enter a dBASE III PLUS command.

the two dBASE tables are the same for corresponding fields. For example, both tables have fields named *ID* and *phone*. If the field was named *telephone* in one table and *phone* in the other, the next step would not work.

So, create a temporary table using the same field names as the final target dBASE table, and perform the APPEND command to import data from the data file.

Once the data is brought into the FIRST table, you can easily move it to the FINAL1 table. The task is simple because the field names are the same.

First, make the target table active with this command:

```
USE FINAL1
```

Now, append the records from the FIRST table, and the field names will be matched between the two structures. If there is a corresponding field in the FIRST table, then the data will be placed in the FINAL1 record. If there is no corresponding field, as with the EXTRA1 field, then that field will remain empty for that record. Here is the command:

APPEND FROM FIRST

The screen in Figure 5–16 displays the records in the FINAL1 table. The data has been moved over successfully; now return and edit the records to update the EXTRA1, EXTRA2, and

FIGURE 5–16
FINAL1 Table in BROWSE View with Appended Records

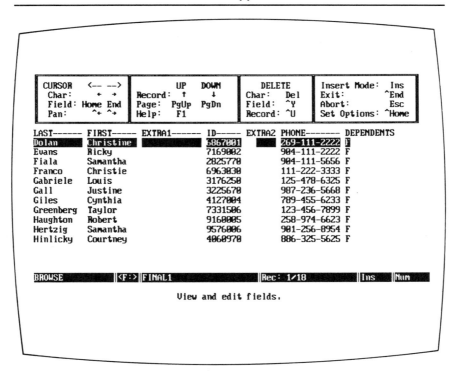

EXTRA3 fields for the newly added records. With these techniques, you can bring in any data in a supported format and add it to a new or existing database table.

SKIPPING RECORDS

Only one other fine point remains. There may be times when you do not want to bring in all the records in a certain data file. Perhaps the file contains information about all states, but you only want data on a single state. Maybe the file covers many departments, but you only need to know about your department. Perhaps the file has data on a year's worth of transactions, but you only want to know about a specific month.

dBASE makes this sort of selection easy to manage. Certainly, you could bring in all the data and then use the dBASE selection facilities to extract the records you want, and even delete what you don't want.

But why take the extra time and disk space for this approach when the same end can be achieved in a single step? Both the APPEND and COPY commands used in the above examples accept a FOR condition as part of the command syntax. The syntax for APPEND is as follows:

```
APPEND FROM filename FOR condition TYPE filetype
```

Conditions are explained thoroughly in the dBASE documentation if you are not familiar with them, but they are simple to use. If you wished to bring in fixed-length records for only the employees living in California, you could issue this command:

```
APPEND FROM SAMPLE.SDF FOR STATE="CA" TYPE SDF
```

dBASE would ignore all lines of data except those that had "CA" in the state field. You can create more complex commands that combine conditions using the dBASE .AND., .OR., and .NOT. logical operators. As a result, you can winnow good data from the chaff before it gets to your database file.

SUMMARY

As you have seen in this chapter, dBASE offers a range of simple yet powerful features that make it fairly easy to bring data into its database tables.

When you combine these capabilities with the corresponding techniques for moving data out of dBASE, you end up with a system that offers an attractive intermediary when trying to move data between two other programs that may not be as easy on transfers. All you need to know is how to move the data out, and this is covered in Chapter 6.

CHAPTER 6

MOVING DATA OUT
OF dBASE III

There is probably more data stored in microcomputers in dBASE .DBF format files than any other type of file. For the most part, these files contain lists, accounting details, and a wealth of other information. The dBASE applications that use this data often make enough difference in a company's operation that these benefits alone justify an entire microcomputer system.

Yet, how much more valuable would that information be if its owners could access it in different ways, and use it with different programs?

If you have dBASE files, this chapter shows how easy it is to move data out of dBASE files and into other formats that you can use for various purposes. As with the last chapter, the focus is on dBASE III, and additional features offered by dBASE IV are mentioned.

THE dBASE EXPORT COMMAND

The EXPORT command is the inverse of the IMPORT command discussed at the start of the last chapter. It creates a PFS:File data base file from a dBASE .DBF file.

If anything, this command is less practical than its counterpart. PFS:File is a simple program of limited capability, and most users outgrow its constraints and turn to a more powerful program such as dBASE. As a result, using the dBASE EXPORT command might appear like trying to convert a power lawn mower into a manual push-mower.

Still, you may have colleagues who need access to your data in a PFS format, so here is how the EXPORT command works. Figure 6–1 shows how to execute the EXPORT command from the dBASE ASSIST mode. It makes the entire process quick and easy.

As with IMPORT, you can also execute the command from the dot-prompt mode using the following syntax:

```
EXPORT TO filename TYPE PFS
```

where "filename" is the name of a PFS:file data file. Note that there are no conditions permitted, and you may specify only

FIGURE 6–1
dBASE ASSIST Mode: Export

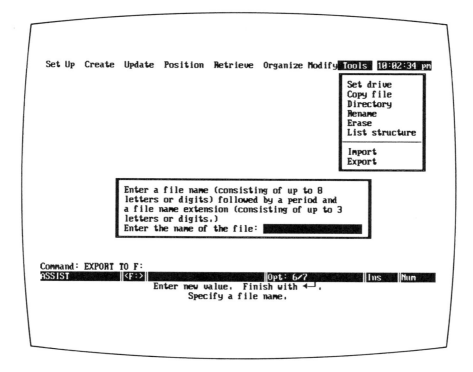

certain field names. The entire dBASE table, including all fields and all records, will appear in the resulting PFS file.

Also, as with the IMPORT command, dBASE IV offers additional options here, as shown in Figure 6–2; you can also create dBASE II, Framework II, or RapidFile data files from dBASE IV tables with this command.

EXPORTING dBASE FILES WITH COPY

The dBASE COPY command is more powerful and flexible than the EXPORT command. It can create a variety of different data-transfer text-file formats, and can create some files that are immediately useful.

FIGURE 6–2
dBASE IV Export Options

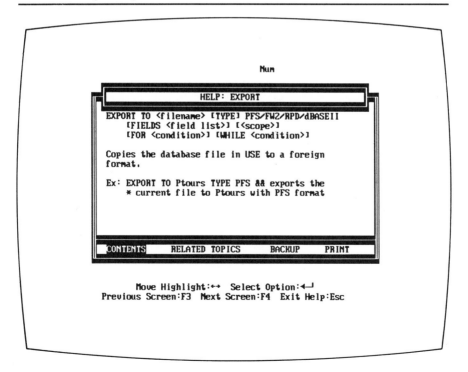

In addition to the choice of formats, you can also control the fields and records that are exported. These factors can save valuable hours when trying to clean up data that you are moving between applications.

In fact, you can handle so many data-transfer chores with the COPY command that you may want to use dBASE as an intermediate stop between two other programs. It is conceivable, however, that you may not accomplish everything with the COPY command, which is why other tips involving simple dBASE procedure files are covered at the end of this chapter.

FIGURE 6–3
Sample dBASE File Structure

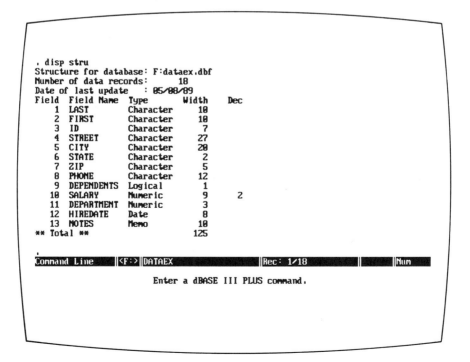

```
. disp stru
Structure for database: F:dataex.dbf
Number of data records:      18
Date of last update   : 05/08/89
Field  Field Name  Type        Width    Dec
    1  LAST        Character      10
    2  FIRST       Character      10
    3  ID          Character       7
    4  STREET      Character      27
    5  CITY        Character      20
    6  STATE       Character       2
    7  ZIP         Character       5
    8  PHONE       Character      12
    9  DEPENDENTS  Logical         1
   10  SALARY      Numeric         9      2
   11  DEPARTMENT  Numeric         3
   12  HIREDATE    Date            8
   13  NOTES       Memo           10
** Total **                      125
```

Command Line ║<F:>║DATAEX ║Rec: 1/18 ║ ║Num

Enter a dBASE III PLUS command.

Basic Syntax for the COPY Command

The syntax for the COPY command is similar to its companion
command, APPEND.

```
COPY TO filename [scope] [FIELDS fieldlist] [FOR condition]
[WHILE condition] [TYPE filetype] [DELIMITED <WITH BLANK/
delimiter>]
```

Any item in the square brackets is optional. Note that if you do
not mention a TYPE or DELIMITED at the end of the command,
your output ends up in a new .DBF file. This is the technique
used at the end of the last chapter to create a temporary table
with the appropriate fields in its table structure. The TYPE options are the same as for APPEND.

FIGURE 6–4
COPY TO . . . TYPE WKS Command Example

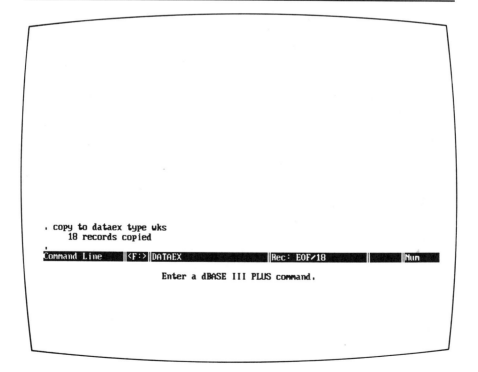

```
. copy to dataex type wks
    18 records copied
```

```
Command Line    |<F:>|DATAEX                    |Rec: EOF/18          |Num
```

```
            Enter a dBASE III PLUS command.
```

COPY TO File TYPE WKS

The TYPE WKS option creates Lotus 1–2–3 Release 1A .WKS worksheet files. A demonstration with the sample data file shows the results of this command.

Figure 6–3 shows the structure of the original DATAEX.DBF table. Note that it has character, numeric, logical, date, and memo fields.

While this table is in use, we issue the COPY TO command, as shown in Figure 6–4. dBASE responds by reporting how many records have been copied, and it then returns to the dot prompt when finished.

FIGURE 6–5
First Part of the DATAEX.WKS File in 1–2–3

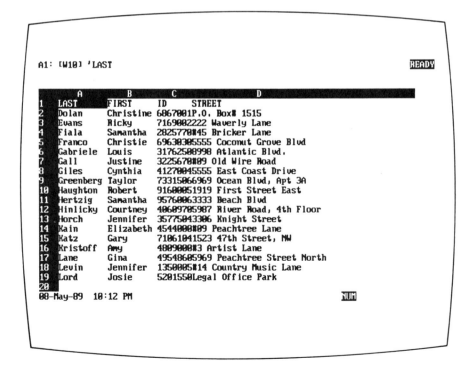

This process creates a file called DATAEX.WKS, which we can call up in 1–2–3. Figure 6–5 shows how this file appears on the screen.

Notice important details on this screen. For example, the field names are entered as labels at the top of each column. Column widths have been automatically adjusted to match the field lengths of the original dBASE table structure definition.

It is not until you examine the next set of columns to the right that you encounter some limitations with this process. Figure 6–6 shows the second half of the worksheet.

Note that the zip and phone fields are correctly entered as labels. Also, the column widths have been adjusted to match

FIGURE 6–6
Second Part of the DATAEX.WKS File in 1–2–3

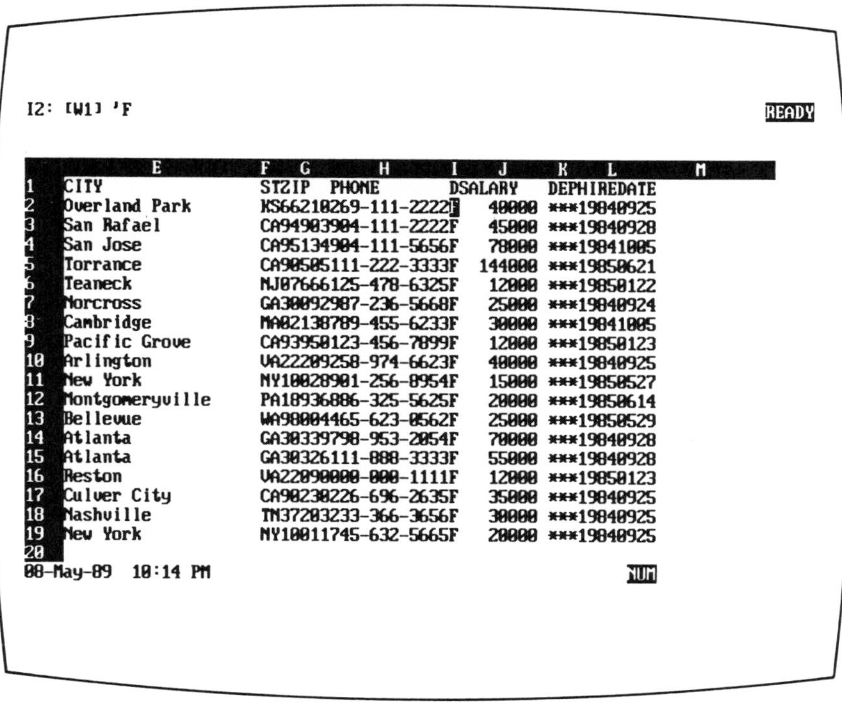

field lengths. The right-hand columns show some problems, however.

First, look at Column *I*. The label at the top is just *D*, which is DEPENDENTS truncated to a single character due to the fact that the column width has been set to 1. In the rows below, the values are either *F* or *T*, which are reasonable considering that DEPENDENTS was a logical field in the dBASE table. Unfortunately, the values are entered as labels. This form can be used for logical evaluations, but it takes some work.

You might use the Lotus @IF command to convert the contents of this column into something more useful. For example, we might use Column *M* and enter the following formula:

```
M2;    @IF(I2="T",@TRUE,@FALSE)
```

and then copy this formula into the other cells of the column. This would put a 1 in every row of Column *M* where there is a *T* in Column *I*, and a 0 in the others.

There is a smaller, tidier formula that you can use, however, that yields the same effect. Enter the following formula:

```
M2:    +I2="T"
```

This formula offers the same results: a 1 for a *T* and a 0 for an *F*.

Column *J* does not present any problems, but Column *K* illustrates a small difficulty. Instead of department codes, all we see are asterisks. This is the result of automatic column-width settings. The dBASE structure defined this as a three-character numeric field. The resulting worksheet allocated only three characters for the column width, and defined the cell entries as numeric. Since 1–2–3 requires room for the numeric-value sign indicator (such as a − for negative numbers) whether it uses it or not, there is not enough room to display a three-digit value in a three-character column.

To get rid of the asterisks, use the /WORKSHEET COLUMN SET-WIDTH command, and expand the column width by a character.

The next to last problem is Column *L:* HireDate. In Figure 6–6, the date is in the dBASE format of YYYYMMDD. What may not be apparent is the fact that the cell contents are considered a label, not numeric. This leads to some work before you can convert this into a format that 1–2–3 can recognize as a date.

The solution is a complex formula that is similar to one mentioned in Chapter 3. Again, rather than discuss its inner workings, it is presented for your use; you can figure it out on your own. Simply enter it in a column and refer to the column of cells that contain the dBASE date-format data in a label format, which is Column *L* in this case.

```
@DATE(@VALUE(@MID(L2,2,2)),@VALUE(@MID(L2,4,2)),@VALUE(@RIGHT
(L2,2)))
```

This returns a value in the Lotus date format, and you can then format the cell using the /RANGE FORMAT command to select one of the various 1–2–3 date-display format options.

The only remaining problem is a hidden one, and it is shown in Column *M*. You can see in Figure 6–6 that there is nothing in this column. If you refer back to the original dBASE table structure, however, you will find that there was one more field, a memo field named notes. Memo fields are not converted with the TYPE WKS command, or with any of the COPY TO commands. If you need to convert memo-field information you will find relevant tips at the end of this chapter.

The bottom line on dBASE to WKS conversions is that there are some aspects that are done better by the Lotus 1–2–3 Release 2.01 Translate utility, such as handling dates and logical fields. Translate does not offer the ability to select specific fields or records from your dBASE table, however, so dBASE may offer the extra control needed when extracting certain information from a large data base for use in a Lotus worksheet.

COPY TO File TYPE DIF

The COPY TO . . . TYPE DIF command is straightforward with one significant limitation.

The syntax and results of this command look much like the TYPE WKS example above. Notice that there is no choice given in terms of whether you wish to create a row-wise or column-wise DIF file. dBASE will create a column-wise file only. If you need to transpose the data, rely on the receiving program to make the change or use an intermediate utility (such as Lotus 1–2–3 Release 2.01 Translate) to make the conversion.

The DIF file will format the data as labels, values, or a logical true or false. Dates are converted to values in the dBASE YYYYMMDD format. Memo fields are not converted.

COPY TO File TYPE SYLK

The COPY TO . . . TYPE SYLK uses the same syntax. Character, logical, and date fields are all brought in as labels. The dates are in the dBASE YYYYMMDD format. Numeric fields come in as values. As with other examples in this section, the notes memo field was ignored.

COPY TO File TYPE SDF

As mentioned in Chapter 2, fixed-length records are perhaps the most common data file format. dBASE refers to this format as "SDF," or Standard Data Format. The COPY TO command makes it simple to create such a file from a dBASE table.

The next illustration, Figure 6–7, shows the resulting output. In this screen, the individual lines wrap at the edge of the screen so that each record takes up one-and-a-half lines. In fact, there are Carriage Returns only at the end of the half-line, which ends with the eight-digit date field.

Notice how the data was formatted in the conversion process. First, the character fields have been padded with spaces to the right to fill out the field lengths. Numeric values, as seen in the salary field, are padded with spaces to the left. There are no separators between fields, and no special treatment of character, logical, or date information. The logical values come through as a simple *F* or *T,* and the date appears in the typical dBASE format: YYYYMMDD.

Note that the memo field notes has been ignored.

COPY TO File DELIMITED

There are a number of options available for the DELIMITED version of the COPY TO command. You will rarely have any use for the alternatives beyond the basic version. Using the same ex-

FIGURE 6–7
Sample SDF File

```
Dolan      Christine 6867001P.O. Box# 1515              Overland Park     KS6621
8269-111-2222F 40000.0036019040925
Evans      Ricky     7169002222 Waverly Lane            San Rafael        CA9490
3904-111-2222F 45000.0036019040928
Fiala      Samantha  2825770#45 Bricker Lane            San Jose          CA9513
4904-111-5656F 70000.0036019041005
Franco     Christie  69630305555 Coconut Grove Blvd     Torrance          CA9050
5111-222-3333F144000.0010019050621
Gabriele   Louis     31762500990 Atlantic Blvd.         Teaneck           NJ0766
6125-478-6325T 12000.0024019050122
Gall       Justine   3225670#09 Old Wire Road           Norcross          GA3009
2987-236-5668F 25000.0036019040924
Giles      Cynthia   41270045555 East Coast Drive       Cambridge         MA0213
8789-455-6233F 30000.0036019041005
Greenberg  Taylor    73315066969 Ocean Blvd, Apt 3A     Pacific Grove     CA9395
0123-456-7899T 12000.0024019050123
Haughton   Robert    91600051919 First Street East      Arlington         VA2220
9258-974-6623T 40000.0036019040925
Hertzig    Samantha  95760063333 Beach Blvd             New York          NY1002
8901-256-8954F 15000.0012019050527
Hinlicky   Courtney  40609705987 River Road, 4th Floor  Montgomeryville   PA1893
6806-325-5625F 20000.0010019050614
Horch      Jennifer  35775043306 Knight Street           Bellevue          WA9800
```

ample dBASE table, you get the file shown in Figure 6–8. As
in the last section, the lines wrap at the edge of the screen, so
each record appears to take up one-and-a-half lines. There is
only a Carriage Return at the end of the half-line, which ends
in the eight-digit date field.

This command produces a quoted-string, comma-delimited
file. The fields are not padded with spaces, and the character
fields are surrounded by quotation marks. Note that the employee ID, zip code, and social security fields are all in quotes,
since these are special fields that contain digits but are not
intended to be evaluated as numeric values.

The logical field dependents appears right after the social
security field data. You should see that it contains character
data, either an *F* or a *T*. Also notice, however, that these char-

FIGURE 6–8
Sample Delimited File

```
"Dolan","Christine","6867001","P.O. Box# 1515","Overland Park","KS","66210","269
-111-2222",F,40000.00,360,19840925
"Evans","Ricky","7169002","222 Waverly Lane","San Rafael","CA","94903","904-111-
2222",F,45000.00,360,19840928
"Fiala","Samantha","2825770","#45 Bricker Lane","San Jose","CA","95134","904-111
-5656",F,78000.00,360,19841005
"Franco","Christie","6963030","5555 Coconut Grove Blvd","Torrance","CA","90585",
"111-222-3333",F,144000.00,100,19850621
"Gabriele","Louis","3176250","8990 Atlantic Blvd.","Teaneck","NJ","07666","125-4
78-6325",T,12000.00,240,19850122
"Gall","Justine","3225670","#09 Old Wire Road","Norcross","GA","30092","987-236-
5668",F,25000.00,360,19840924
"Giles","Cynthia","4127004","5555 East Coast Drive","Cambridge","MA","02138","78
9-455-6233",F,30000.00,360,19841005
"Greenberg","Taylor","7331506","6969 Ocean Blvd, Apt 3A","Pacific Grove","CA","9
3950","123-456-7899",T,12000.00,240,19850123
"Haughton","Robert","9160005","1919 First Street East","Arlington","VA","22209",
"258-974-6623",T,40000.00,360,19840925
"Hertzig","Samantha","9576006","3333 Beach Blvd","New York","NY","10020","901-25
6-8954",F,15000.00,120,19850527
"Hinlicky","Courtney","4060970","5987 River Road, 4th Floor","Montgomeryville","
PA","18936","886-325-5625",F,20000.00,100,19850614
"Horch","Jennifer","3577504","3306 Knight Street","Bellevue","WA","98004","465-6
```

acters are not surrounded by quotes. This has significant implications, as was seen in Chapter 3 when we tried to bring this file into 1–2–3. Most programs will not recognize this data as character data, since it is not in quotes. Since the data is in the form of letters and not digits, however, it will not be recognized as numeric values. As a result, you will probably lose dBASE logical-field data when trying to transfer it from a dBASE table to another program using the delimited format.

There are a number of steps that you can use here. One solution would be to write a dBASE program that would output a 1 or a 0 instead of T or F for those fields, which could then be correctly evaluated by the receiving program as a numeric value. The programming skills required are covered in the last section of this chapter. Another approach would be to use the text-file tips and tricks covered in Part 3 to search and replace the occurrences of ,T, with ,"T", (and make a similar change for the *F* fields). Note that the memo field notes was ignored again.

COPY TO . . . DELIMITED offers some options. If we used the same command as above, except with the format of COPY TO . . . DELIMITED WITH BLANK, we would get the file shown in Figure 6–9.

Notice that instead of commas between the fields, we now see single blank spaces instead. A few programs require spaces instead of commas between fields, and this format produces that result. This is of little use with a data file such as this one, since there are already spaces between words in the ad-

FIGURE 6–9
Example of DELIMITED WITH BLANK File

```
Dolan Christine 6867001 P.O. Box# 1515 Overland Park KS 66210 269-111-2222 F 400
00.00 360 19040925
Evans Ricky 7169002 222 Waverly Lane San Rafael CA 94903 904-111-2222 F 45000.00
   360 19040928
Fiala Samantha 2825770 #45 Bricker Lane San Jose CA 95134 904-111-5656 F 78000.0
0 360 19041005
Franco Christie 6963030 5555 Coconut Grove Blvd Torrance CA 98505 111-222-3333 F
   144000.00 100 19050621
Gabriele Louis 3176250 8998 Atlantic Blvd. Teaneck NJ 07666 125-478-6325 T 12000
   .00 240 19050122
Gall Justine 3225670 #09 Old Wire Road Norcross GA 30092 987-236-5668 F 25000.00
   360 19040924
Giles Cynthia 4127004 5555 East Coast Drive Cambridge MA 82138 789-455-6233 F 30
000.00 360 19041005
Greenberg Taylor 7331506 6969 Ocean Blvd, Apt 3A Pacific Grove CA 93950 123-456-
7899 T 12000.00 240 19050123
Haughton Robert 9160005 1919 First Street East Arlington VA 22209 250-974-6623 T
   40000.00 360 19040925
Hertzig Samantha 9576006 3333 Beach Blvd New York NY 10028 901-256-8954 F 15000.
00 120 19050527
Hinlicky Courtney 4060970 5987 River Road, 4th Floor Montgomeryville PA 18936 88
6-325-5625 F 20000.00 100 19050614
Horch Jennifer 3577504 3306 Knight Street Bellevue WA 98004 465-623-0562 F 25000
```

dress fields, and many first or last names have spaces in them. Still, if you have straight numeric data, the blank-delimited format may be useful.

Figure 6–10 shows an example of the other DELIMITED variation. You can specify a character-field delimiter, provided that it is a single printable character. In this case, the command was COPY TO . . . DELIMITED WITH \.

Here, you see the resulting file with the backslash character between fields. You can use this approach to insert nearly any character as the string-field delimiter. Note that the field contents are still separated by commas. It is simply the character around the string data that you can specify.

The character must be a single character. You cannot specify a Control character, such as with the dBASE CHR() func-

FIGURE 6–10
Example of DELIMITED WITH \ File

```
\Dolan\,\Christine\,\6867001\,\P.O. Box# 1515\,\Overland Park\,\KS\,\66210\,\269
-111-2222\,F,40000.00,360,19040925
\Evans\,\Ricky\,\7169002\,\222 Waverly Lane\,\San Rafael\,\CA\,\94903\,\904-111-
2222\,F,45000.00,360,19040928
\Fiala\,\Samantha\,\2825770\,\#45 Bricker Lane\,\San Jose\,\CA\,\95134\,\904-111
-5656\,F,70000.00,360,19041005
\Franco\,\Christie\,\6963030\,\5555 Coconut Grove Blvd\,\Torrance\,\CA\,\90505\,
\111-222-3333\,F,144000.00,180,19050621
\Gabriele\,\Louis\,\3176250\,\9998 Atlantic Blvd.\,\Teaneck\,\NJ\,\07666\,\125-4
78-6325\,T,12000.00,240,19050122
\Gall\,\Justine\,\3225670\,\#09 Old Wire Road\,\Norcross\,\GA\,\30092\,\987-236-
5668\,F,25000.00,360,19040924
\Giles\,\Cynthia\,\4127004\,\5555 East Coast Drive\,\Cambridge\,\MA\,\02138\,\78
9-455-6233\,F,30000.00,360,19041005
\Greenberg\,\Taylor\,\7331506\,\6969 Ocean Blvd, Apt 3A\,\Pacific Grove\,\CA\,\9
3950\,\123-456-7899\,T,12000.00,240,19050123
\Haughton\,\Robert\,\9160005\,\1919 First Street East\,\Arlington\,\WA\,\22209\,
\250-974-6623\,T,40000.00,360,19040925
\Hertzig\,\Samantha\,\9576006\,\3333 Beach Blvd\,\New York\,\NY\,\10028\,\901-25
6-8954\,F,15000.00,120,19050527
\Hinlicky\,\Courtney\,\4060970\,\5907 River Road, 4th Floor\,\Montgomeryville\,\
PA\,\18936\,\886-325-5625\,F,20000.00,100,19050614
\Horch\,\Jennifer\,\3577504\,\3306 Knight Street\,\Bellevue\,\WA\,\90004\,\465-6
```

FIGURE 6–11
High-Order Character in DELIMITED WITH Æ Example

```
ÆDolanÆ,ÆChristineÆ,Æ6867001Æ,ÆP.O. Box# 1515Æ,ÆOverland ParkÆ,ÆKSÆ,Æ66210Æ,Æ269
-111-2222Æ,F,40000.00,360,19040925
ÆEvansÆ,ÆRickyÆ,Æ7169002Æ,Æ222 Waverly LaneÆ,ÆSan RafaelÆ,ÆCAÆ,Æ94903Æ,Æ904-111-
2222Æ,F,45000.00,360,19040928
ÆFialaÆ,ÆSamanthaÆ,Æ2825770Æ,Æ#45 Bricker LaneÆ,ÆSan JoseÆ,ÆCAÆ,Æ95134Æ,Æ904-111
-5656Æ,F,70000.00,360,19041005
ÆFrancoÆ,ÆChristieÆ,Æ6963030Æ,Æ5555 Coconut Grove BlvdÆ,ÆTorranceÆ,ÆCAÆ,Æ90505Æ,
Æ111-222-3333Æ,F,144000.00,100,19050621
ÆGabrieleÆ,ÆLouisÆ,Æ3176250Æ,Æ8998 Atlantic Blvd.Æ,ÆTeaneckÆ,ÆNJÆ,Æ07666Æ,Æ125-4
78-6325Æ,T,12000.00,240,19050122
ÆGallÆ,ÆJustineÆ,Æ3225670Æ,Æ#09 Old Wire RoadÆ,ÆNorcrossÆ,ÆGAÆ,Æ30092Æ,Æ987-236-
5660Æ,F,25000.00,360,19040924
ÆGilesÆ,ÆCynthiaÆ,Æ4127004Æ,Æ5555 East Coast DriveÆ,ÆCambridgeÆ,ÆMAÆ,Æ02130Æ,Æ78
9-455-6233Æ,F,30000.00,360,19041005
ÆGreenbergÆ,ÆTaylorÆ,Æ7331506Æ,Æ6969 Ocean Blvd, Apt 3AÆ,ÆPacific GroveÆ,ÆCAÆ,Æ9
3950Æ,Æ123-456-7899Æ,T,12000.00,240,19050123
ÆHaughtonÆ,ÆRobertÆ,Æ9160005Æ,Æ1919 First Street EastÆ,ÆArlingtonÆ,ÆVAÆ,Æ22209Æ,
Æ258-974-6623Æ,T,40000.00,360,19040925
ÆHertzigÆ,ÆSamanthaÆ,Æ9576006Æ,Æ3333 Beach BlvdÆ,ÆNew YorkÆ,ÆNYÆ,Æ10020Æ,Æ901-25
6-8954Æ,F,15000.00,120,19050527
ÆHinlickyÆ,ÆCourtneyÆ,Æ4060970Æ,Æ5987 River Road, 4th FloorÆ,ÆMontgomeryvilleÆ,Æ
PAÆ,Æ18936Æ,Æ886-325-5625Æ,F,20000.00,100,19050614
ÆHorchÆ,ÆJenniferÆ,Æ3577504Æ,Æ3306 Knight StreetÆ,ÆBellevueÆ,ÆWAÆ,Æ98004Æ,Æ465-6
```

tion, but you can specify a character not on the keyboard. Figure 6–11 shows the result of entering a high-order character as the delimiter.

This character has a decimal ASCII value of 146. You can enter it by holding down the Alt and Left Shift keys, then using the numeric keypad to enter the decimal ASCII value. You can use this technique to enter any of the higher ASCII values. One reason to do this is so that you can later search and replace the string-delimiting character and know that you are using a character that does not appear as data in any of the records. In this case, it is unlikely that the Æ character appears in any of the fields.

COPY TO WITH FIELD LISTS
AND CONDITIONS

In all the examples in the earlier sections on the COPY TO variations, you have the same general options available. You can specify which fields to use, and you can specify which records are to be included.

As mentioned earlier, the full syntax for this command is:

```
COPY TO filename [scope] [FIELDS fieldlist] [FOR condition]
[WHILE condition] [TYPE filetype] [DELIMITED <WITH BLANK/
delimiter]
```

There are three selection criteria to use: the scope, the field list, and the FOR or WHILE conditions.

Scope Options

The scope selection describes the records to be considered. If no scope is specified, as in all the examples so far, all the records are processed. You can also specify a single record with its physical record number. For example, to create an SDF file of the 17th record of the dBASE table, issue this command:

```
COPY TO filename RECORD 17 TYPE SDF
```

You can also specify that only a given number of records are to be processed using the NEXT option. This starts with the current record, and it includes as many records as specified. To export the next 10 records, use this command:

```
COPY TO filename NEXT 10 TYPE SDF
```

Remember that it starts with the current record, and it does not jump the record pointer back up to the start of the table. If you run out of records by reaching the end of the file before processing the specified number of records, the COPY command will end without an error message—having used only the records it found before it got to the end of file.

The remaining scope option is REST, and this will process all records from the current record to the end of the table. Again, to create an SDF file from the current record to the end, issue this command:

```
COPY TO filename REST TYPE SDF
```

The scope options take the records in their logical sequence. If you want to extract certain records according to selection criteria, use the FOR or WHILE options.

FOR and WHILE Options

These two parts of the command evaluate a comparison, and then decide whether or not to include that record's data. For example, to create a file for just those employees from California, you might use the selection criteria "STATE = "CA"."

If you wanted to search through the entire table to get all employees from California, you would use the FOR condition. To create an SDF file from the results, issue this command:

```
COPY TO filename FOR STATE="CA" TYPE SDF
```

The WHILE option works similarly, except it only processes records until it finds one that does not match the selection criteria. At the first record where the selection criteria do not match, it halts the processing. If you are working with a table where the records wanted are sprinkled throughout, use the FOR option. This forces dBASE to search through the entire file to ensure that you receive all requested records.

If your table is ordered so that all the desired records are grouped together, such as if you had an active index on the selection field, you could move the record pointer to the first record that matches your criteria and then use the WHERE option. In this case, the processing would finish faster because the COPY command would work only with that group of records, and it stops when the selection criteria no longer match.

The choice between FOR and WHILE only makes a difference when you work with large tables. If you have a small table, or you are not concerned with how long the COPY command will run, use the FOR option to make your selection. If you are not sure how to use the WHILE option, you run a greater risk of missing records that you want to find.

Also remember that selection criteria may be combined using the dBASE logical operators. For example, we could modify the earlier command to find all the California employees in Department 360 with the following change:

```
COPY TO filename FOR STATE="CA" .AND. DEPT = 360 TYPE SDF
```

You could have a file of all the employee data for people in California or Connecticut with this command:

```
COPY TO filename FOR STATE="CA" .OR. STATE = "CT" TYPE SDF
```

And, to find all employees who do not live in California, you can use:

```
COPY TO filename FOR .NOT. STATE="CA" TYPE SDF
```

Combined with the different logical operators, the FOR and WHILE selection options give great flexibility and control over what records are extracted and placed in the export file created with the COPY command.

FIELDS Options

Just as the scope and FOR/WHILE options permit you to select the records transferred to the new file, the FIELDS option permits you to control the fields included in the file.

If you do not use the FIELDS option, you will get data from all fields in each record of your output file, such as in the examples used so far in this chapter. There may be circumstances when you do not want all this data. For example, if we used the sample dBASE table to create an employee ID list in a word processor, we might not want to waste time erasing all the extraneous information from each record. All we want is the name and the employee ID number.

Here is where the FIELDS option comes into play. To create a fixed-length format text file of this information, use this command:

```
COPY TO filename FIELDS FIRST, LAST, ID TYPE SDF
```

Figure 6–12 shows the file created from this command.

This technique works with any of the COPY TO file formats, and you can use it to rearrange the field sequence. In this case,

FIGURE 6–12
Name and ID List Extracted by COPY TO . . . FIELDS

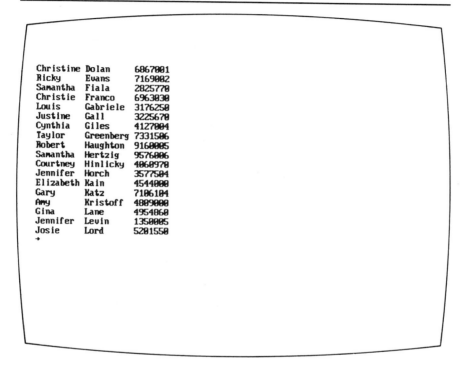

we have reversed the first and last names from their original order in the dBASE table structure.

Selection Options

Between the scope, FOR/WHILE, and FIELDS options, you can exert great control over the records, fields, and sequence of fields that appear in your COPY TO export files. Using them decreases the time required to clean up data on the receiving end, which makes it easier for the other program to import the information so that it will be closer to your desired end result.

But what if this is not enough control? What if you need to change names to all upper-case letters, reformat date information, or use other transformations? Are you stuck? Must you turn to another program or utility? The answer is no, and you don't need a computer science degree to make the solutions work.

THE SET ALTERNATE APPROACH

The secret to success is the SET ALTERNATE command in dBASE. The command comes in three parts.

SET ALTERNATE TO FILENAME opens a file to receive output from dBASE commands. SET ALTERNATE ON causes anything that would appear on the screen to be sent to the file as well. (There are ways to turn off the screen display and only have the output go to the file; this can hasten performance.) The information continues to be stored in the file until the SET ALTERNATE OFF command is given.

This has an interesting implication. The output is stored as a text file. Since it is formatted for screen (or in some cases, printer) output in straight columns, the fields are neatly padded so that each field begins in the same position as the corresponding field in the record before and after. If this sounds like the definition of a fixed-length record format, you are on target.

The easiest way to use this approach is to interact from the dBASE dot-prompt mode. Figure 6–13 illustrates a simple session in which the sample dBASE table is already active. In this case, let's find a list of the employee names and phone numbers. Eventually, the names all will be in capitals, but for now, here is the simplest approach.

Start by setting the alternate output file to NAMES.TXT. Then, SET ALTERNATE ON and use the LIST command to show the first, last, and phone fields. Finally, use SET ALTERNATE OFF to stop the rerouting of output to the file.

The syntax for the LIST command is almost identical in selection options as the COPY TO command described in the previous section:

```
LIST [scope] [expression list] [FOR condition] [WHILE
condition] [OFF] [TO PRINT]
```

FIGURE 6–13
Simple SET ALTERNATE Example

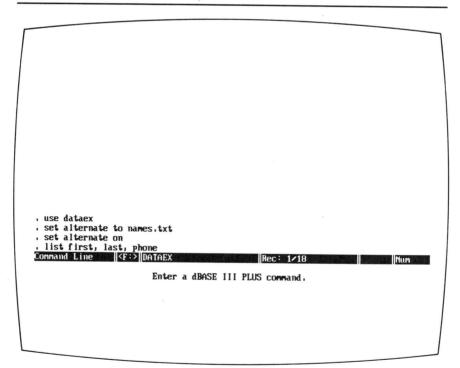

```
. use dataex
. set alternate to names.txt
. set alternate on
. list first, last, phone
Command Line      <F:> DATAEX                    Rec: 1/18            Num
             Enter a dBASE III PLUS command.
```

The scope and FOR/WHILE options are the same as COPY TO, and the TO PRINT option does exactly as it sounds—routes the output to the printer. Instead of a FIELDS option, LIST offers something that dBASE refers to as an "expression list," and there is also the mysterious OFF option. More on these last two options in a minute, but first let's see the results of the list command given in the above example.

Figure 6–14 shows the results of our SET ALTERNATE experiment. It isn't perfect, but it is easy enough to clean up. All you need is to delete the extra beginning and ending lines, and you will have what you want; you still have the record numbers, however, and nothing has been done to put the names in capitals.

FIGURE 6–14
Results of SET ALTERNATE and LIST Commands

```
. list first, last, phone
Record#  first     last       phone
     1   Christine Dolan      269-111-2222
     2   Ricky     Evans      904-111-2222
     3   Samantha  Fiala      904-111-5656
     4   Christie  Franco     111-222-3333
     5   Louis     Gabriele   125-478-6325
     6   Justine   Gall       987-236-5668
     7   Cynthia   Giles      789-455-6233
     8   Taylor    Greenberg  123-456-7899
     9   Robert    Haughton   258-974-6623
    10   Samantha  Hertzig    901-256-8954
    11   Courtney  Hinlicky   886-325-5625
    12   Jennifer  Horch      465-623-8562
    13   Elizabeth Kain       798-953-2054
    14   Gary      Katz       111-888-3333
    15   Amy       Kristoff   000-000-1111
    16   Gina      Lane       226-696-2635
    17   Jennifer  Levin      233-366-3656
    18   Josie     Lord       745-632-5665

. set alternate off→
```

The record numbers succumb to a simple solution. The OFF option in the LIST command suppresses the record number.

Putting the names in capitals is not much harder. As seen in the first LIST example, the expression list behaves similarly to the FIELDS option in the COPY TO command. This is because field names are valid expressions in dBASE.

An expression can be much more, however. You can use any dBASE function in an expression, and they are evaluated as the LIST command is executed.

Of interest in our particular example is the dBASE UPPER() command. This command converts character data to uppercase letters. As a result, we can use UPPER(FIRST) and UPPER(LAST) instead of just the field names to achieve the desired result.

This technique has other valuable uses. For example, we could LIST SALARY*1.1 and see what people's salaries would be with a 10 percent raise. LIST IIF(DEPENDENTS,1,0) would return a 1 for a true entry, and a 0 for a false one, which is a useful conversion to prepare for import into some programs, such as 1–2–3.

While cleaning up, issue another command: SET HEADINGS OFF. This suppresses listing of the field names at the top of the columns. As a result, the new command looks like this:

```
LIST UPPER(FIRST), UPPER(LAST), PHONE OFF
```

Figure 6–15 shows the entire revised sequence of commands used to create a text file of the employee names and phone numbers with the names in upper-case letters.

FIGURE 6–15
Revised SET ALTERNATE Example

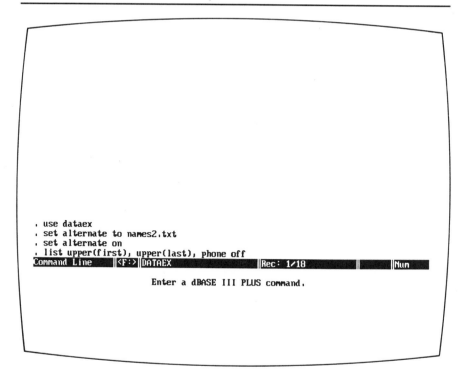

```
. use dataex
. set alternate to names2.txt
. set alternate on
. list upper(first), upper(last), phone off
Command Line      <F:> DATAEX                   Rec: 1/18                    Num
          Enter a dBASE III PLUS command.
```

The results are shown in Figure 6–16, and there is less work to clean up the unwanted data. Once the extra lines are removed, there is a perfectly formatted fixed-length record file.

This approach also offers some additional important assistance. None of the methods mentioned has helped extract the contents of a memo field. The SET ALTERNATE and LIST approach solves this problem.

If a simple LIST command with no options or qualifiers is issued, you get a listing of all the fields in the entire table with the exception of memo fields. These appear as a consistent memo notation that indicates the field is a memo field and may or may not contain data. This effect is illustrated in Figure 6–17.

FIGURE 6–16
Revised Results of SET ALTERNATE and LIST Commands

```
. list upper(first), upper(last), phone off
upper(first) upper(last) phone
CHRISTINE    DOLAN       269-111-2222
RICKY        EVANS       904-111-2222
SAMANTHA     FIALA       904-111-5656
CHRISTIE     FRANCO      111-222-3333
LOUIS        GABRIELE    125-478-6325
JUSTINE      GALL        987-236-5668
CYNTHIA      GILES       789-455-6233
TAYLOR       GREENBERG   123-456-7899
ROBERT       HAUGHTON    258-974-6623
SAMANTHA     HERTZIG     901-256-8954
COURTNEY     HIMLICKY    886-325-5625
JENNIFER     HORCH       465-623-8562
ELIZABETH    KAIN        798-953-2054
GARY         KATZ        111-888-3333
AMY          KRISTOFF    000-000-1111
GINA         LANE        226-696-2635
JENNIFER     LEVIN       233-366-3656
JOSIE        LORD        745-632-5665

. set alternate off⁺
```

FIGURE 6–17
LIST of the Sample dBASE Table

```
Record# LAST      FIRST     ID      STREET                          CITY
        STATE ZIP  PHONE            DEPENDENTS      SALARY DEPARTMENT HIREDATE NOTES
      1 Dolan     Christine 6867001 P.O. Box# 1515                  Overland Park
        KS    66210 269-111-2222 ,F,              40000.00          360 09/25/84 Memo
      2 Evans     Ricky     7169002 222 Waverly Lane                San Rafael
        CA    94903 904-111-2222 ,F,              45000.00          360 09/28/84 Memo
      3 Fiala     Samantha  2825770 #45 Bricker Lane                San Jose
        CA    95134 904-111-5656 ,F,              78000.00          360 10/05/84 Memo
      4 Franco    Christie  6963030 5555 Coconut Grove Blvd         Torrance
        CA    90505 111-222-3333 ,F,             144000.00          100 06/21/85 Memo
      5 Gabriele  Louis     3176250 8998 Atlantic Blvd.             Teaneck
        NJ    07666 125-478-6325 ,F,              12000.00          240 01/22/85 Memo
      6 Gall      Justine   3225670 #09 Old Wire Road               Norcross
        GA    30092 987-236-5668 ,F,              25000.00          360 09/24/84 Memo
      7 Giles     Cynthia   4127004 5555 East Coast Drive           Cambridge
        MA    02138 789-455-6233 ,F,              30000.00          360 10/05/84 Memo
      8 Greenberg Taylor    7331506 6969 Ocean Blvd, Apt 3A         Pacific Grove
        CA    93950 123-456-7899 ,F,              12000.00          240 01/23/85 Memo
      9 Haughton  Robert    9160005 1919 First Street East          Arlington
        VA    22209 258-974-6623 ,F,              40000.00          360 09/25/84 Memo

Command Line    <F:> DATAEX                    Rec: 9/18            Num
              Enter a dBASE III PLUS command.
```

If the name of a memo field is issued, as shown in Figure 6–18, the memo data appears on the screen. Note that it is formatted to appear in a specific column width. This will destroy any hopes of creating a fixed-length format, but you can't expect the free-form text of a memo to fit comfortably in a fixed-length format.

The width of the memo-line format defaults to 30 characters, but this can be changed with the dBASE environmental SET MEMOWIDTH command. This command allows you to set the width as needed. You can use the SET ALTERNATE procedure to reroute the output to a text file, which you can bring into a word processing program for editing, formatting, and further manipulation.

FIGURE 6–18
LIST with the NOTES Field to Show Memo Contents

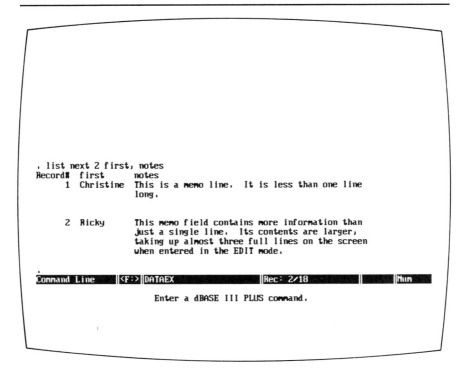

```
. list next 2 first, notes
Record# first    notes
      1 Christine This is a memo line. It is less than one line
                 long.

      2 Ricky    This memo field contains more information than
                 just a single line. Its contents are larger,
                 taking up almost three full lines on the screen
                 when entered in the EDIT mode.

Command Line     ||<F:>||DATAEX              ||Rec: 2/18        ||      ||Num

            Enter a dBASE III PLUS command.
```

You can eliminate the need to edit the SET ALTERNATE results entirely if you resort to dBASE programming files. The SET CONSOLE command allows you to turn off the screen display for faster performance. You can also use the dBASE ? output command with pointer-control commands to control the records and data that are sent to the text file. These are more complex procedures, and the dot-prompt techniques covered here will handle almost any task without programming.

dBASE IV COPY TO OPTIONS

dBASE IV offers all the above, plus a few twists for creating new data-file formats. As you might expect from seeing the related commands, dBASE IV also supports dBASE II, Framework II, and RapidFile formats. It also offers a dBASE III format so that you can turn a table back into a format that dBASE III can read.

SUMMARY

dBASE offers a powerful selection of tools for extracting data from .DBF tables and placing the information in various file formats. Considering its flexible-import capabilities, dBASE is a useful alternative whenever you must move columnar data—where the information can be made to conform to a data base record and field structure. There are times, however, when you must deal with free-form information such as letters and reports. These are grist for the word-processing mills, and the techniques of moving this type of information is covered in the next chapter.

CHAPTER 7

MOVING DATA IN AND OUT OF POPULAR WORD-PROCESSING PROGRAMS

Word-processing data requires different treatment than data base and spreadsheet files. While much of the information that people work with on computers conforms to the rows-and-columns orientation of spreadsheets and data base files, at least an equal amount of information fits no pattern. Reports, memos, letters, and other written communication is free-form, and it cannot be forced easily to fit into tidy fields.

As a result, word processing is an application providing specific tools that are often different from the tools of more organized spreadsheets and data base managers. Word processors are more concerned with giving control over the output's appearance than most other applications. Typically, there are neither complex margin and indents control; nor ranges of type pitches and fonts; nor various print attributes such as bold, underline, or italic with a spreadsheet or data base program. Yet, you expect these features and much more from a good word-processing program.

You also can expect to find support for headers and footers, flush or ragged-right justification, varying line spacing, and more. Many word-processing programs also maintain document data such as creation date, author, operator, number of revisions, and latest revision date. Expect to be able to automatically number pages, show the system date in a header, and create form letters by merging a document with a mailing list.

There is one major problem with word processors; there are so many in use. Unlike spreadsheets where 1–2–3 reigns supreme (at least for the moment), or data base programs where dBASE III has a mammoth lead on the others, there is no word-processing program that dominates the marketplace.

As a result, you cannot count on any individual to use the same word-processing program that you use. To make matters worse, there are few standards for word-processing file formats, and each program seems to have the best way to store text, so other programs must make their data accessible.

This chapter makes the most of this difficult situation. The ideal solution is to get everyone that you work with to agree on a single word processor so that there is no problem with exchanging files. The following pages teach what you can and cannot expect from five major word-processing programs, and how to work with their limitations.

SOME GENERAL ADVICE ON WORD-PROCESSING FILES

The remainder of this chapter is divided into five sections: WordPerfect 5.0, WordStar Professional, MultiMate Advantage II, Microsoft Word 4.0, and DisplayWrite 4. These five packages represent the vast majority of installed word-processing programs.

Each section covers the same topics for each program. You will see how to bring an ASCII text file into a document for each program, and how to convert a document into pure ASCII text format. You will see the effect of different Carriage Return/Line Feed text formats on the import process, and how to deal with them.

You will also see how the program can import other formats (if any), and what you need to know about the limitations of these procedures. Finally, you will learn about the form-letter merge-file structures, so that you can create appropriately formatted files from your spreadsheet or data base files. Before covering specific programs, however, there is some general information that needs to be addressed.

Formatting and Print Attributes

In researching this chapter, I created a simple three-page document. It contains sections with different left and right margins, a hanging-outdent for one paragraph, bold and underlined text, and centered text. It also contains a forced page break, a two-line header that includes the system date, and a footer that prints the page number centered at the bottom of the page. Finally, I did my best to set up the program to work with the HP LaserJet Series II printer, and called on a number of different proportional fonts stored in a ROM font cartridge in the printer.

I created two ASCII text versions of the file, one with a Carriage Return at the end of each line, and another with Carriage Returns only between paragraphs. I then imported each into the five word-processing programs and worked with the easiest one to create the fully formatted version.

I then tried available export format options. After the export files were created, I tried importing them into the five programs that could convert other formats.

There was not a single translation utility contained within the word-processing programs that correctly translated the test file. The different programs come with varying translation capabilities—practically nonexistent in some cases—but none was perfect.

Not even the DCA formats worked reliably. As discussed in Part 1, DCA stands for "Document Content Architecture." It comes in two varieties: RFT ("Revisable Format Text") and FFT ("Final Form Text"). They were invented by IBM to move formatted text between different word-processing programs. Unfortunately, the bugs have not been worked out, and it is not yet the reliable, fool-proof system that we need.

As a result, no matter what path you choose, you face some amount of editing or reformatting. For example, you will probably need to recreate any header or footer in the imported document. You will usually lose any specific font control such as selecting the right point size of a certain typestyle.

The Text-File Approach

Since some editing is involved anyway, consider instead a strategy of surrender. Rather than finding all the hidden and tricky faults introduced by the translation process, think about controlling the process even if it means a little more work.

Achieve this strategy by planning on using text files as the exchange medium from the start. All programs listed here (and most word processors) can move text files in and out with relative ease. Instead of the program's native formatting commands, you can use *pseudocodes* to represent different formatting attributes.

For example, it you want to mark text for bold printing, bracket it with a pseudocode that represents where the bold face printing will start and then stop. For example, your text might include this line:

This sentence has two words set in BF>bold type<BF and the rest in normal type.

In this example, use the receiving program's search and replace options to change the "BF>" to the appropriate command to start bold face printing, and "<BF" for the command to stop it.

Similar codes can be developed for other attributes. For example, "IT>" can start italics, "UL>" can start underlining, "<LM = 10>" can represent a change to a left margin of 10, and "<JU>" can mark where fully justified text starts.

These codes have no effect on your printout in either the sending or receiving program. They are shorthand that specify how you expect the page to be formatted, and you use the search and replace function to replace the fake codes with ones that work for the program.

Preparing a Document for Conversion to Text

In general, when you try to create a text file from a document, simplicity is the best guiding principle. Set your left margin to 0, and set the right margin to a reasonable line length (typically 65). This prevents a column of spaces to the left of each line, which is a nuisance to remove.

Set the program to use the simplest printer driver available; often this is called *Line Printer* or *DOS File*. Many word processors send massive amounts of printer-control commands whether the formatting of the document requires it or not, so a simple driver avoids this problem. Do not use bold or underlined text, since they are often handled by backspacing and retyping, which can cause headaches when cleaning up the imported file later.

Do something special to mark the start of a new paragraph. Either indent each paragraph with a tab or a certain number of spaces, or skip a line between paragraphs. By identifying the start of a new paragraph, difficulty and agony are spared when you clean up the file.

Eliminate all headers and footers, and print as many lines to the page as possible. If the program is set up for 11-inch paper, try to format the page so that there is no top or bottom margin—to print 66 lines per page. This eliminates extra Carriage Returns from the text file, meaning that there are fewer extraneous characters to clean up.

The guiding principle for ASCII conversion between word processors is keeping the original document simple. In many cases, it is easier to enter the print attributes and formatting commands later than it is to hassle with the conversions.

WORDPERFECT 5.0

The latest version of WordPerfect expands on the original program's power and ease of use. WordPerfect is often cited as one of the easier programs to learn, as far as writing a simple letter is concerned. It also boasts a range of features for macros, form letters, and complex formatting.

The last versions did an adequate but imperfect job of handling laser-printer proportional fonts; they were better suited for straightforward business-document production. The newest release expands greatly, however, on the formatting and font control features, which makes WordPerfect 5.0 a candidate for many simple to moderately complex desktop-publishing tasks. WordPerfect offers a range of ways to move data in and out.

How to Bring in a Text File

It is easy to bring a text file into WordPerfect 5.0, just like prior versions. It is done from within the program; there is no need to rely on any external conversion utility.

Text files can be brought into an empty workspace, or they may be appended to an existing document. Figure 7–1 illustrates an empty document. At the bottom of the screen, there is a row of choices. They were called by pressing the "Text In/Out" function key: Ctrl-F5.

FIGURE 7–1
WordPerfect 5.0 Text In/Out Menu

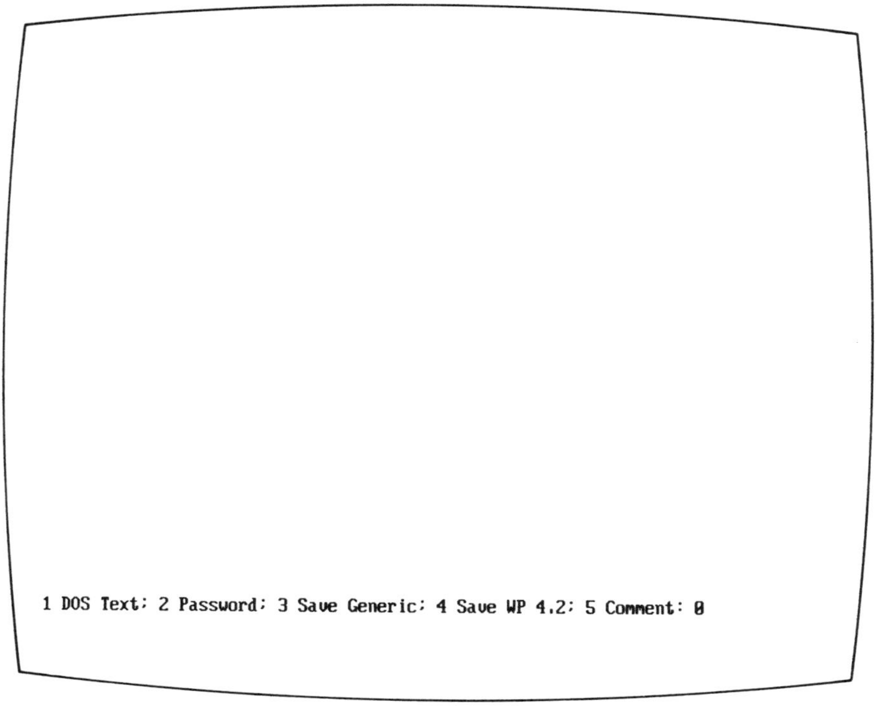

```
1 DOS Text: 2 Password: 3 Save Generic: 4 Save WP 4.2: 5 Comment: 0
```

There are a number of choices on the menu, and we want the first selection: DOS TEXT. Figure 7–2 shows the next menu that appears when you press 1.

This menu offers three choices. The first choice is used to save a WordPerfect document as a text file. Presently, however, we are most concerned with the other two selections. There are two options for retrieving text. The first translates all Carriage Return/Line Feed combinations into hard carriage returns (coded as [HRt] in a WordPerfect file). The second converts Carriage Return/Line Feed combinations to soft returns (coded [SRt]) if they fall within the defined *hot zone,* which Word-Perfect uses to define the end of a line in a paragraph; the hot zone is the area used to determine hyphenation and word wrap.

FIGURE 7–2
WordPerfect DOS Text Menu

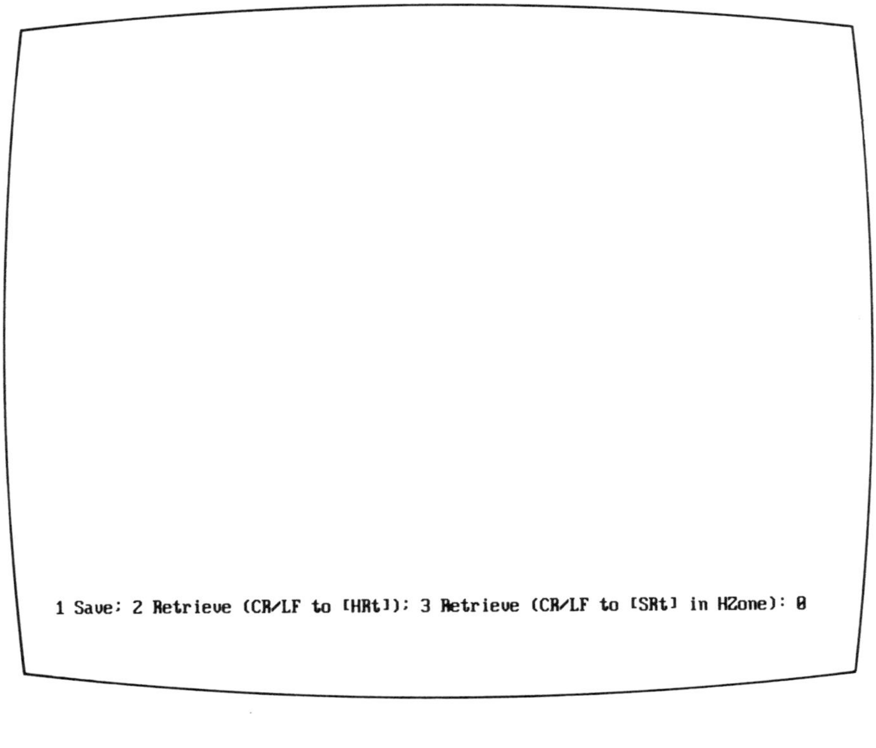

```
1 Save: 2 Retrieve (CR/LF to [HRt]); 3 Retrieve (CR/LF to [SRt] in HZone): 0
```

If your text file only has Carriage Returns at the end of each paragraph, then you are better off using the option that converts them all to hard returns (#2 on the menu.) This is the choice to make if your file has lots of tabular material where the lines are as long as the page is wide.

On the other hand, if you have textual material in paragraph form with Carriage Returns at the end of each line, then the conversion to soft returns in the hot zone (#3 on the menu) is the best choice.

Figure 7–3 shows the effect of bringing in a file under the hard-return option. The original file had Carriage Return and Line Feed characters at the end of each paragraph.

FIGURE 7–3
Text In with Hard Returns

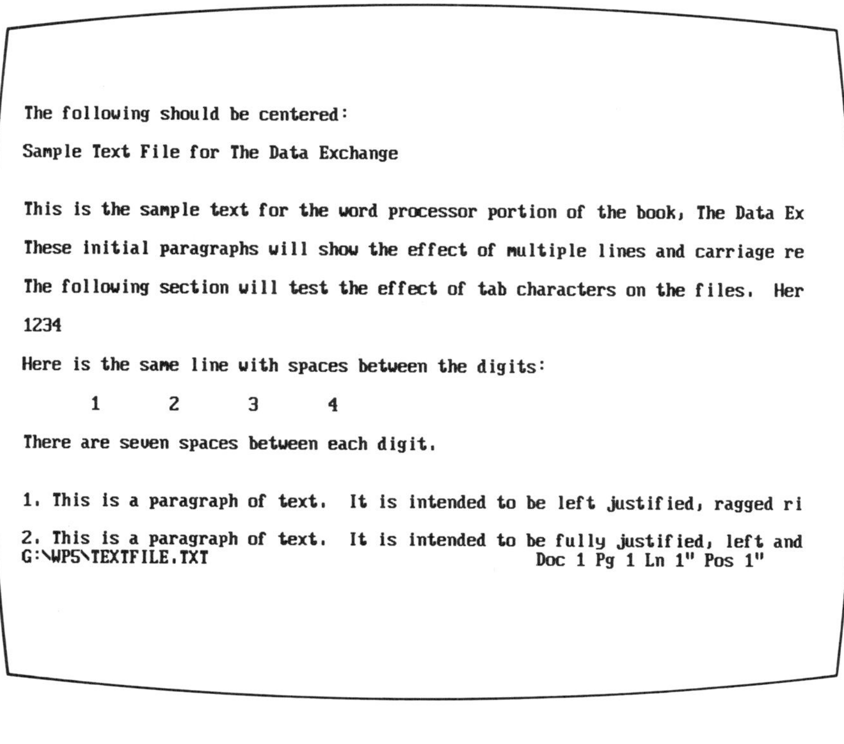

```
The following should be centered:

Sample Text File for The Data Exchange

This is the sample text for the word processor portion of the book, The Data Ex

These initial paragraphs will show the effect of multiple lines and carriage re

The following section will test the effect of tab characters on the files.  Her

1234

Here is the same line with spaces between the digits:

     1      2      3      4

There are seven spaces between each digit.

1. This is a paragraph of text.  It is intended to be left justified, ragged ri

2. This is a paragraph of text.  It is intended to be fully justified, left and
G:\WP5\TEXTFILE.TXT                          Doc 1 Pg 1 Ln 1" Pos 1"
```

Note that the lines of text for each paragraph extend beyond the right edge of the screen display. This is because WordPerfect has not reformatted the file completely.

To fix this situation, move the cursor down through the file. Figure 7–4 shows the effect of moving the cursor past the first long line.

WordPerfect automatically adjusts the word wrap for all lines on the screen, and it updates the display. You can now edit the file, and the paragraphs will reformat automatically. Figure 7–5 illustrates the results of importing a print file with the soft-return option.

As shown in Figure 7–5, it is formatted from the start—ready for editing. The soft returns are already in place and so

FIGURE 7–4
Text In with Hard Returns after Reformat

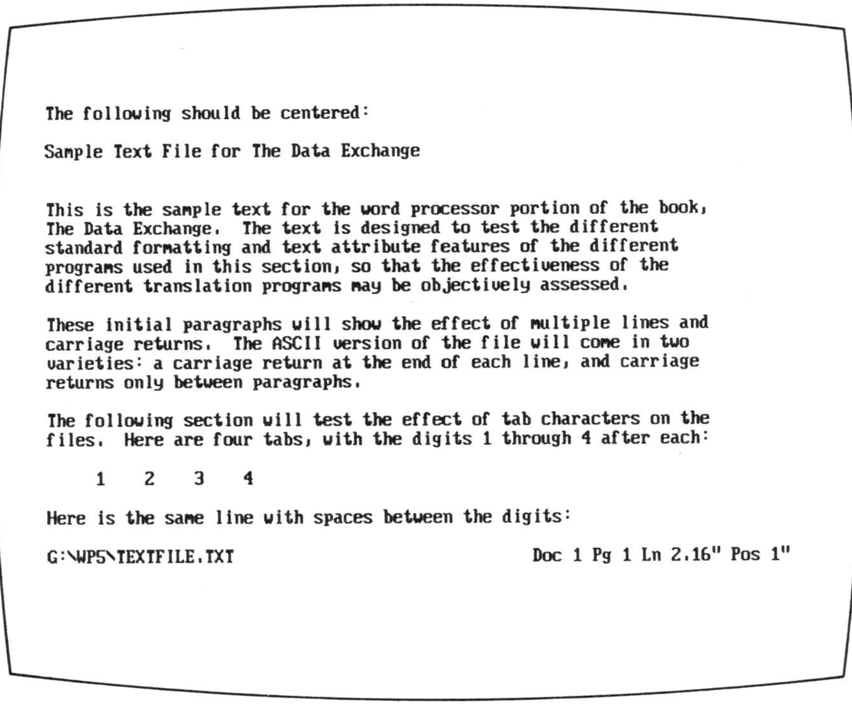

```
The following should be centered:

Sample Text File for The Data Exchange

This is the sample text for the word processor portion of the book,
The Data Exchange. The text is designed to test the different
standard formatting and text attribute features of the different
programs used in this section, so that the effectiveness of the
different translation programs may be objectively assessed.

These initial paragraphs will show the effect of multiple lines and
carriage returns. The ASCII version of the file will come in two
varieties: a carriage return at the end of each line, and carriage
returns only between paragraphs.

The following section will test the effect of tab characters on the
files. Here are four tabs, with the digits 1 through 4 after each:

        1    2    3    4

Here is the same line with spaces between the digits:

G:\WP5\TEXTFILE.TXT                          Doc 1 Pg 1 Ln 2.16" Pos 1"
```

are the word wraps. Although it cannot be seen on this screen, there is tabular material later in the file, but the line endings were maintained in the proper places. The implication of this is that the soft-return feature is much more useful and powerful than the text import of other programs—where you have to use search and replace to get rid of Carriage Returns at the end of lines.

There is one other place where you can easily import text files, and that is the List Files screen, which is called by the F5 Function Key. Figure 7–6 shows an example of this screen.

Note at the bottom of the screen that the #5 menu choice is TEXT IN. Selecting this option is equivalent to the Ctrl-F5 TEXT IN/OUT, 1 DOS TEXT, 2 RETRIEVE (CR/LF TO [HRT]) sequence

FIGURE 7–5
Text In with Soft Return

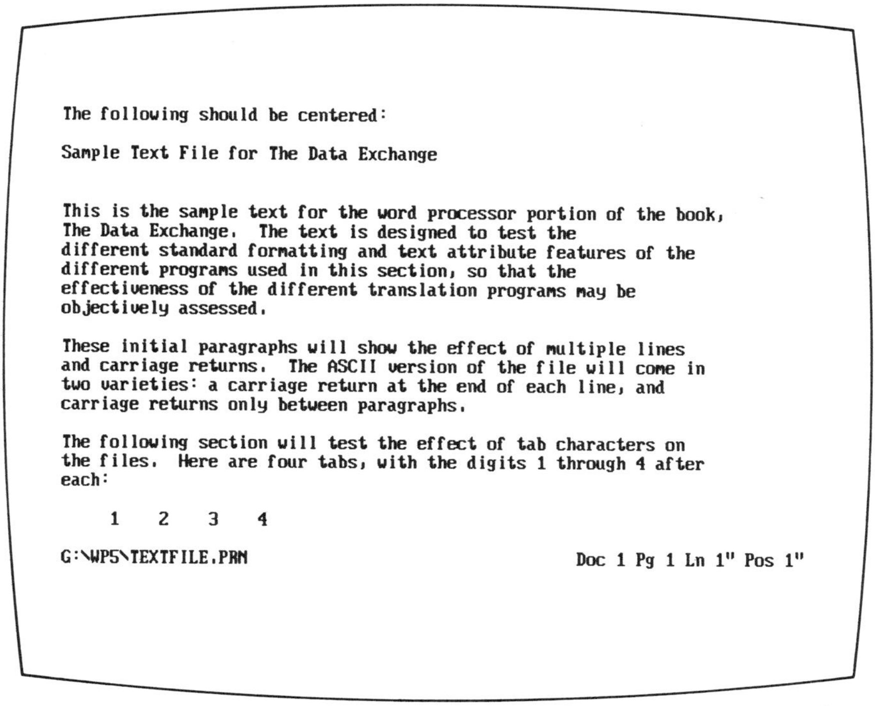

The following should be centered:

Sample Text File for The Data Exchange

This is the sample text for the word processor portion of the book,
The Data Exchange. The text is designed to test the
different standard formatting and text attribute features of the
different programs used in this section, so that the
effectiveness of the different translation programs may be
objectively assessed.

These initial paragraphs will show the effect of multiple lines
and carriage returns. The ASCII version of the file will come in
two varieties: a carriage return at the end of each line, and
carriage returns only between paragraphs.

The following section will test the effect of tab characters on
the files. Here are four tabs, with the digits 1 through 4 after
each:

    1   2   3   4

G:\WP5\TEXTFILE.PRN   Doc 1 Pg 1 Ln 1" Pos 1"

FIGURE 7–6
WordPerfect 5.0 List Files Screen

```
04/28/89  10:59              Directory G:\WP5\*.*
Document size:        0   Free:   104448   Used:  2206000      Files:  90

MMPROF   .        3460  01/28/89 12:42  ▲  MMPROF   .SAM     4003  01/28/89 12:25
MULTISMC.WPD      4010  04/27/88 14:24  |  NEWSPAPR.WPG     1388  04/27/88 14:24
M01      .WPG     3234  04/27/88 14:24  |  PC       .WPG     2586  04/27/88 14:24
PENCIL   .WPG     3510  04/27/88 14:24  |  PHONE    .WPG     4100  04/27/88 14:24
PRESENT  .WPG     1430  04/27/88 14:24  |  PRINTER  .TST    21367  05/18/88 00:28
QUILL    .WPG     1310  04/27/88 14:24  |  README   .       10757  05/18/88 00:28
README   .WP     12742  05/18/88 00:28  |  RPTCARD  .WPG     6054  04/27/88 14:24
SPELL    .EXE    37888  04/27/88 14:13  |  STANDARD .CRS     1932  05/18/88 00:28
STANDARD .PRS     1025  05/05/88 12:47  |  TEST     .OUT        0  04/28/89 09:08
TEXTFILE .PRN     4761  05/18/88 12:00  |  TEXTFILE .TXT     4702  05/18/88 12:00
TEXTFILE .XY      5105  05/18/88 12:17  |  THINKER  .WPG     4626  04/27/88 14:24
USAMAP   .WPG     9082  04/27/88 14:24  |  WP       .DRS    73356  04/27/88 14:24
WP       .EXE   244736  05/05/88 12:47  |  WP       .FIL   298884  05/05/88 12:47
WP       .MRS     3756  05/05/88 12:47  |  WPHELP   .FIL    47507  05/05/88 12:47
WPHELP2  .FIL    52121  05/05/88 12:47  |  WPSMALL  .DRS    13022  05/05/88 12:47
WP{WP}   .SET     2144  04/28/89 09:14  |  WP{WP}EN.LEX    292095  04/27/88 14:13
WP{WP}EN.THS    362269  04/27/88 14:17  |  WP}WP{   .BU1        0  04/28/89 09:35
WP}WP{   .CHK        0  04/28/89 09:35  |  WP}WP{   .SPC     4096  04/28/89 09:35
WP}WP{   .TU1        0  04/28/89 09:35  |  WYSE700  .WPD     3568  04/27/88 14:24

1 Retrieve; 2 Delete; 3 Move/Rename; 4 Print; 5 Text In;
6 Look; 7 Other Directory; 8 Copy; 9 Word Search; N Name Search: 6
```

on the main editing screen. The important fact to remember is that it converts all Carriage Returns to hard returns; you do not get the extra options offered by the TEXT IN/OUT command.

How to Export a Text File

Exporting a text file is simple. The TEXT IN/OUT command (called by Ctrl-F5 on the main editing screen) offers a SAVE option in the DOS TEXT option, as shown in Figure 7–1 earlier in this section.

The TEXT IN/OUT also offers another option, #3, which is called SAVE GENERIC. This option removes all WordPerfect formatting codes, but saves the text.

There is an important difference between these two commands. The DOS TEXT SAVE command puts a Carriage Return/ Line Feed combination at the end of each line. This makes it less suitable for import into another word-processing program where you might have to search for and replace the pairs except between paragraphs. On the other hand, this type of file is ideal for transmitting via electronic-mail systems.

The SAVE GENERIC option is the reverse. It only puts Carriage Return/Line Feed pairs at the end of paragraphs. This can simplify importing the file for other word processors, but it causes problems for electronic-mail systems because of the long, unbroken lines in each paragraph.

Other Supported Formats

WordPerfect has a conversion utility called CONVERT. Call the program from the DOS prompt (not from within the WordPerfect program), and you are greeted with a title screen and then a blank screen with a single prompt asking for the input-file name. After a response, it asks for an output-file name. After that, it responds with a screen similar to Figure 7–7.

WordPerfect 5.0 converts from six different formats including DCA RFT (Document Content Architecture Revisable Format Text), which is now offered by many major word-processing programs. The last three options on the list relate to mail-merge files, which are covered in the next section.

If you convert from an existing WordPerfect 5.0 file to another format, select the first choice on the menu, which produces a screen similar to the one in Figure 7–8.

Note that the output formats include both the DCA RFT and FFT (Final Format Text) file formats. Also, the Navy DIF format is not the same as the Data Interchange Format discussed in this book. The typical DIF files are data files produced by data base programs or spreadsheets. Navy DIF is a word-processing format that is not widely used, but Word-Perfect evidently had a large U.S. Navy contract at one point and built the feature into the regular program.

FIGURE 7–7
Convert Input File Format List

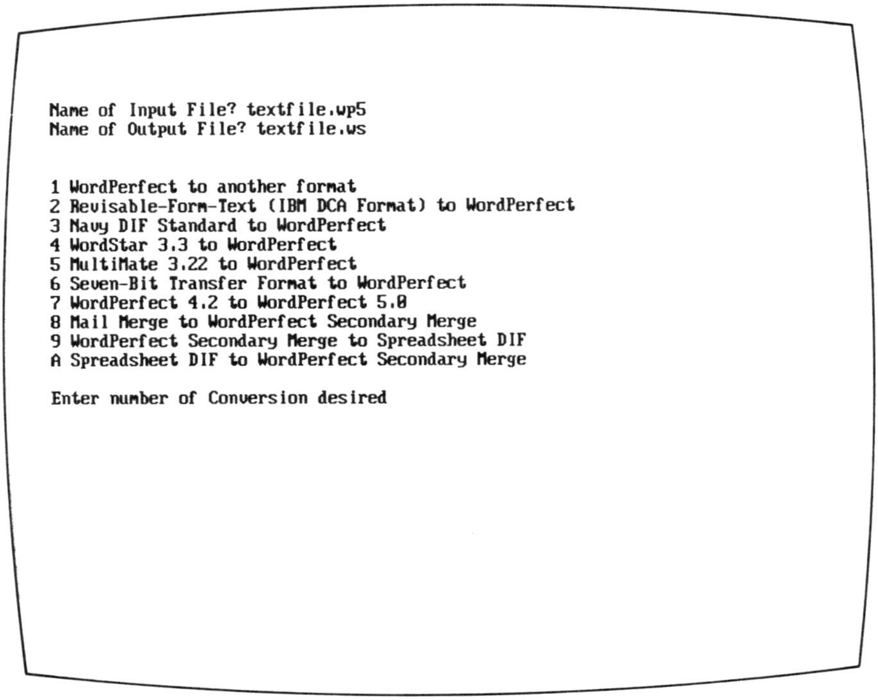

```
Name of Input File? textfile.wp5
Name of Output File? textfile.ws

1 WordPerfect to another format
2 Revisable-Form-Text (IBM DCA Format) to WordPerfect
3 Navy DIF Standard to WordPerfect
4 WordStar 3.3 to WordPerfect
5 MultiMate 3.22 to WordPerfect
6 Seven-Bit Transfer Format to WordPerfect
7 WordPerfect 4.2 to WordPerfect 5.0
8 Mail Merge to WordPerfect Secondary Merge
9 WordPerfect Secondary Merge to Spreadsheet DIF
A Spreadsheet DIF to WordPerfect Secondary Merge

Enter number of Conversion desired
```

Overall, WordPerfect has limited conversion abilities regarding other program formats. As a result, you will want to rely on either text-format transfers, or use one of the third-party conversion programs discussed in Part 4.

Mail-Merge Files

In the world of unusual file formats, the WordPerfect mail-merge data file takes the cake. WordPerfect calls it a *secondary-merge file;* it is the file that contains the data used to "fill in the blanks" on a form letter.

Figure 7–9 illustrates the contents of such a file. Each field's data appears on its own line. There is a hard-return [HRt] code embedded at the end of each one.

FIGURE 7–8
Convert Output File Format List

```
Name of Input File? textfile.wp5
Name of Output File? textfile.ws

1 Revisable-Form-Text (IBM DCA Format)
2 Final-Form-Text (IBM DCA Format)
3 Navy DIF Standard
4 WordStar 3.3
5 MultiMate 3.22
6 Seven-Bit Transfer Format
7 ASCII text file

Enter number of output file format desired
```

Also notice that each data line ends in a "^R." This is an on-screen representation of Ctrl-R, which is a single character, as opposed to separate "^" and "R" characters. This Ctrl-R marks the end of a data field. The end of each record is marked by a Ctrl-E on its own line.

There are few data base programs that support this format. Fortunately, a number of alternatives are available if you need to put data in this format.

If your data base program supports custom-report formats and print-to-disk, you may define a format that prints each field on a line, inserts the Ctrl-R at the end, and then puts the Ctrl-E on the line by itself between records. You can also use the WordPerfect CONVERT utility to translate from comma-delimited or DIF data-file formats.

FIGURE 7–9
WordPerfect Secondary-Merge File

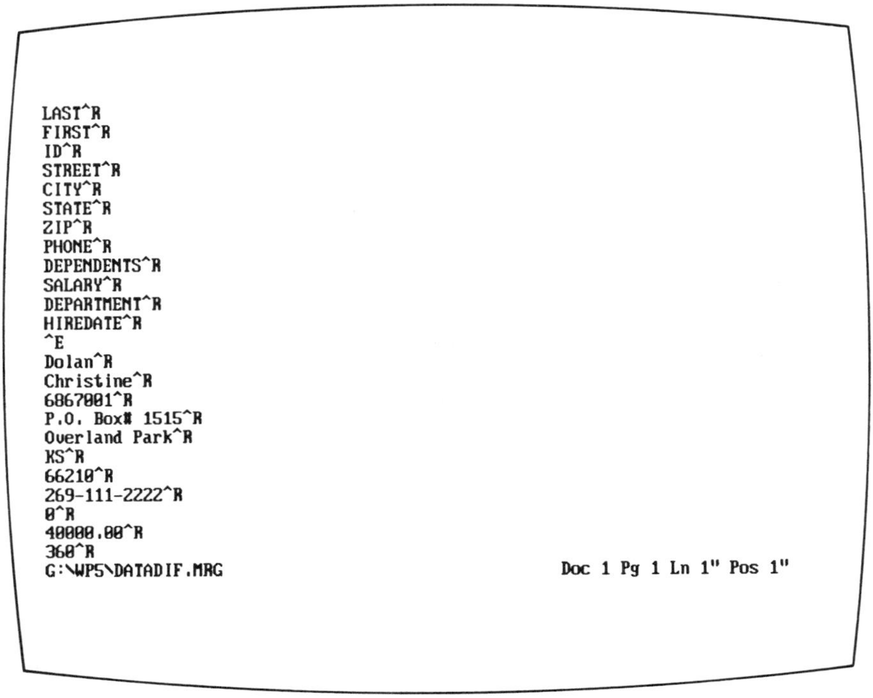

```
LAST^R
FIRST^R
ID^R
STREET^R
CITY^R
STATE^R
ZIP^R
PHONE^R
DEPENDENTS^R
SALARY^R
DEPARTMENT^R
HIREDATE^R
^E
Dolan^R
Christine^R
6867001^R
P.O. Box# 1515^R
Overland Park^R
KS^R
66210^R
269-111-2222^R
0^R
40000.00^R
360^R
G:\WP5\DATADIF.MRG                    Doc 1 Pg 1 Ln 1" Pos 1"
```

To convert comma-delimited files, select the "Mail Merge to WordPerfect Secondary Merge" option as shown in Figure 7–7. Mail merge refers to the WordStar mail-merge format, which is the same as comma-delimited. The CONVERT program will ask for the field delimiter, which is a comma (,), and a record delimiter, which is a Carriage Return/Line Feed combination. This last pair must be entered as decimal ASCII values, namely {013}{010}. Note that the curly brackets (the "squiggly parentheses") are required by CONVERT. Finally, if the string fields are quoted, you must tell CONVERT to strip the quote marks from the file during conversion. If there are commas inside a string field surrounded by quotes, the CONVERT program will not split the field at the comma.

The CONVERT program works well with the comma-delimited files except for one hitch. You need to have a comma at the end of the line after the last data field or else the Ctrl-E will not appear on a line by itself.

The DIF conversion works more smoothly—since there are no options or choices to make. The CONVERT program knows how to change into the WordPerfect mail-merge format with no trouble. As a result, you may want to use DIF when moving data from a data base or spreadsheet to a form letter in WordPerfect.

WORDSTAR RELEASE 5.5

If there is a revered elder in the word-processor market, it is WordStar. Originally written for the CP/M operating system,

FIGURE 7–10
WordStar Opening Menu

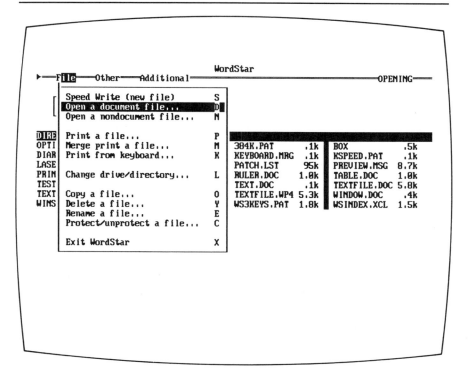

FIGURE 7–11
WordStar Document File Prompt

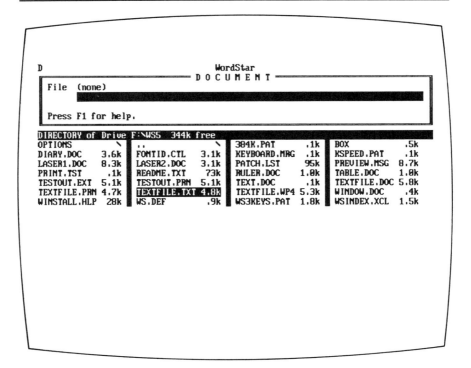

it has survived the rise and fall of a half-dozen microcomputer models and is used widely.

Today, there are a variety of versions when purchasing WordStar. The latest version (as this is written) is WordStar 5.5, and it offers modern features while maintaining close ties to past versions. It has many useful programs (like outlining, merging graphics with documents, and more), and it has pull-down menus that make it easy to use.

Like its predecessors, WordStar is not fancy with file formats. There are two choices: document and nondocument modes. This can limit your flexibility in manipulating files for use with other programs, but chances are that this deficiency will be compensated for by import and export capabilities of the other program.

FIGURE 7–12
Sample Text File in WordStar before Reformat

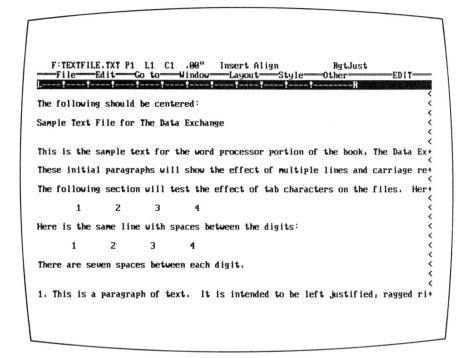

How to Bring in a Text File

Bringing a text file into WordStar is easy. If you do not want to use the WordStar formatting features, such as when you edit program code, you can edit text files in the nondocument mode and they will remain text files.

However, you will want the paragraph formatting and print attribute controls that are part of a word-processing program. In this case, use the document mode.

Figure 7–10 shows the WordStar Release 5.5 opening menu. The "*F*" key has been pressed to pull down the File command menu. Note that the second and third options are "*D*" and "*N*." These select whether you will work with the file in a document or nondocument mode.

FIGURE 7–13
WordStar Quick Menu

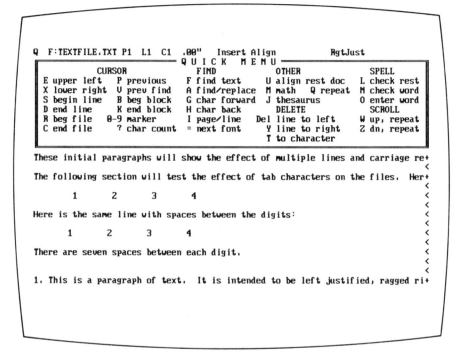

The next screen, Figure 7–11, shows the effects of select-ing the "*D*" option and entering the filename when prompted. WordStar allows use of the cursor control keys to select a file-name from the displayed directory listing without having to retype the entire filename.

Figure 7–12 shows how the sample file appears when brought into WordStar. The less-than symbols ("<") at the right margin of the screen indicate an end-of-line character or a Carriage Return. Four lines of text end in a "+" instead; this indicates that the lines extend past the right edge of the screen.

The reason that these lines go past the edge of the screen is that this file was formatted without a Carriage Return at

FIGURE 7–14
Sample Text File in WordStar after Reformat

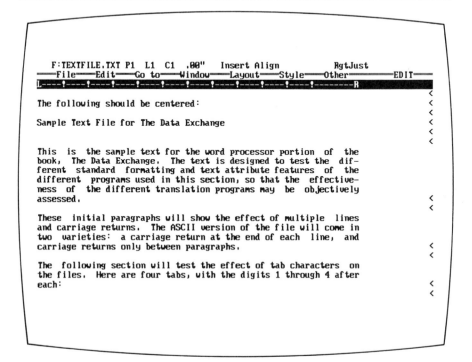

the end of each line. All it takes is the reformat command to fix the paragraphs. You can use the Ctrl-B command to reformat on a paragraph-by-paragraph basis, or you can use a Quick command. Figure 7–13 shows the Quick command menu, which was called by pressing Ctrl-Q.

The first option in the other column is "*U*," which will reformat all document paragraphs. Figure 7–14 shows how the file looks after the Ctrl-Q U command is given and the cursor has been moved back to the start of the file.

The file can now be formatted and manipulated as if it was entered directly into WordStar. The text is fully justified left and right on the screen; this is a result of default settings and

FIGURE 7–15
DOS List of WordStar 5.5 Sample File

```
•} Uhplaser     ⊊§
The following should be centered:

•
       ~       ~        !
•Sample Text File for The Data Exchange

.OJ OFF

This is the sample text for the word processor portion of the ⌐
book, The Data Exchange.  The text is designed to test the dif▾⌐
ferent standard formatting and text attribute features of the ⌐
different programs used in this section, so that the effective▾⌐
ness of the different translation programs may be objectively ⌐
assessed.

These initial paragraphs will show the effect of multiple lines ⌐
and carriage returns.  The ASCII version of the file will come in ⌐
two varieties: a carriage return at the end of each line, and ⌐
carriage returns only between paragraphs.

The following section will test the effect of tab characters on ⌐
the files.  Here are four tabs, with the digits 1 through 4 after ⌐
```

can be overridden for the whole document or individual paragraphs as needed.

To format the file so that it matched the desired formatting and font attributes for the test document, WordStar embedded-dot commands and other commands were used. Figure 7–15 shows the final result with a DOS listing of the actual file. The WordStar format places an unusual garbage character at the end of each line. It is a decimal 141 ASCII character, which is 128 more than the normal Carriage Return character. This character is followed by a normal Line Feed character. This combination of characters is used by WordStar 5.5 to identify line breaks within a paragraph—sometimes referred to as a *soft return*.

FIGURE 7–16
Older Version of WordStar Document File

```
The following should be centered:

            Sample Text File for The Data Exchange
                Wordsta² Professiona⁻ Version

Thi⟨ i⟨ th⁻ sampl⁻ tex⟨ fo² th⁻ wor∑ processo² portio€ o⊭ th⁻ ⟩
book⅛ Th⁻ Dat⁻ Exchange⟨ Th⁻ tex⟨ i⟨ designe∑ t⋂ tes⟨ th⁻ ⟩
differen⟨ standar∑ formattin⊤ an∑ tex⟨ attribut⁻ feature⟨ o⊭ th⁻ ⟩
differen⟨ program⟨ use∑ i€ thi⟨ section⅛ s⋂ tha⟨ th⁻ ⟩
effectivenes⟨ o⊭ th⁻ differen⟨ translatio€ program⟨ ma· b⁻ ⟩
objectivel· assessed.

Thes⁻ initia⁻ paragraph⟨ wil⁻ sho⁼ th⁻ effec⟨ o⊭ multipl⁻ line⟨ ⟩
an∑ carriag⁻ returns⟨ Th⁻ ASCI⊮ versio€ o⊭ th⁻ fil⁻ wil⁻ com⁻ i€ ⟩
tw⋂ varieties⫼ ⊭ carriag⁻ retur⟨ a⟨ th⁻ en∑ o⊭ eac⧗ line⅛ an∑ ⟩
carriag⁻ return⟨ onl· betwee€ paragraphs.

Th⁻ followin⊤ sectio€ wil⁻ tes⟨ th⁻ effec⟨ o⊭ ta⟨ character⟨ o€ ⟩
th⁻ files⟨ Her⁻ ar⁻ fou² tabs⅛ wit⧗ th⁻ digit⟨ ⫿ throug⧗ ⫰ afte² ⟩
each:

        1       2       3       4
```

The extra 128 added to the Carriage Return character at the end of each line is a vestige of the original, classic Word-Star file format. Figure 7–16 shows a similar file created with WordStar 4. WordStar changes the last character of each word so that the file is sprinkled with garbage characters. This is normal, and these characters are how WordStar used to identify the breaks between words for wrapping lines in paragraphs. The weird characters are generated by adding 128 to the character's decimal ASCII value; often this is described as "setting the high bit," since the 8th bit in the eight-bit byte used for the character is set to 1, which adds 128 to the total value.

FIGURE 7–17
Sample File with Carriage Returns at Each Line

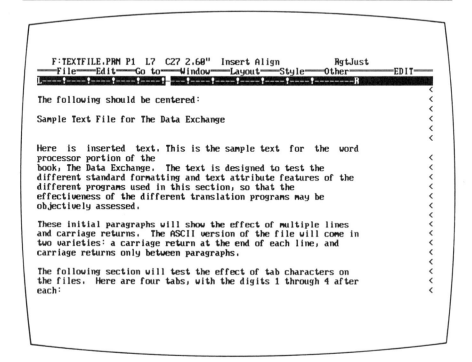

There are utility programs available that can turn an older-version WordStar file into a straight-text file. They simply subtract 128 from any character that has a value greater than 128, and this returns the character to its "normal" value.

It is more work to bring in a text file that has Carriage Returns at the end of each line. Again, it is easier to accomplish if you have some way to distinguish the end of a paragraph from the end of a line. You may use a tab or a certain number of spaces, or, as in the sample file, you may use two Carriage Returns between paragraphs.

Figure 7–17 shows the effect of editing the sample file with the Carriage Returns at the end of each line as a WordStar document file. Note that the second line in the first paragraph

FIGURE 7–18
WordStar Search and Replace Two Carriage Returns with Asterisk

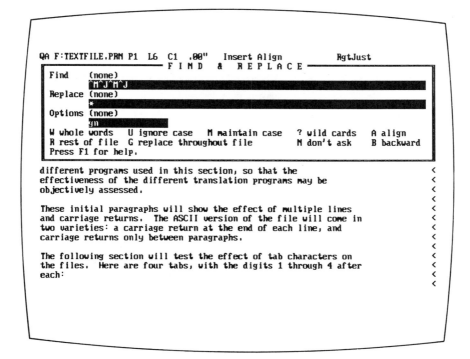

```
QA F:TEXTFILE.PRN P1  L6  C1  .00"   Insert Align            RgtJust
─────────────────────── F I N D  &  R E P L A C E ───────────
 Find    (none)
         ^M^J^M^J
 Replace (none)
         *
 Options (none)
         jn
 W whole words   U ignore case   M maintain case   ? wild cards   A align
 R rest of file  G replace throughout file         N don't ask    B backward
 Press F1 for help.

 different programs used in this section, so that the              <
 effectiveness of the different translation programs may be        <
 objectively assessed.                                             <
                                                                   <
 These initial paragraphs will show the effect of multiple lines   <
 and carriage returns.  The ASCII version of the file will come in <
 two varieties: a carriage return at the end of each line, and     <
 carriage returns only between paragraphs.                         <
                                                                   <
 The following section will test the effect of tab characters on   <
 the files.  Here are four tabs, with the digits 1 through 4 after <
 each:                                                             <
```

ends abruptly; WordStar does not reformat the paragraph properly because of the Carriage Returns at the end of each line.

The first step is to replace all the breaks between paragraphs with something distinctive so that you can later reinsert the Carriage Returns. An asterisk or any unusual character will do the job.

The WordStar command to start a search and replace operation is Ctrl-Q A. Figure 7–18 shows how the screen appears to replace the pairs of Carriage Returns with an asterisk.

Note that the "Find what?" prompt is followed by "^M^J^M^J." Ctrl-M is a Carriage Return, and Ctrl-J is a Line Feed character. This means that the search portion of the command will look for a pair of Carriage Return/Line Feed

FIGURE 7–19
WordStar Replacement Complete Message

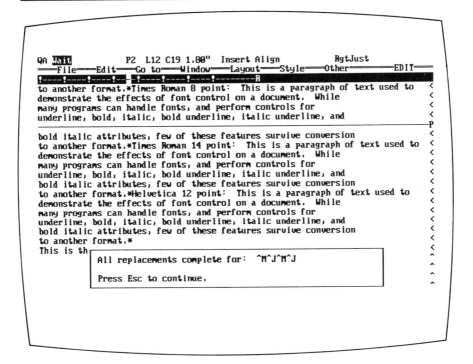

characters. Also notice the prompt to signal WordStar that you are finished entering the string is the Return Key. How can you enter a Carriage Return so that WordStar doesn't take it to mean that you have ended the command?

The answer is that there are some special codes for WordStar search strings. One is Ctrl-N, which is interpreted by WordStar as a Carriage Return/Line Feed pair. The string in this example was entered by pressing Ctrl-N twice.

The "Replace with?" prompt shows a simple asterisk— use any character as long as it doesn't appear elsewhere in the text.

Finally, WordStar asks about some options. In this case, the replacements start at the beginning and they replace in

FIGURE 7–20
WordStar Strip Carriage Returns Command

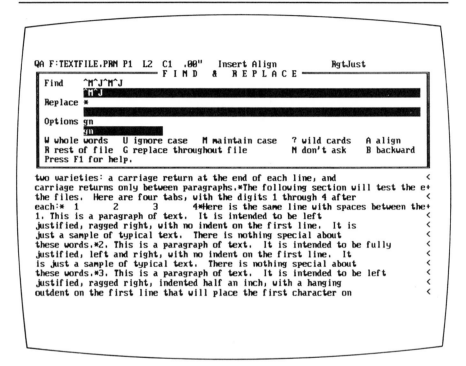

```
QA F:TEXTFILE.PRN P1  L2  C1  .00"    Insert Align              RgtJust
                    ========= F I N D  &  R E P L A C E ========
 Find    ^M^J^M^J
         ^M^J
 Replace *

 Options gn
         gn
 W whole words   U ignore case   M maintain case   ? wild cards   A align
 R rest of file  G replace throughout file         N don't ask    B backward
 Press F1 for help.

two varieties: a carriage return at the end of each line, and               <
carriage returns only between paragraphs.*The following section will test the e+
the files. Here are four tabs, with the digits 1 through 4 after            <
each:*  1       2       3       4*Here is the same line with spaces between the+
1. This is a paragraph of text.  It is intended to be left                  <
justified, ragged right, with no indent on the first line.  It is           <
just a sample of typical text.  There is nothing special about              <
these words.*2. This is a paragraph of text.  It is intended to be fully    <
justified, left and right, with no indent on the first line.  It            <
is just a sample of typical text.  There is nothing special about           <
these words.*3. This is a paragraph of text.  It is intended to be left     <
justified, ragged right, indented half an inch, with a hanging              <
outdent on the first line that will place the first character on            <
```

every instance without asking. As a result, the screen shows the responses of *GN* to this prompt. The *A* align option is not selected—the process runs faster without it.

When you press Return on this screen, the search and replace occurs, which ends with the message shown in Figure 7–19; it states that the replacement is complete.

Now, strip out all remaining Carriage Returns. By moving the cursor at the end of a line, it may appear that WordStar has a space between the last word and the end of the line. As a result, you might not add a space when stripping the end-of-line characters to keep the last word from joining the first word on the next line. This is a mistake—since that apparent space does not exist. Create a search and replace command as shown in Figure 7–20, and note that while it does not show in the illustration, there is a single space in response to the "Replace with?" prompt. Also, use the *A* align command in addition to the *GN* options.

Your file should look like Figure 7–21—collapsed into a single paragraph. Now, all you need to do is reverse the search and replace the command that eliminated the paragraph breaks to put them back.

Reformat the document and you get the same results as after opening the other version of the sample text file at the start of the chapter. The only difference is that you can lose the end-of-line characters if there is a list of short lines with this technique. If there are many of them, it will take some effort to reinsert them. It may be easier to double-space lists before bringing them into WordStar with this technique. Then, delete the blank lines between them later. In either case, it is simple to bring in a text file for editing with WordStar.

How to Export a Text File

Exporting a text file is also easy. You do it through the Print options and then reroute the output to disk. WordStar uses different printer drivers so formatting commands are correctly interpreted by different printers. The program also has special drivers that are not intended for use with a specific printer, however. The driver we are most concerned about is called ASCII. As expected, it creates a text file from your WordStar document. Figure 7–22 shows a print-option screen. The printer driver is the last option, and that is where you must specify the different driver.

If you simply specify the ASCII driver, WordStar will create a file called ASCII.WS that will contain the output. Since it will overwrite older files with the same name, remember to rename these files as they are produced or you may lose them.

A better way is to give the output file a new name from the start. As shown in Figure 7–22, you can put a symbol followed by a filename and the output will be routed to that file.

Figure 7–23 shows what the resulting output file looks like when it is typed from DOS. It is formatted with Carriage Re-

FIGURE 7–21
Search and Replace to Put Back the Carriage Returns

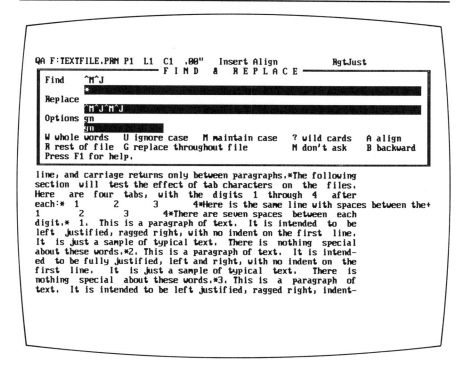

turns at the end of each line, but it contains no bold, underlining, or other print attributes.

There is no easy way to create a text file that only has Carriage Returns at the end of paragraphs, but as discussed elsewhere in this chapter and in Parts 3 and 4, there are other programs that overcome this limitation.

Other Supported Formats

The WordStar program does not recognize or produce any file formats other than its own or text file. Rely on other programs to perform the transformation or use text-file format as an intermediary.

FIGURE 7–22
Print Options Showing the ASCII Print Driver with File Redirection

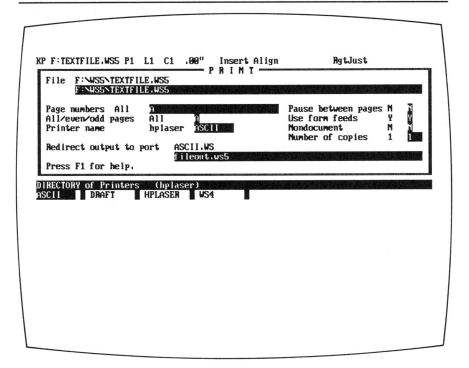

Fortunately, Micropro now bundles such a program with WordStar 5.5: Star Exchange. This is a private-label version of the Software Bridge, which is discussed in more detail in Part 4 of this book. It is one of the best document-file converters available. This version supports five formats: DCA RFT, Microsoft Word 4.0, MultiMate Advantage II 3.6, Word-Perfect 5.0, and WordStar 2000 version 3.0. You can only convert them to and from WordStar format; you can't use this program to go directly from WordPerfect to MultiMate, for example. For that, you need the full-blown version of Software Bridge.

Star Exchange offers many options to make the conversion process more accurate. These are documented well in the

FIGURE 7–23
WordStar Document Printed to Disk

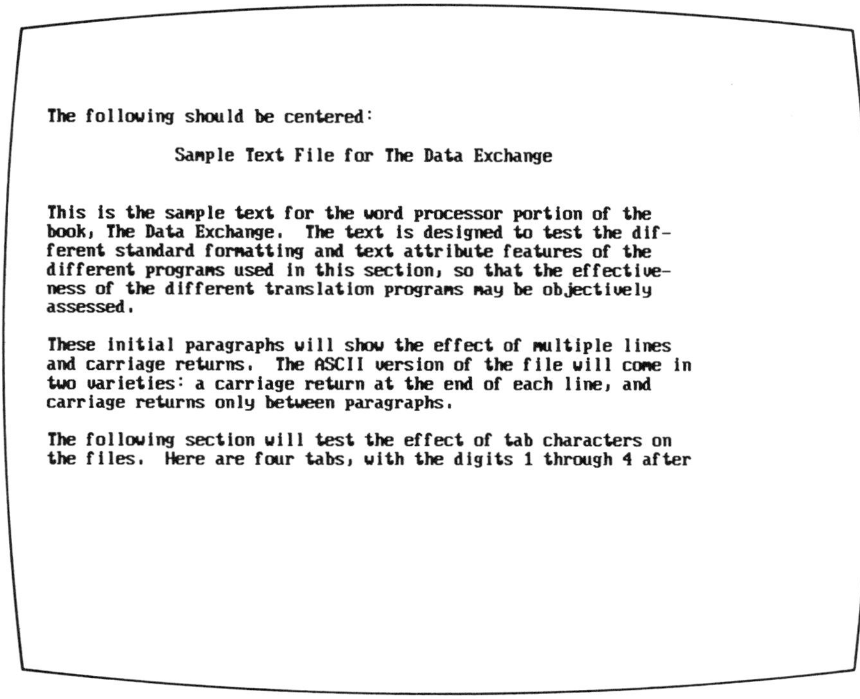

The following should be centered:

　　　　　Sample Text File for The Data Exchange

This is the sample text for the word processor portion of the
book, The Data Exchange. The text is designed to test the different standard formatting and text attribute features of the
different programs used in this section, so that the effectiveness of the different translation programs may be objectively
assessed.

These initial paragraphs will show the effect of multiple lines
and carriage returns. The ASCII version of the file will come in
two varieties: a carriage return at the end of each line, and
carriage returns only between paragraphs.

The following section will test the effect of tab characters on
the files. Here are four tabs, with the digits 1 through 4 after

WordStar manual, although most users will never need to
make changes from the default settings.

Mail-Merge Files

Mail-merge files couldn't be simpler than WordStar. All you
need is a standard quoted-string, comma-delimited text-file
format. In fact, it doesn't even need quoted strings as long as
the fields do not contain commas, but it's always safer to have
a quoted-string format. It doesn't matter if the records contain
more fields than needed for your merge document; name each
field at the start of the document but do not use them all in the
body of the text.

There are many ways to create a comma-delimited data file. Second only to fixed-length record format, it is a common data-file format and it works without modification as a Word-Star merge data file.

WordStar 5.5 has additional capabilities in this area, however. It also uses Lotus 1–2–3 worksheets and ranges in worksheets, and it uses dBASE II or III data files as mail-merge data files without having to first convert them.

When you combine WordStar's flexible reading of data files with its powerful MERGE DOCUMENT commands, you will find many creative and useful applications for these features.

MULTIMATE ADVANTAGE II

MultiMate sprang to the forefront in the early days of the IBM PC. Businesses adopted the new microcomputers by the thousands, and they needed good software. Word processing was a likely application, but many companies made major investments of time and money in training staff to work on dedicated word-processing systems. One of the most popular dedicated systems was the Wang, and MultiMate was an attempt to create a PC word-processing program that Wang users could operate with little additional training.

MultiMate is now published by Ashton-Tate, but it remains true to its Wang-inspired heritage. It has dozens of brightly hued stickers that attach to your keyboard's key caps so that you can relabel the keys for the various MultiMate commands and functions.

MultiMate is a polyglot among word processors; through its conversion utilities, it recognizes as many different word-processor formats as you can find in a single program. With varying degrees of success, expect to get most of your text either into or out of MultiMate without much difficulty.

How to Bring in a Text File

The MultiMate Advantage conversion utility offers numerous ways to deal with ASCII text files, but you don't need to bother with it. You can bring text files directly into a MultiMate document.

Start by opening your document from the main menu. Either edit an existing document or create a new one. Here is a demonstration of how to bring a text file into a new, empty document. Figure 7–24 shows the empty edit screen. After the edit screen appeared, I pressed Ctrl-6, which is the IMPORT ASCII keystroke command. I also could have used MultiMate Advantage's pull-down menu system by pressing Alt-L to call up the menu, then selecting the SPECIAL menu, then selecting IMPORT ASCII FILE. The menus are handy if you can't find the command on the keyboard template, but it is faster if you press Ctrl-6 instead.

In the upper-right hand corner of the display, the program is ready to "Import ASCII File." A set of options appears in the

FIGURE 7–24
MultiMate Advantage Import ASCII File Screen

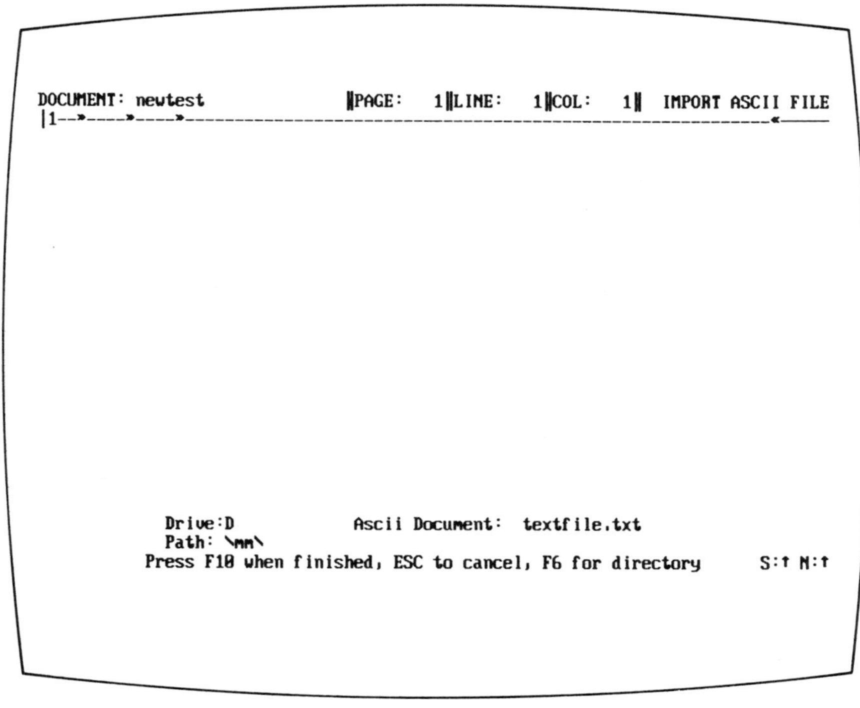

```
DOCUMENT: newtest              ‖PAGE:   1‖LINE:   1‖COL:   1‖  IMPORT ASCII FILE
|1--»----»----»--------------------------------------------------------«------




                Drive:D            Ascii Document:  textfile.txt
                Path: \mm\
                Press F10 when finished, ESC to cancel, F6 for directory    S:↑ M:↑
```

bottom three lines of the screen, which I have already filled. You can access a different directory and a different drive through these options. You also have the choice of displaying a file directory so that you can locate a specific file.

Once the F10 Function Key is pressed, MultiMate will start the import process. In this example, I use the file that contains Carriage Returns only between paragraphs, and Figure 7–25 shows the initial results of the import.

Notice that MultiMate Advantage inserted a new format ruler with the imported text. To clean up the file and its formatting, modify the top format line to suit your needs (using F9), delete the inserted format line (using Del F9 F10), and then reorganize the document with the repagination option

FIGURE 7–25
Immediate Result of MultiMate Import of .TXT Sample ASCII File

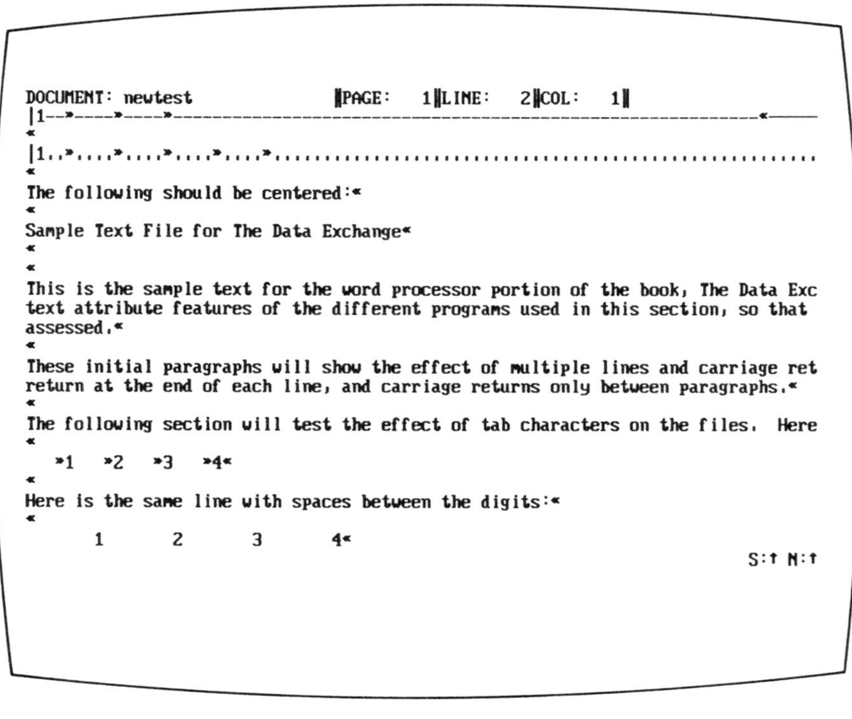

```
DOCUMENT: newtest              ‖PAGE:   1‖LINE:   2‖COL:   1‖
|1-->----->----->------------------------------------------------------------<------
«
|1..».....».....».....».....».....................................................
«
The following should be centered:«
«
Sample Text File for The Data Exchange«
«
«
This is the sample text for the word processor portion of the book, The Data Exc
text attribute features of the different programs used in this section, so that
assessed.«
«
These initial paragraphs will show the effect of multiple lines and carriage ret
return at the end of each line, and carriage returns only between paragraphs.«
«
The following section will test the effect of tab characters on the files. Here
«
   »1   »2   »3   »4«
«
Here is the same line with spaces between the digits:«
«
      1      2      3      4«

                                                              S:↑ N:↑
```

(using Ctrl-F2 F10). Figure 7–26 shows the results of these three steps.

At this point, I can go about the finer formatting points including centering, indents, justification, headers, footers, and different print attributes and fonts.

The process for the text file with Carriage Returns at the end of each line is the same—with a few steps added to eliminate the extra end-of-line characters within paragraphs.

As mentioned before, ensure there is a way to distinguish the end of a paragraph from the end of a regular text line. Do this with a Tab or spaces at the start of the first line of a paragraph, or by using a pair of Carriage Returns to skip a line between paragraphs. Without some way to distinguish between

FIGURE 7–26
Formatted Result of MultiMate Import of .TXT Sample ASCII File

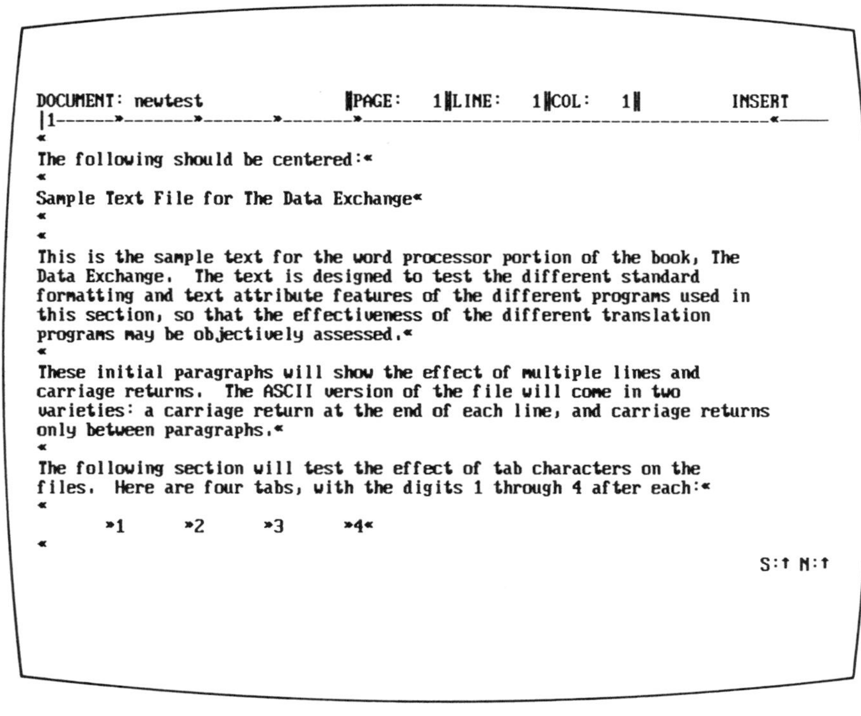

```
DOCUMENT: newtest              |PAGE:   1|LINE:   1|COL:   1|           INSERT
|1------>-------->-------->-------->--------------------------------------<------
«
The following should be centered:«
«
Sample Text File for The Data Exchange«
«
«
This is the sample text for the word processor portion of the book, The
Data Exchange.  The text is designed to test the different standard
formatting and text attribute features of the different programs used in
this section, so that the effectiveness of the different translation
programs may be objectively assessed.«
«
These initial paragraphs will show the effect of multiple lines and
carriage returns.  The ASCII version of the file will come in two
varieties: a carriage return at the end of each line, and carriage returns
only between paragraphs.«
«
The following section will test the effect of tab characters on the
files.  Here are four tabs, with the digits 1 through 4 after each:«
«
      »1      »2      »3      »4«
«
                                                              S:↑ N:↑
```

the different lines, you can't use a search-and-replace procedure to eliminate line endings.

Figure 7–27 shows the initial results of bringing in the
sample file that has a Carriage Return at the end of each line.
As before, modify the top format line, delete the second format
line, and reorganize the document.

Then, there is the problem of Carriage Returns at the end
of each line. This file is formatted with a pair of Carriage Returns between paragraphs, so they must be replaced before
stripping the rest of the Carriage Returns from the document.

Figure 7–28 shows the screen after pressing Shift-F6 to
start the replace function. The menu of options has been set so

FIGURE 7–27
MultiMate Import of .PRN Sample File

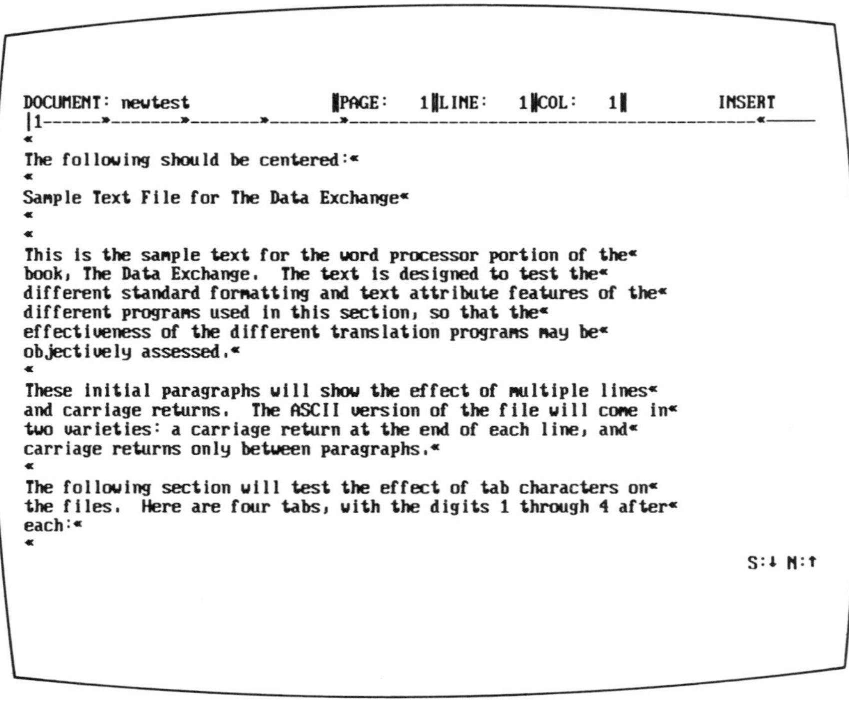

```
DOCUMENT: newtest              |PAGE:   1|LINE:   1|COL:   1|           INSERT
|1------»--------»--------»--------»--------------------------------------«------
«
The following should be centered:«
«
Sample Text File for The Data Exchange«
«
«
This is the sample text for the word processor portion of the«
book, The Data Exchange.  The text is designed to test the«
different standard formatting and text attribute features of the«
different programs used in this section, so that the«
effectiveness of the different translation programs may be«
objectively assessed.«
«
These initial paragraphs will show the effect of multiple lines«
and carriage returns.  The ASCII version of the file will come in«
two varieties: a carriage return at the end of each line, and«
carriage returns only between paragraphs.«
«
The following section will test the effect of tab characters on«
the files.  Here are four tabs, with the digits 1 through 4 after«
each:«
«
                                                              S:↓ N:↑
```

FIGURE 7–28
MultiMate Advantage Replace What? Prompt

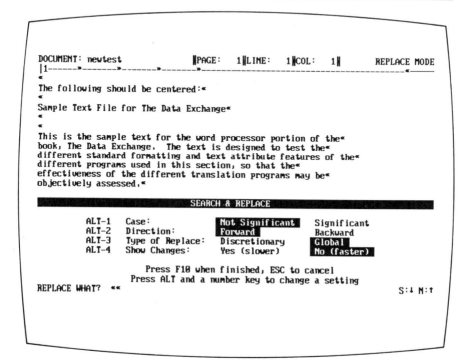

that the replace will be global without showing the changes; these are the fastest-performance settings.

Note that there are two end-of-line characters entered in response to the "REPLACE WHAT?" prompt. Unlike most other editors, MultiMate does not use the Return Key to trigger the execution of a command. Instead, it uses the F10 Function Key. As a result, you can specify an end-of-line in a search-or-replace string by pressing the Return Key. In this case, press the key twice.

Press the F10 Key and MultiMate Advantage responds with the prompt shown in Figure 7–29, "REPLACE WITH?." I have entered an asterisk in this example; you can use any

FIGURE 7–29
MultiMate Advantage Replace With? Prompt

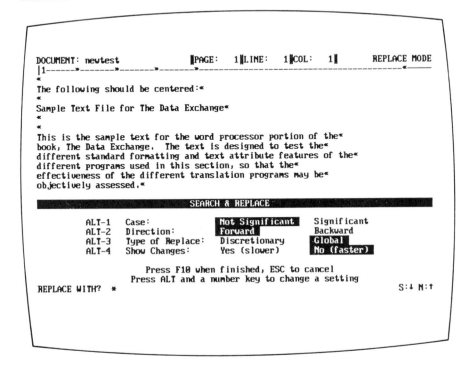

character or combination of characters as long as they do not appear elsewhere in the document. At the end, we will replace this character with the pair of Carriage Returns to restore paragraph breaks.

Press the F10 Key again to execute the command. Return to the top of the document and replace all remaining Carriage Returns with a single space. When that is complete, again return to the top of the file and replace all the asterisks with two Carriage Returns. Figure 7–30 shows the final result of this three-step, search-and-replace sequence.

Thus, it is simple to bring text files into MultiMate Advantage without relying on the conversion utility. It is easier with-

FIGURE 7–30
Final Format of Imported .PRN File after the
Search-and-Replace Sequence

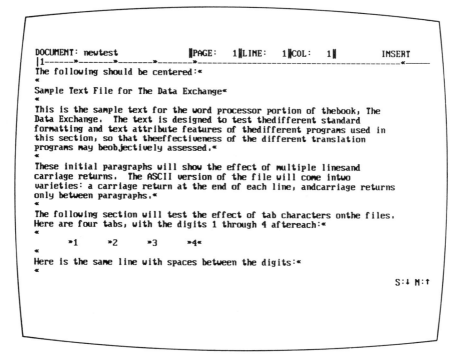

```
DOCUMENT: newtest              |PAGE:   1|LINE:   1|COL:   1|          INSERT
 |1------>-------->--------->--------->----------------------------------<------
 The following should be centered:«
 «
 Sample Text File for The Data Exchange«
 «
 This is the sample text for the word processor portion of thebook, The
 Data Exchange. The text is designed to test thedifferent standard
 formatting and text attribute features of thedifferent programs used in
 this section, so that theeffectiveness of the different translation
 programs may beobjectively assessed.«
 «
 These initial paragraphs will show the effect of multiple linesand
 carriage returns. The ASCII version of the file will come intwo
 varieties: a carriage return at the end of each line, andcarriage returns
 only between paragraphs.«
 «
 The following section will test the effect of tab characters onthe files.
 Here are four tabs, with the digits 1 through 4 aftereach:«
 «
         »1      »2      »3      »4«
 «
 Here is the same line with spaces between the digits:«
 «
                                                              S:↓ M:↑
```

out Carriage Returns at the end of each line, but either format works.

The conversion utility (described later in this chapter) offers some advantages for a Carriage Return at the end of each line format file. It eliminates the extra end-of-line characters automatically; there is no need for the search-and-replace sequence. On the other hand, this conversion inserts extra format lines that must be modified or deleted. Depending on the source document, the conversion approach may mean less clean-up work, but for most cases, the direct-text import through the Ctrl-6 keystroke command is most efficient and useful.

How to Export a Text File

Any document is quickly converted to a text file. As in the last section, you can use the conversion utility, but there is a more direct and efficient method. All you need to do is print the file to disk.

Figure 7–31 shows the print menu in MultiMate Advantage. Note that the draft-print option is set to "Y," the left and top margins are set to 0, and the output device is set to "F" for file. The Printer Action Table is set to "TTYCRLF," which is a simple driver.

Note that the bottom of the screen contains prompts for an output-file name. The program defaults to the document name and the current directory, but you can override any of them.

FIGURE 7–31
MultiMate Advantage Print Menu for Print to Disk

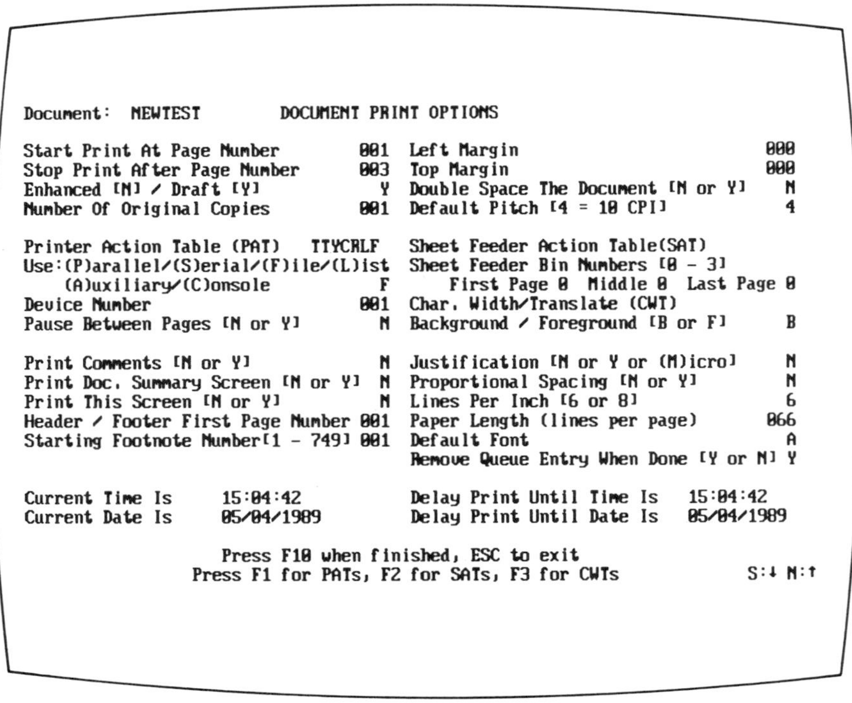

```
Document: NEWTEST        DOCUMENT PRINT OPTIONS

Start Print At Page Number        001  Left Margin                          000
Stop Print After Page Number      003  Top Margin                           000
Enhanced [N] / Draft [Y]            Y  Double Space The Document [N or Y]     N
Number Of Original Copies         001  Default Pitch [4 = 10 CPI]             4

Printer Action Table (PAT)   TTYCRLF   Sheet Feeder Action Table(SAT)
Use:(P)arallel/(S)erial/(F)ile/(L)ist  Sheet Feeder Bin Numbers [0 - 3]
    (A)uxiliary/(C)onsole          F      First Page 0  Middle 0  Last Page 0
Device Number                     001  Char. Width/Translate (CWT)
Pause Between Pages [N or Y]        N   Background / Foreground [B or F]       B

Print Comments [N or Y]            N   Justification [N or Y or (M)icro]      N
Print Doc. Summary Screen [N or Y] N   Proportional Spacing [N or Y]          N
Print This Screen [N or Y]         N   Lines Per Inch [6 or 8]                6
Header / Footer First Page Number 001  Paper Length (lines per page)        066
Starting Footnote Number[1 - 749] 001  Default Font                          A
                                       Remove Queue Entry When Done [Y or N] Y

Current Time Is     15:04:42          Delay Print Until Time Is    15:04:42
Current Date Is     05/04/1989        Delay Print Until Date Is    05/04/1989

              Press F10 when finished, ESC to exit
          Press F1 for PATs, F2 for SATs, F3 for CWTs                S:↓ N:↑
```

MultiMate Advantage II automatically gives the file a .PRN extension.

A message appears on the screen stating that a document is being printed, and the disk-access light goes on periodically. Using a sample document, Figure 7–32 shows the results of this process.

The file is fully formatted, and you can use the DOS COPY command to send it to a printer. All the headers, footers, and extra lines for page breaks are included. Also, bold and underlined text is repeated with a Carriage Return, but no Line Feed Character is paired with it so that the characters will overprint the same line. This formatting means that you will face some work to clean out extraneous material.

FIGURE 7–32
DOS Listing of Print-to-Disk Result of MultiMate

The following should be centered:

            Sample Text File for The Data Exchange
                  MultiMate Advantage Version

This is the sample text for the word processor portion of the
book, The Data Exchange. The text is designed to test the
different standard formatting and text attribute features of the
different programs used in this section, so that the
effectiveness of the different translation programs may be
objectively assessed.

These initial paragraphs will show the effect of multiple lines
and carriage returns. The ASCII version of the file will come in
two varieties: a carriage return at the end of each line, and
carriage returns only between paragraphs.

The following section will test the effect of tab characters on
the files. Here are four tabs, with the digits 1 through 4 after
each:

        1   2   3   4

The MultiMate conversion utility offers an advantage in that it doesn't format the file, but it includes the header and footer command information to be modified or deleted as desired. The conversion utility tries to produce bold and underlined text using backspace characters to doublestrike the individual characters. If you do not want this, erase the extra characters.

Other Supported Formats

MultiMate Advantage supports many file formats in its file-conversion utility—some common and others obscure.

Use the utility to convert to and from the formats listed in Table 7–1. Not all features and formatting options are supported in all the conversions, but they move text across without too much trouble.

Note that some conversions only work in one direction. For example, Lotus 1–2–3 and DIF files can be converted into MultiMate documents, but the process cannot be reversed.

To illustrate the conversion process, we will convert the sample document formatted with MultiMate Advantage and put in a form read by WordStar. Start by selecting the conversions and utilities option on the main menu, as shown in Figure 7–33.

Next, select the convert-documents option, as shown in Figure 7–34.

TABLE 7–1
Supported-File Conversions in MultiMate Advantage

ASCII
COMM
DCA
DIF
GSA
Honeywell
Just Write
WKS and WK1
Wang PC
Wang WPS
WordStar

FIGURE 7–33
MultiMate Advantage Main Menu

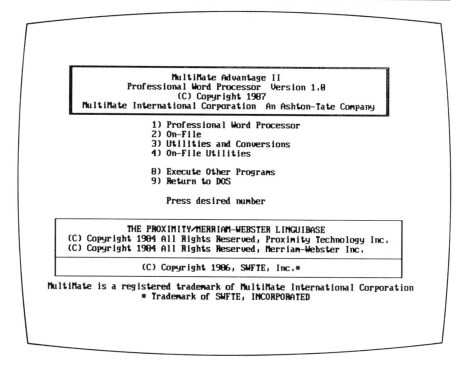

MultiMate then will read information from three directories: the source file, the target file, and the conversion-program directories. These can all be the same directory, as seen in this example. It takes a moment to reach a screen that looks similar to Figure 7–35, but the lower three windows will fill when the program has found all the files.

This screen has already been filled out. The first window lists the files available in the source-file directory, and in this case, we use a file named "NEWFILE.DOC." The source format is "MM," which means that the file is in MultiMate format. We want to create a WordStar file, so the output type is "WST," as seen at the bottom of the window. Finally, I have given the output file the name "NEWMULTI.WST" so I can tell it came from MultiMate and is now in a WordStar format.

FIGURE 7–34
Conversion Menu

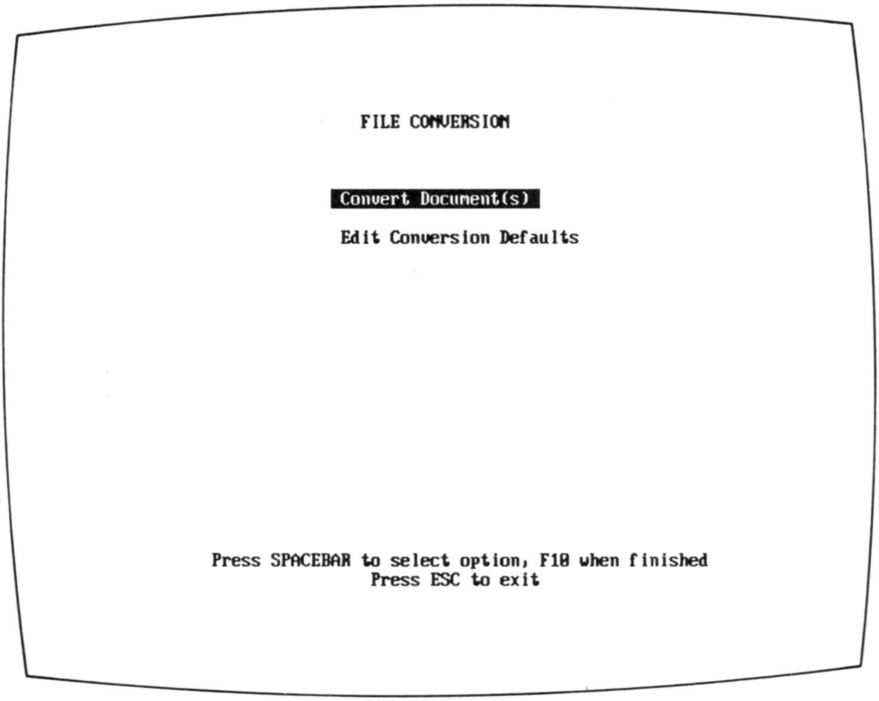

```
                    FILE CONVERSION


                 █ Convert Document(s) █

                 Edit Conversion Defaults










       Press SPACEBAR to select option, F10 when finished
                    Press ESC to exit
```

When you press the F10 Function Key, the program will load the required conversion program and produce the output file. When it is complete, you may continue by converting another file, or you may press the Escape Key to return to the previous menu.

Figure 7–36 shows the result of this conversion. The file has been called up in WordStar to show what details have and have not been converted.

Note that MultiMate starts by inserting a long string of dot commands to take explicit control over certain page-formatting features. There are some successes and shortcomings in the results.

FIGURE 7–35
Conversion Screen

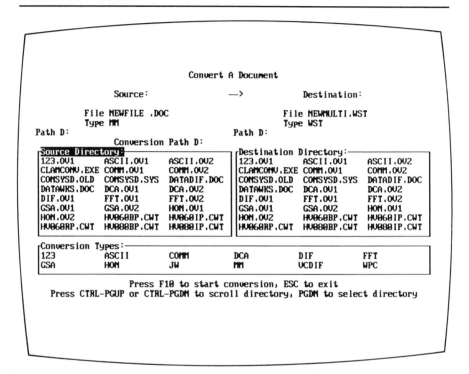

First, the heading remains properly centered above the text. Not shown on this screen is the fact that underline is translated properly, and bold is translated to the WordStar "double strike" attribute instead of "bold." All text was moved over successfully.

Everything is not perfect, however. Note the empty space to the left of the text. As seen from the ruler at the top of the screen, WordStar thinks the left margin is at the edge of the screen. MultiMate has created the file with extra blank spaces to the left of each text line as if it were a print file.

Also, each line ends in a Carriage Return, as indicated by the < symbols on the right edge of the screen. These end-of-

FIGURE 7–36
MultiMate Converted File in WordStar

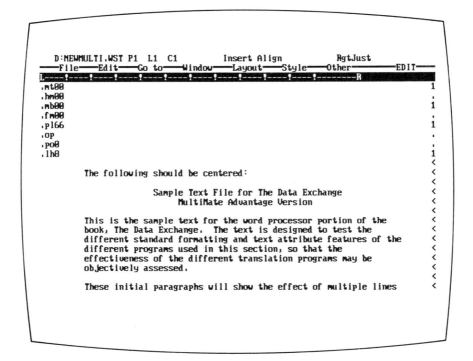

line characters must be searched and replaced, since the document will not reformat properly without help.

Figure 7–37 illustrates what happens to this first paragraph of the sample file when you use the Ctrl-Q U command to reformat the document.

Since each line has a Carriage Return, it is treated as a separate paragraph; the end result is that lines that are too long are split into two lines without joining the following lines. The document ends up a jumbled mess.

Other conversion problems are that blank lines for top and bottom margins are included, and header and footer information is brought over—but only as lines of text buried in the body of the document with no indication that they are meant to be headers or footers.

FIGURE 7–37
Reformat Test Import from MultiMate

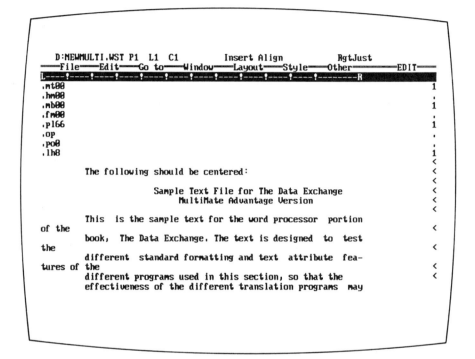

Moving a file in the other direction is not much better. MultiMate does not deal with WordStar dot commands that it does not understand, and it leaves them littered about the document as shown in Figure 7–38. The header lines are shown, but not as MultiMate headers; they still have the WordStar dot-command prefix.

MultiMate converts footer information correctly, and bold and underline print attributes also come across. Paragraphs do not have Carriage Returns on each line, so editing and reformatting work as expected.

Figure 7–39 shows an unusual side effect of the translation; MultiMate puts in many formatting rulers, sometimes even in the middle of a paragraph. It appears to be a result of trying to match the line lengths of different paragraphs, but it

FIGURE 7–38
WordStar File Converted by MultiMate Shown in MultiMate

```
DOCUMENT: textwst            |PAGE:  1||LINE:  1||COL:  1||
|1--»»--»_____»_____»_____»_____«_____
.u.j«
.o.j off«
«
The following should be centered:«
«
    »»  »     Sample Text File for The Data Exchange«
    »»  »       » Wordstar Professional Version«
.h1 Sample Word Processing Document«
.h2 No Automatic System Date«
«
This is the sample text for the word processor portion of the
book, The Data Exchange.  The text is designed to test the
different standard formatting and text attribute features of the
different programs used in this section, so that the
effectiveness of the different translation programs may be
objectively assessed.«
«
These initial paragraphs will show the effect of multiple lines
and carriage returns.  The ASCII version of the file will come in
two varieties: a carriage return at the end of each line, and
carriage returns only between paragraphs.«
«
                                                         S:↑ N:↑
```

has the unfortunate consequence of adding an end-of-line character to some lines in the middle of a paragraph, which makes editing and reformatting more difficult.

Similar results are obtained with some other conversion formats. When you convert to a DCA format and bring it into DisplayWrite 4, tabs appear at the start of each line and a Carriage Return appears at the end of each line. Formatting details are lost in the other direction, along with extra pages inserted as MultiMate attempts to handle the header and footer information.

With the MultiMate conversion utility, there is extra work in using it to move from one file format to another. In many ways, you are better off using text-file techniques.

FIGURE 7–39
Multiple Rulers in a MultiMate Conversion of WordStar File

```
DOCUMENT: textwst              ‖PAGE:   2‖LINE:  18‖COL:  32‖

|1--»»--»---------»---------»---------»-----------------------------«---------
«
|1..».................................................«
 →4. This is a paragraph of text. It is intended to be
 indented a half inch from the left and right margins,
 left justified, ragged right, with no indent on the
 first line. It is just a sample of typical text. There
 is nothing special about these words.«
.lm 8«
|1..».................................................«
.rm 65«
«
5. This is a paragraph of text. It is intended to be the same as
the paragraph 1. in this sequence, left justified, ragged right, «
|1.................................................«
with no indent on the first line. It is just a sample of typical
text. There is nothing special about these words.«
«
«
Print Attributes:«
«
The following are to be printed in the Courier 10 pitch font:«
                                                              S:↑ M:↑
```

Mail-Merge Files

MultiMate Advantage merge files are unwieldy and cumbersome. Each field must have its field name entered along with it, plus some weird formatting characters entered from the keyboard. The result is a file structure that could probably be duplicated by some clever programming, but is it worth the effort? Most people would expect it is easier than this to merge data in a word processor published by the makers of dBASE.

Well, Ashton-Tate did not let us down, although the MultiMate documentation is poor at helping you discover the powerful and flexible merge features that are supported. In fact, MultiMate Advantage II accepts three different standard data-file formats: dBASE .DBF, comma-delimited, and fixed-length record.

These features are documented in the "Advanced Topics" manual, but there are confusing holes and a little misinformation. Each is used similarly; you must first enter a "define block" at the start of your merge document to tell it about the merge file to be used.

The easiest one is the dBASE format: add three lines at the top of the file, as shown in Figure 7–40. The high-order ASCII characters that look like the left half of a capital *H* are ASCII 195, and it is the MultiMate "merge" character produced on the MultiMate keyboard with an Alt-M keystroke.

If you define the merge file as a dBASE-type file, MultiMate does the rest. Use the same field names in your merge

FIGURE 7–40
MultiMate dBASE Merge Document

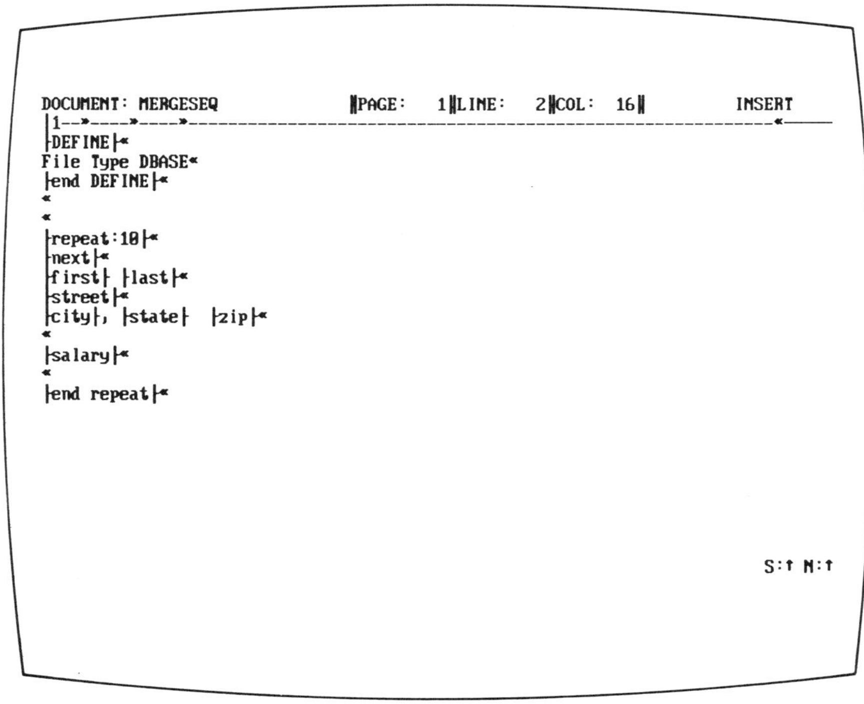

```
 DOCUMENT: MERGESEQ              ‖PAGE:   1‖LINE:   2‖COL:  16‖          INSERT
 |1-->----->----->---------------------------------------------------------<-----
 ├DEFINE├<
 File Type DBASE<
 ├end DEFINE├<
 <
 <
 ├repeat:10├<
 ├next├<
 ├first├ ├last├<
 ├street├<
 ├city├, ├state├ ├zip├<
 <
 ├salary├<
 <
 ├end repeat├<




                                                              S:↑ N:↑
```

document as in the dBASE table-structure definition since MultiMate reads this information from the .DBF file to determine field names and locations.

The other two types of merge formats are more confusing; a circumstance that is puzzling since Ashton-Tate owns MultiMate. Rather than using standard file nomenclature, or at least adhering to dBASE usage, the manual refers to "Random" and "Sequential" file types. They correspond to the more familiar "fixed-length" and "comma-delimited" formats.

In both cases, the define blocks at the start of a merge document are more complex. You must name the file type and list the field names.

Figure 7–41 shows the define block for a comma-delimited merge file. The merge file is the same one used earlier in the chapters on dBASE and Lotus.

FIGURE 7–41
MultiMate Advantage Merge File for Comma-Delimited

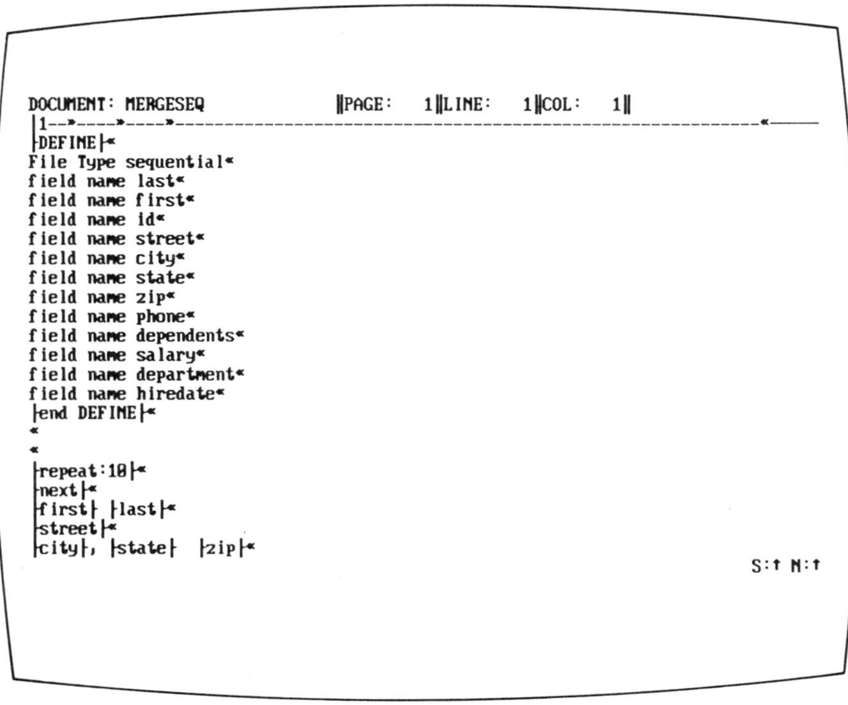

```
DOCUMENT: MERGESEQ              ‖PAGE:   1‖LINE:   1‖COL:   1‖
 |1-->---->---->--------------------------------------------------«------
 |DEFINE|«
 File Type sequential«
 field name last«
 field name first«
 field name id«
 field name street«
 field name city«
 field name state«
 field name zip«
 field name phone«
 field name dependents«
 field name salary«
 field name department«
 field name hiredate«
 |end DEFINE|«
 «
 «
 |repeat:10|«
 |next|«
 |first| |last|«
 |street|«
 |city|, |state| |zip|«
                                                          S:↑ N:↑
```

There are some confusing and misleading points in the documentation at this point. The first one is that the field names are *case sensitive*. This means that if you refer to a field as "FIRSTNAME" in your define block and "firstname" as a merge field in your document, nothing will appear in that space in the final printout. This is well hidden in the manual.

The second point is that the documentation states that the merge file must have a "record separator," a "field separator," and a "field delimiter." The default values are a Carriage Return/Line Feed combination for the record separator, a comma for the field separator, and double quotes for the field delimiter.

These default values are identical to a standard quoted-string, comma-delimited format in every way save one. In the comma-delimited format, there is no need to put quotes around numeric values. The MultiMate documentation states the requirements: you need quotes around all fields. However, you don't need quotes on numeric fields, and they will come into the MultiMate merge document without a hitch.

On the plus side, you can use the define block to specify other characters as "separators" and "delimiters" if you have a file from another program with an unusual format. Macintosh programs typically use a Tab Character instead of a comma between fields, for example.

Things get just one step more complex with a fixed-length record format, which MultiMate refers to as a "Random" file type. Figure 7–42 shows the merge document and the define block for this type of data file.

The define block is nearly identical to the last case, except you must also define the length of each field. The same case-sensitivity applies to the field names as it did for the comma-delimited format.

A new "gotcha" appears in the last line of the list of fields in the define block. There is a new field named "NEWLINE" with a size of two characters. MultiMate Advantage II doesn't assume you are working with a fixed-length file that separates the records with a Carriage Return and Line Feed character pair. Instead, it assumes that there are no record delimiters. If you fail to account for these two "extra" characters, which ap-

FIGURE 7–42
MultiMate Advantage Merge File for Fixed Length

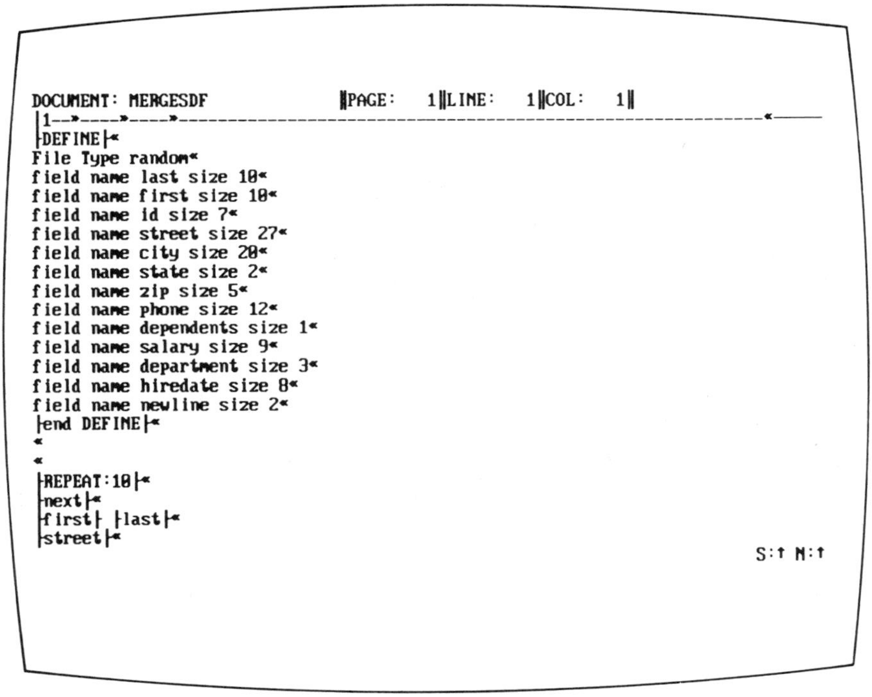

```
DOCUMENT: MERGESDF           ┃PAGE:   1┃LINE:   1┃COL:   1┃
|1--»----»----»-------------------------------------------------«----
┝DEFINE┝«
File Type random«
field name last size 18«
field name first size 18«
field name id size 7«
field name street size 27«
field name city size 28«
field name state size 2«
field name zip size 5«
field name phone size 12«
field name dependents size 1«
field name salary size 9«
field name department size 3«
field name hiredate size 8«
field name newline size 2«
┝end DEFINE┝«
«
«
┝REPEAT:18┝«
┝next┝«
┝first┝ ┝last┝«
┝street┝«
                                                      S:↑ M:↑
```

pear in most fixed-length format files, you get a barberpole effect with the data. Each field's data will be offset to the right
by two additional characters for each new record merged. The
results quickly deteriorate into a garbled mess. If you assign a
fake field name to the two characters in your define block, however, your merge will proceed correctly.

Once you have created a merge document and have its associated data file ready, you can either print from the main
menu or give the Alt-F5 Function Key command while editing
the merge document.

While MultiMate Advantage II does not have conversion
utilities to change data files into a native-format merge-data
file, its ability to read and merge data from dBASE, comma-

delimited, and fixed-length record-format files means that you can probably bring data from any source to use with merge documents.

MICROSOFT WORD 4.0

In spite of its generic name, Word from Microsoft is not a plain word processor. It was one of the first major products to offer both text and graphic display formats. If you have a graphics display, you can see the underlining, the bold, and the italics of your text right on the screen. It does not show different type-styles or sizes on the screen, however.

Word is also one of the best at making sensible use of a mouse for word processing. It is one of the few where I actually feel that the mouse saves time and effort.

As for file transfers, there is one interesting fact about Word 4.0 when compared with earlier versions. It's not a matter of new features; instead it's what is missing. In earlier versions, there was an extra utility that converted documents between Word and a half-dozen other formats. This utility is no longer included with the program.

How to Bring in a Text File

Importing a text file is simple with Word. Use the same command sequence that brings in a Word format file: TRANSFER LOAD.

Figure 7–43 shows the Word editing screen after the TRANSFER LOAD command has been given and the file name has been entered. Once the Return Key is pressed, Word will load the file and you will be ready to format and edit the file.

If the file you bring in only has Carriage Returns at the end of each paragraph, you will see a file on the screen that will look and act as if you had typed in the text yourself. Figure 7–44 shows the sample file after it has been brought into Word in this manner.

To make it easier to see the formatting commands, I have set the Options so that all the codes are "Visible," although

FIGURE 7–43
Word Transfer Load Screen

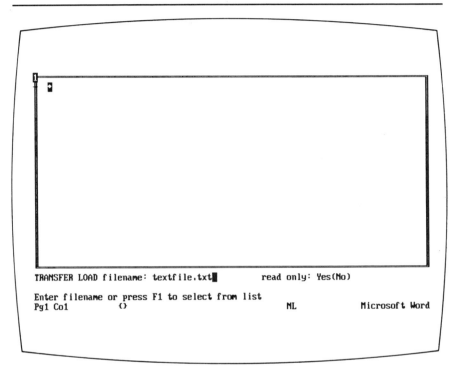

TRANSFER LOAD filename: textfile.txt█   read only: Yes(No)

Enter filename or press F1 to select from list
Pg1 Co1   {}   ML   Microsoft Word

most users prefer to leave this set to "None." The spaces are shown as dots between words, and the paragraph symbol, ¶, marks the location of Carriage Return characters.

Figure 7–45 shows the sample file that has the Carriage Returns at the end of each line as it appears after being brought into Word. Again, with the formatting characters visible, you can see where the Carriage Return characters appear.

Here, the lines break in strange places because the sample file was formatted with a longer line length than the default settings on this Word screen. To fix this, use the same search-and-replace sequences as described for the other word processors.

FIGURE 7–44
Sample .TXT File in Word

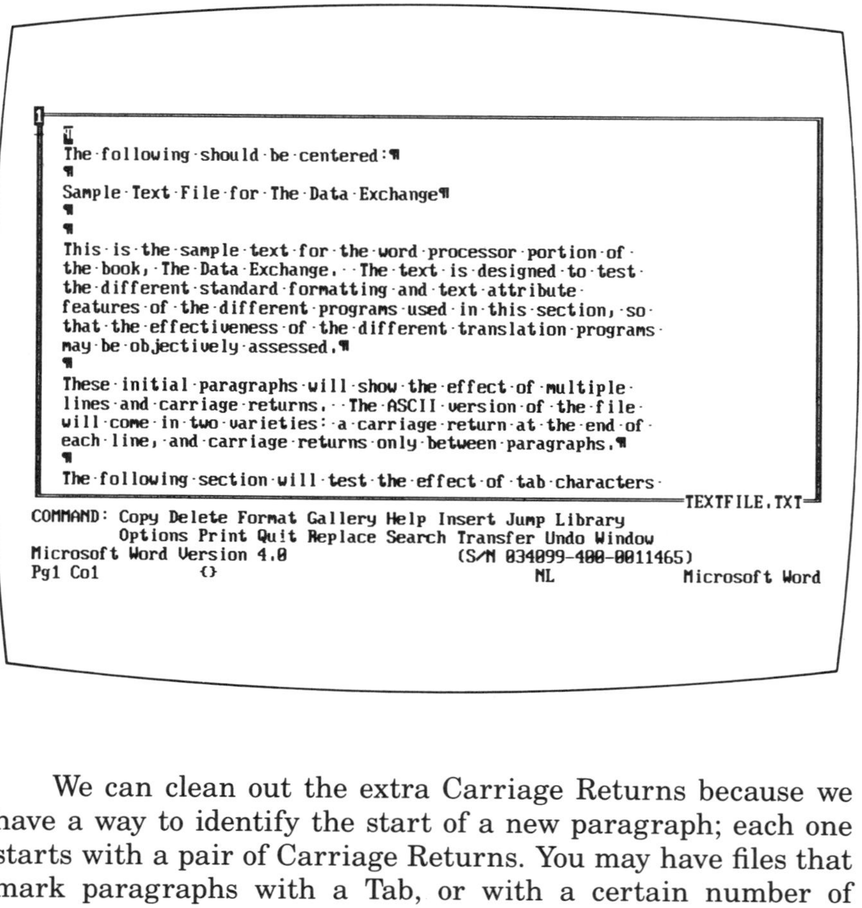

```
The·following·should·be·centered:¶
¶
Sample·Text·File·for·The·Data·Exchange¶
¶
¶
This·is·the·sample·text·for·the·word·processor·portion·of·
the·book,·The·Data·Exchange,··The·text·is·designed·to·test·
the·different·standard·formatting·and·text·attribute·
features·of·the·different·programs·used·in·this·section,·so·
that·the·effectiveness·of·the·different·translation·programs·
may·be·objectively·assessed.¶
¶
These·initial·paragraphs·will·show·the·effect·of·multiple·
lines·and·carriage·returns,··The·ASCII·version·of·the·file·
will·come·in·two·varieties:·a·carriage·return·at·the·end·of·
each·line,·and·carriage·returns·only·between·paragraphs.¶
¶
The·following·section·will·test·the·effect·of·tab·characters·
                                                        TEXTFILE.TXT
COMMAND: Copy Delete Format Gallery Help Insert Jump Library
         Options Print Quit Replace Search Transfer Undo Window
Microsoft Word Version 4.0              (S/N 034099-400-0011465)
Pg1 Col         {}                      NL          Microsoft Word
```

We can clean out the extra Carriage Returns because we have a way to identify the start of a new paragraph; each one starts with a pair of Carriage Returns. You may have files that mark paragraphs with a Tab, or with a certain number of spaces for a first-line indent, but as long as it is consistent, you can use the same technique.

Figure 7–46 shows the first step in the process, where we search for all pairs of Carriage Returns and replace them with an asterisk. You can use any character in place of the asterisk; it must be a character that doesn't appear elsewhere in the document.

Notice that the REPLACE text is "^p^p." This is because Word uses the Enter Key as a signal that the command is com-

FIGURE 7–45
Sample .PRN File in Word

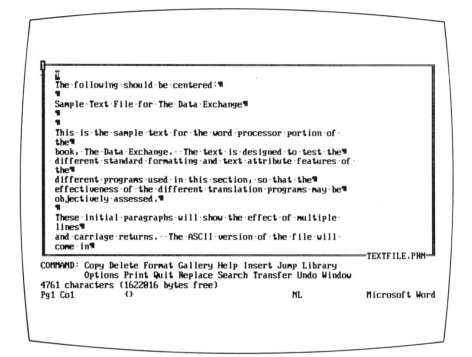

```
The·following·should·be·centered:¶
¶
Sample·Text·File·for·The·Data·Exchange¶
¶
¶
This·is·the·sample·text·for·the·word·processor·portion·of·
the¶
book,·The·Data·Exchange,··The·text·is·designed·to·test·the¶
different·standard·formatting·and·text·attribute·features·of·
the¶
different·programs·used·in·this·section,·so·that·the¶
effectiveness·of·the·different·translation·programs·may·be¶
objectively·assessed.¶
¶
These·initial·paragraphs·will·show·the·effect·of·multiple·
lines¶
and·carriage·returns,··The·ASCII·version·of·the·file·will·
come·in¶
                                                    TEXTFILE.PRN
COMMAND: Copy Delete Format Gallery Help Insert Jump Library
         Options Print Quit Replace Search Transfer Undo Window
4761 characters (1622016 bytes free)
Pg1 Co1        {}                        ML           Microsoft Word
```

plete and that execution should start. As a result, Word needs a code to represent the Carriage Return. It uses the two characters of the carat ^ and the letter *p*. Word has other codes for items such as Tab characters and page breaks. Notice that the replacement confirmation is off to speed the process.

The results are shown in Figure 7–47, and they may appear jumbled. At the bottom of the screen, the second REPLACE command is ready, in which all remaining Carriage Returns are replaced with a single space. You cannot see it from looking at this screen, but there is a single space in the "with text:" field.

This further collapses the document, and we are ready for the final step. The REPLACE command shown at the bottom of

FIGURE 7–46
Word Replace for a Pair of Carriage Returns

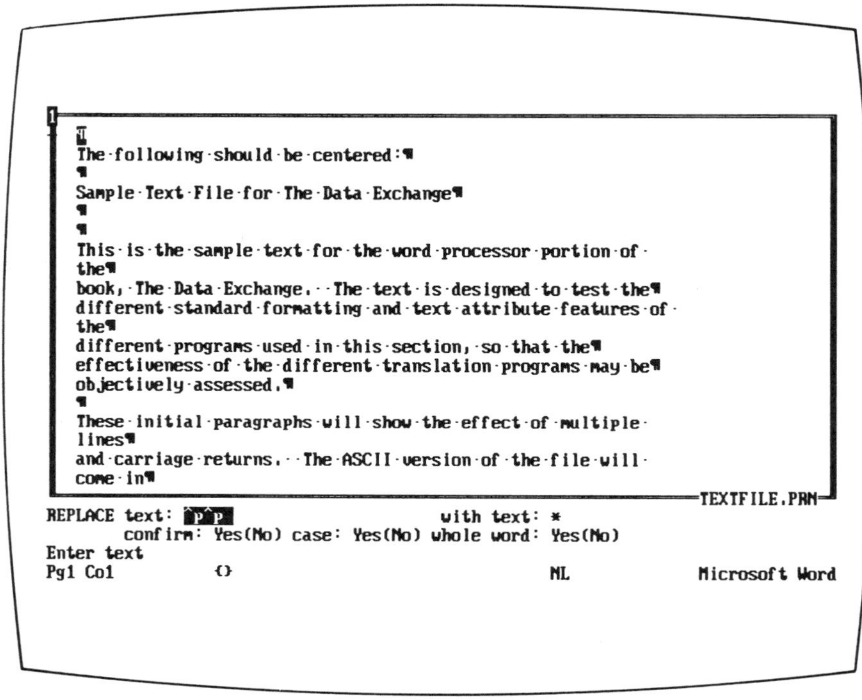

Figure 7–48 puts back the pairs of Carriage Returns between paragraphs.

The asterisk character is replaced with two "^p" combinations, which puts two Carriage Returns back between the paragraphs. The results are shown in Figure 7–49, and you can now edit and format the file. When you finish, save the final version as a Word format file with the TRANSFER SAVE command.

How to Export a Text File

Creating a text file from a Word document is as easy as bringing one in. There are two options. To create a version that has a Carriage Return at the end of each line, print the document

FIGURE 7–47
Word—Ready to Replace Carriage Returns with Space

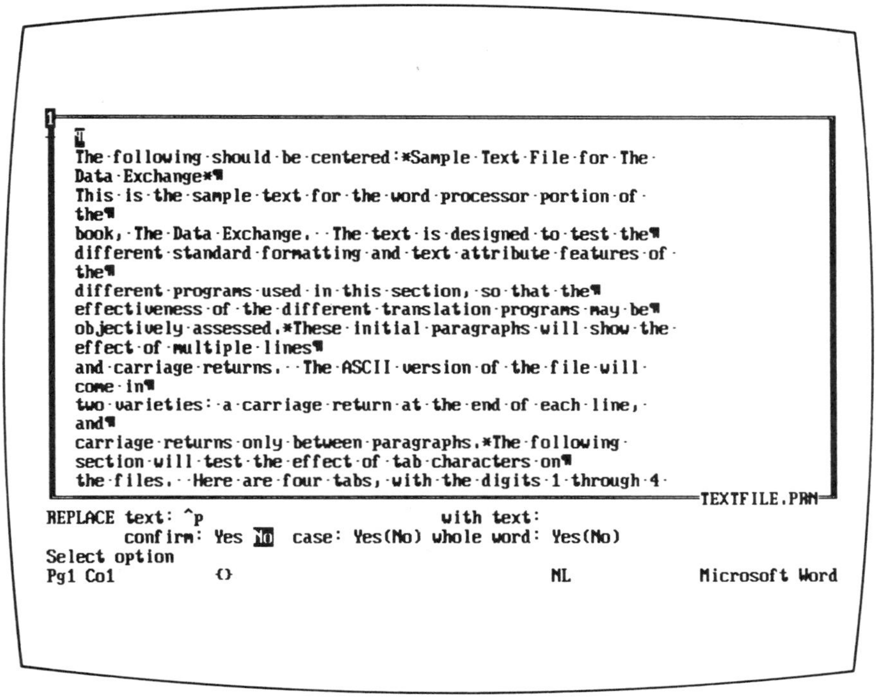

```
¶
The·following·should·be·centered:*Sample·Text·File·for·The·
Data·Exchange*¶
This·is·the·sample·text·for·the·word·processor·portion·of·
the¶
book,·The·Data·Exchange,··The·text·is·designed·to·test·the¶
different·standard·formatting·and·text·attribute·features·of·
the¶
different·programs·used·in·this·section,·so·that·the¶
effectiveness·of·the·different·translation·programs·may·be¶
objectively·assessed.*These·initial·paragraphs·will·show·the·
effect·of·multiple·lines¶
and·carriage·returns,··The·ASCII·version·of·the·file·will·
come·in¶
two·varieties:·a·carriage·return·at·the·end·of·each·line,·
and¶
carriage·returns·only·between·paragraphs,*The·following·
section·will·test·the·effect·of·tab·characters·on¶
the·files.··Here·are·four·tabs,·with·the·digits·1·through·4·
                                              TEXTFILE.PRN
REPLACE text:·^p                   with text:
     confirm: Yes NO  case: Yes(No)  whole word: Yes(No)
Select option
Pg1 Col        {}                         NL        Microsoft Word
```

to a disk file instead of a printer. This adds extra lines for page formatting, margins, and so forth, but they can be adjusted by changing margin settings.

If you want a file with carriage returns only at the end of paragraphs, it is even easier. Go to the Transfer Save screen, as shown in Figure 7–50. Use the file's existing name, or save it under a new name.

Note that there is a single option on the Transfer Save screen—formatted. If you select yes on this option, the file is stored in a Word format file. On the other hand, if you select no, you get an ASCII format with Carriage Returns only at the end of paragraphs. Header and footer information are included in the final file, but only once. There are no margins, print

FIGURE 7–48
Word—Put Back Pairs of Carriage Returns

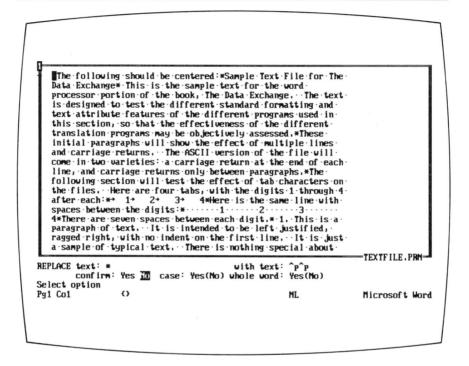

attributes, or special formatting features such as justified columns.

The result of an unformatted TRANSFER SAVE is a clean ASCII file that is easy to bring into most word processors.

Other Supported Formats

Again, Microsoft Word 4.0 has dropped a conversion program that appeared in earlier versions. Now, you can convert back and forth between only two other formats.

One is called RTF, which stands for Rich Text Format (not to be confused with the Revisable Format Text of the DCA for-

FIGURE 7–49
Final Version of .PRN Sample File in Word

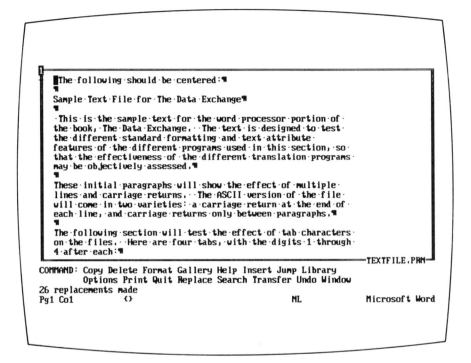

```
█The·following·should·be·centered:¶
¶
Sample·Text·File·for·The·Data·Exchange¶
¶
·This·is·the·sample·text·for·the·word·processor·portion·of·
the·book,·The·Data·Exchange,··The·text·is·designed·to·test·
the·different·standard·formatting·and·text·attribute·
features·of·the·different·programs·used·in·this·section,·so·
that·the·effectiveness·of·the·different·translation·programs·
may·be·objectively·assessed.¶
¶
These·initial·paragraphs·will·show·the·effect·of·multiple·
lines·and·carriage·returns.··The·ASCII·version·of·the·file·
will·come·in·two·varieties:·a·carriage·return·at·the·end·of·
each·line,·and·carriage·returns·only·between·paragraphs.¶
¶
The·following·section·will·test·the·effect·of·tab·characters·
on·the·files.··Here·are·four·tabs,·with·the·digits·1·through·
4·after·each:¶
                                              ═TEXTFILE.PRN═
COMMAND: Copy Delete Format Gallery Help Insert Jump Library
         Options Print Quit Replace Search Transfer Undo Window
26 replacements made
Pg1 Col      {}                        NL         Microsoft Word
```

mat). This is a Microsoft creation, and it is rare, so you may have little use for it.

Word 4.0 also converts to and from DCA format using the Revisable Format Text (RFT) format. Use the WORD_ DCA.EXE utility, which is separate from the Word program.

I tried converting the sample document using this utility in both directions, using the DCA format as an intermediate step between Word and the other programs in this chapter with mixed results, mostly disappointing. Some programs refused to read the DCA file produced by Word, and they gave various error messages. The other way was not much better, as Word lost all Carriage Returns while sprinkling the file with Tab characters.

FIGURE 7–50
Word Transfer Save

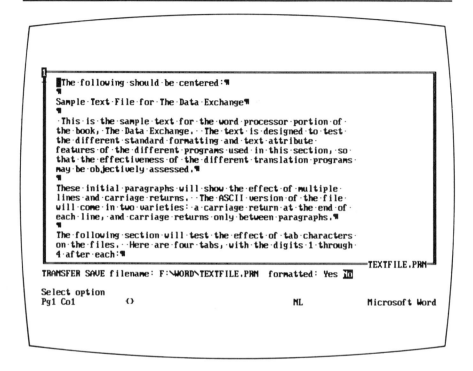

Given the ease in moving ASCII files in and out of Word, don't bother with the DCA conversion, and instead rely on ASCII and formatting pseudocodes.

Mail-Merge Files

Mail-merge files are painless under Word. The data files are delimited-text files. You can use files that have commas, Tab characters, or semicolons as delimiters, and you can use quoted strings or unquoted strings. The easiest approach, however, is to plan on using a typical quoted-string, comma-delimited format.

The only real catch is that the first record of the data file must be what is called a *header record*. Instead of containing information to be merged with the main document, this record must contain the list of field names that correspond to the data elements in the records that follow. This is the only way that Word can match the individual items to the blank fields that appear in the main document.

This may not seem difficult at first. Call up the data file and edit it by inserting the first line and all the field names. But there are times when this is a pain. For example, you may have a certain letter that you send out to different customers each month. It may not be a big deal to export the names and addresses from your data base program, but then you have to go in each time and enter the field names. Also, your data file may have an unwieldy number of similar fields, and it is easy to make a mistake typing in the field names.

There is a way around this problem mentioned in the documentation. You can use two data files with a single main document. The first file must be a header file, and it can contain only the header record, which is the list of field names separated by commas. No spaces are allowed in field names, but they can be as long as 64 characters. Then, the second file can be all the records.

For the monthly letter, you could create a header file called CUSTHEAD.DAT that has only the list of field names. You can then have a comma-delimited file of data, which you might call NAMESJAN.DAT in January, and NAMESFEB.DAT for February, and so forth. They could be merged with the main document—perhaps called MONTHLY.DOC. Figure 7–51 shows what these three files might look like when viewed in Word.

Note that the first line of the main document is "<<DATA CUSTHEAD.DAT, NAMESJAN.DAT>>." Below that, the merge fields are listed in the document. While Word doesn't offer any conversions for data files, it uses such a common format that you can convert other formats to work with Word without difficulty. Methods are discussed in the dBASE and 1–2–3 chapters, as well as in Parts 3 and 4.

FIGURE 7–51
Sample Merge Files

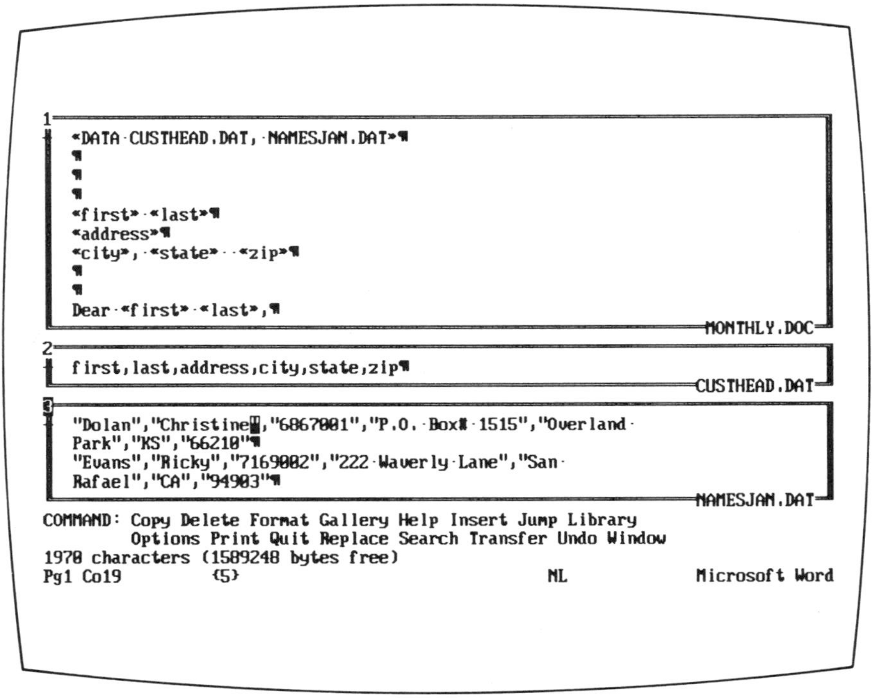

```
1
    «DATA·CUSTHEAD.DAT, ·NAMESJAN.DAT»¶
    ¶
    ¶
    ¶
    «first»·«last»¶
    «address»¶
    «city», ·«state»··«zip»¶
    ¶
    ¶
    Dear··first»·«last»,¶
                                                          MONTHLY.DOC
2
    first,last,address,city,state,zip¶
                                                          CUSTHEAD.DAT
3
    "Dolan","Christine","6867001","P.O.·Box#·1515","Overland·
    Park","KS","66210"¶
    "Evans","Ricky","7169002","222·Waverly·Lane","San·
    Rafael","CA","94903"¶
                                                          NAMESJAN.DAT
COMMAND: Copy Delete Format Gallery Help Insert Jump Library
         Options Print Quit Replace Search Transfer Undo Window
1970 characters (1589248 bytes free)
Pg1 Co19        {5}                        NL         Microsoft Word
```

DISPLAYWRITE 4

DisplayWrite is important in the marketplace, and I recommend it to clients who have invested in training for IBM DisplayWriters, which it emulates. But, I don't recommend it often.

I do not like how it is menu-bound, and the many ways that it channels you through its procedures. I do not like having to explicitly reformat my text rather than have paragraph and pagination handled automatically. I do not like the fact that if IBM doesn't sell it, your printer is not on the driver list.

DisplayWrite is a marked improvement over earlier versions, however. The new pull-down menus are easier to use, and if you have an EGA display and a mouse, you can bring it up in graphics mode (use the DW4APA batch file), which makes it even more tolerable.

However, DisplayWrite exhibits the same attitudes about file formats as it does about printers. It only recognizes DCA and ASCII text files, although it handles them easily.

How to Bring in a Text File

You cannot convert a text file on its own with DisplayWrite 4; instead, bring the text file into a document that is being edited. This is a fine distinction, since you can open a new (and therefore empty) document and bring in the ASCII file. Still, the document must exist first, and understanding that makes it easier to use the DisplayWrite 4 GET command.

Figure 7–52 shows the DisplayWrite 4 editing screen with an empty file.

I pressed the Crtl-F6 Function Key command to initiate the GET command, which produced the window at the bottom of the screen in Figure 7–53. You can also access this window by using the menus; press the F5 Function Key for the Functions Menu, then press *G* or 2 for the GET option.

You can use this command to bring ASCII files, DisplayWrite files, and DCA RFT format files into the file you are editing.

After you bring in the file, repaginate the document using the Ctrl-F7 Function Key command for the Document Options, then use *P* for the paginate command, as shown in Figure 7–54. DisplayWrite 4 puts its own line and characters at the end of each line, and it does not matter if there is a Carriage Return at the end of each line. There's no need to worry about search-and-replace procedures to fix up the file.

This leads to a different problem, however. If you do not have two Carriage Returns between paragraphs, then your text will collapse into a single mass. If you do not use Tab characters or a group of spaces to indent the first line of the paragraph, you risk losing the marking between paragraphs. Double spacing between paragraphs is the most convenient way to avoid the problem. Once the text is brought into the document safely, add formatting and print attributes.

FIGURE 7–52
Empty DisplayWrite 4 Editing Screen

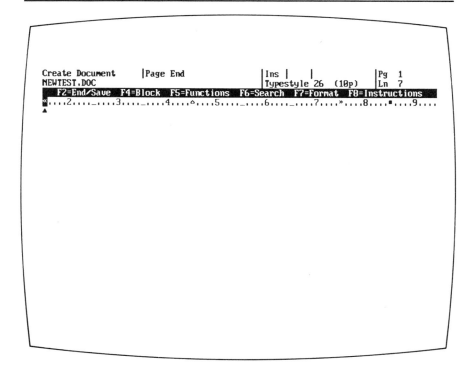

How to Export a Text File

There are two ways to create a text file from a document. One is shown in Figure 7–55. This is the second of two Print Document windows, which appears when you press the PgDn Key at the First Print Document window. Note that the third choice is Output Device; you can route the print output to a disk file. The problem with this approach is that the file will contain all formatting, including printer-control commands that can garble the result and cause lots of clean-up work.

The other way to produce an ASCII copy of your document is to use the Notepad feature in DisplayWrite 4. Start by placing your cursor at the top of the file. Figure 7–56 shows the

FIGURE 7–53
Empty DisplayWrite 4 Editing Screen with Get

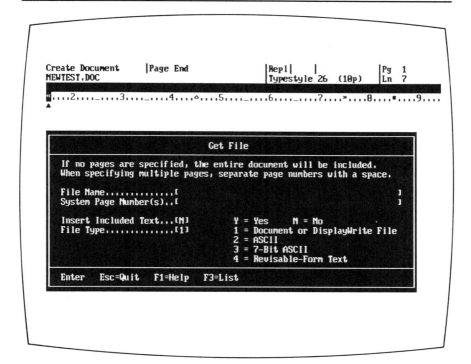

Notepad menu, which you call with the Ctrl-F4 Function Key command, or select from the F5 Function Key Functions Menu.

Select Option 4, ASCII Copy to File, and then mark the text you want to convert to ASCII. After you have finished marking the test, press the Return Key and DisplayWrite 4 will prompt you for a file name. Give a name and press the Return Key again and the program will write the ASCII file.

The file that is produced with this method has the same line length as defined in the original DisplayWrite 4 document. There are no spaces in the left margin, however, there are no top or bottom margins. Form Feed characters (Ctrl-L) are embedded in the file at page-break locations; you may have to remove them before using the file with another program.

FIGURE 7–54
Document Options Menu Showing Repaginate

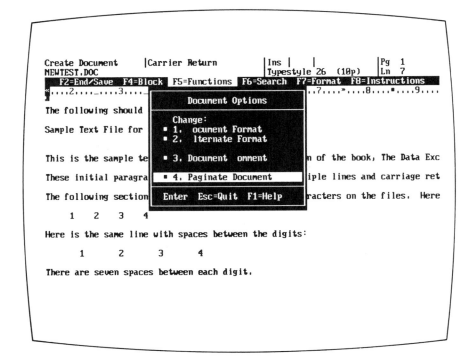

Other Supported Formats

As mentioned earlier, the only other document format supported by DisplayWrite 4 is DCA or Document Content Architecture. DisplayWrite 4 works with either the FFT (Final Format Text) or RFT (Revisable Format Text) formats.

Use the Ctrl-F6 Function Key GET command to read in a DCA RFT file. Also, there is a separate utility to call from the program's main menu that permits file conversion in both directions between DisplayWrite 4 and DCA formats.

Figure 7–57 shows this Document Conversion menu. Enter the name of the file to be converted along with the name of the new file. You can specify different paths for each file.

FIGURE 7–55
DisplayWrite 4 Print Document (2 of 2) Screen

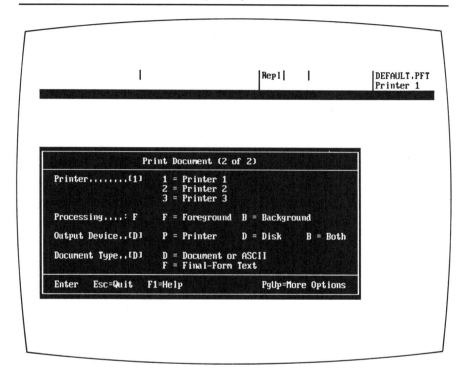

The conversion between DisplayWrite 4 and DCA formats works well; it maintains most formatting and print attributes reliably. Note, however, that not all programs produce reliable DCA formats (see Microsoft Word above), so don't count on this approach too heavily.

Mail-Merge Files

DisplayWrite 4 is much more tolerant of other file formats when it comes to data files for mail-merge documents than it is for document files. While you can create data files directly in DisplayWrite 4, you can also use IBM Personal Decision Series (PDS), Lotus 1–2–3 Release 1A .wks, Symphony 1.0 .wrk, DIF,

FIGURE 7–56
Notepad Menu

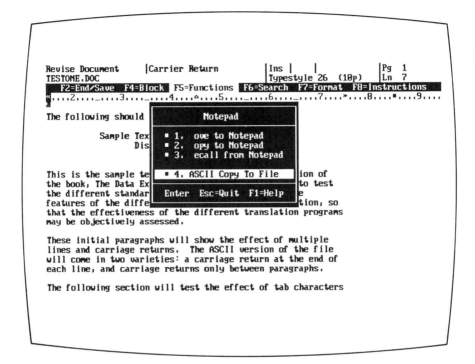

SYLK, dBASE II (not III), comma-delimited, or fixed-length record-format files.

The .WKS, .WRK, DIF, and SYLK formats all have similar requirements. Each record must be on its own row with one field per column. In addition, the first record must be the field name, which must be no more than 16 characters long with no spaces. DisplayWrite 4 field names are case sensitive, so pay attention to upper and lower case in field names.

If you use PDS or dBASE II formats, DisplayWrite 4 receives field names from the data file directly. dBASE II fields automatically occur in all uppercase characters, so use capital letters in your merge document.

For the two ASCII formats (fixed-length and comma-delimited), create a *file description* that defines the fields in the data

FIGURE 7–57
Document Conversion

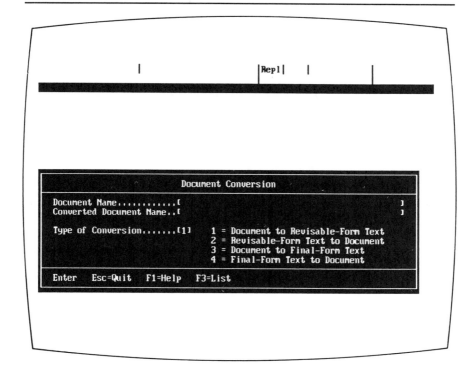

file. Figure 7–58 shows how to start this process; select MERGE from the main menu.

Select the CREATE option under the Data-File Description heading, and give the file description a name. DisplayWrite 4 will give this file a .DES extension (for DEScription) if you do not specify one.

This will bring you to Figure 7–59, where you chose to enter the field descriptions. Select the CREATE option.

You will next see a screen similar to Figure 7–60. Here, you must enter a name, type, and length for each field in the data-file records.

There are a few details to remember about this process. The field names must conform to DisplayWrite 4's requirements: no more than 16 characters and no spaces. Use under-

FIGURE 7–58
Merge Menu in DisplayWrite 4

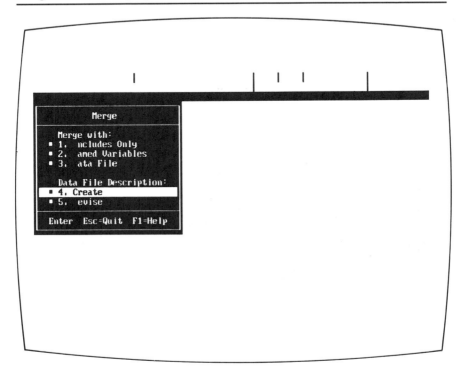

score characters instead of spaces if necessary. Also, name the fields in the same sequence as they appear in the data file.

For a comma-delimited file, ensure that the field length is specified to be *at least* as long as the longest entry in that field.

For fixed-length formats, match the field lengths exactly. If you do not, your merge will not work correctly. Furthermore, if your data file uses Carriage Return/Line Feed combinations at the end of each record, you need to define a separate field. Call it anything you want, such as "EndOfLine," and give it a length of two characters. Without it, your merged data will be jumbled.

FIGURE 7–59
Create/Revise Data File Description Menu, DisplayWrite 4

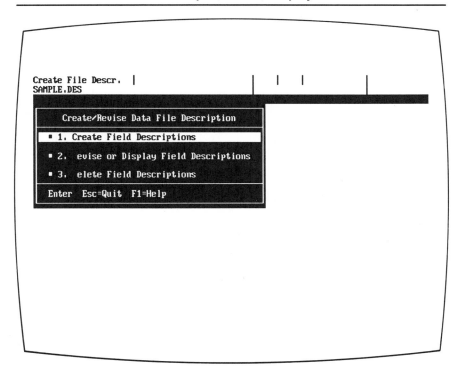

SUMMARY

Most people using microcomputers use a word processor part of the time. If you move data from one program to another often, whether from your machine to another or between programs on your computer, you will probably go to or from a word-processing program before long.

Remember that the text-file approach may often prove most reliable, and that the pseudoformatting codes described earlier eliminate the hassle of reformatting the transferred text.

While most people receive all the formatting they need from their word processor, some want more. They may want

FIGURE 7–60
Adding Field Descriptions

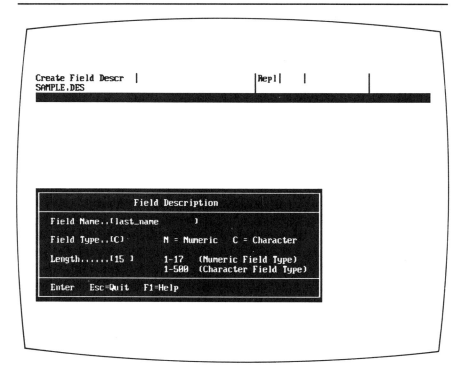

finer control over laser printers and proportional fonts, or the ability to include graphics, or to create carefully crafted pages with boxed text and multiple columns. For this, a full-blown desktop publishing system such as PageMaker or Ventura Publisher is necessary. The next chapter covers ways to move all types of files into these two programs.

CHAPTER 8

MOVING DATA INTO DESKTOP PUBLISHING PROGRAMS

Desktop publishing means different things to different people but whatever your definition may be, this is an application that has injected new excitement into the use of microcomputers.

There are many levels of desktop publishing, and a variety of programs offer a range of complexity from "paint" programs, to drafting, to complex word processors, to stand-alone desktop publishing.

While they are not the most expensive or powerful, the two most popular powerhouse desktop-publishing programs are Xerox's Ventura Publisher and Aldus' PageMaker.

This chapter discusses some commonalities and differences in using both products. Both programs have powerful features that make it possible to bring in data from a large range of file formats.

GENERAL POINTS ABOUT DESKTOP PUBLISHING

The most important concept about these desktop-publishing programs is that they are not designed to create information; they reformat it. In general, you create all the elements of your document outside of the program and then bring them in for assembly and formatting.

These programs have limited facilities for entering and editing text, but you will do better by entering and editing the text in your word processor. Only use the text-manipulation features for making small changes and editing after you have brought the data into your desktop program.

Similarly, these programs can draw simple graphics: lines, boxes, circles, and so on. It is best, however, if you create the graphics in a separate program that gives you more control and options and then import the graphics file for final placement on the page.

Creating Text for Import

When you create text files with a word processor or text editor, do not be concerned about margins and other formatting issues. These details will be stripped before coming into the desktop publishing program, which is where you want to make these decisions in any case.

Print attributes also are generally stripped. Bold and underline are typically imported, but font selection and spacing are left to the desktop-publishing programs. As explained later in the chapter, there are ways to embed codes that will be interpreted by the programs for font and formatting information.

Creating Graphics for Import

Both programs offer various techniques to manipulate and alter graphic images once they are imported. There are a few keys to remember as you prepare the pictures.

The first issue involves cropping. You may create an image that has more on it than you care to show on the final page. If you were working with traditional paper paste-up techniques, you could cut off unwanted portions of the image.

Desktop-publishing programs offer a similar control, but at a price. Instead of cutting off the extra image, you hide unwanted parts. This appears insignificant since the final product appears the same but the difference appears in program performance. If you crop the image file, then the program must load the entire graphic and keep track of what is left out and what is printed. All of this uses processing power, and it can slow the program.

As a result, it is better to plan your graphic at creation, and edit the image to give you the cropping time for the final product. It typically takes the same time or less to make these changes at this time.

The other problem with importing graphics appears in trying to change the image's size. Some programs produce graphic images that are stored as a set of defined lines—such as GEM Draw or CAD programs. These often can be enlarged or reduced without greatly affecting their appearance since the lines can be changed proportionally based on original definitions.

Many images are not defined in this way, however; they are simply a collection of dots, and they are stored as bit-mapped images. When you change the image's size, the desktop-publishing program must guess how to fill in the space created when the dots are moved apart, or guess the dots to eliminate if they are moved closer together.

The problem occurs with any bit-mapped image, but it is most pronounced when working with graphics that include shades of gray. Most printers can only print black ink on white paper, so shades must be produced by spacing the dots closer together or farther apart. There are two basic techniques for making different grays on a printer: dithering and halftones.

Dithering uses a random pattern that puts down dots in a certain density. *Halftones* work by changing the size of the dots to achieve different shades. In either case, the pattern in which shades are produced is neither regular nor obvious.

Figure 8–1 shows a copy of a shaded image printed on a Hewlett Packard LaserJet Series II using Ventura. This is a scanned photograph that was printed without altering the image's scale. While there are limits to the print quality obtained with 300-dot-per-inch resolution, this picture is acceptable for many desktop-publishing uses.

Figure 8–2 shows the same photographic image using the same disk file as the last illustration with a significant difference. Here, the scale has been altered. A checkerboard effect covers the picture. This results from the computer's inability to adequately adjust the shaded areas when the scale is changed.

FIGURE 8–1
Original Scale Photograph from Ventura

The solution to the problem is the same as for cropping: get it right the first time. Ensure that your image is the right size for the space in your document. If you use the same image in various sizes within a single document, either prepare them separately in your graphics program or be prepared for inconsistent results in the final copy.

VENTURA PUBLISHER

It should come as no surprise that I favor some products over the competition. Ventura is a favorite. It does not give as much fine control over page design as PageMaker, but it is superior

FIGURE 8–2
Altered Scale Photograph from Ventura

for long documents and I have been happy with it for everything from two-sided flyers to 100-page documents and longer books.

The current version of Ventura is 1.1, which is an improvement over the original version in terms of data-exchange features. The newer version handles a host of text and graphics formats, and it gives excellent flexibility for moving information into documents. To call the program complex is like saying it's tricky flying a 747.

Ventura is closely tied by heritage to the GEM Desktop environment, although there is now a patch available so that it will run under Windows. Like GEM Draw, it is oriented around frames, which are filled with text or graphics. Text formatting is governed by a set of definitions in a style sheet. These definitions are called *tags*, and they carry information about typestyle, font size, character spacing, and more. Assembling a document means bringing in the appropriate text and graphic files, creating the desired frames, filling the frames with the text and graphics, and then tagging the text so that it takes on the desired characteristics.

Note that Ventura also expects to find the text and graphics files in the same location that they were loaded from originally—namely a specific subdirectory on a certain disk. If you use removable media for some Ventura files, such as a floppy disk or Bernoulli Box, ensure that the right disk is in the correct drive to open a saved Ventura document successfully.

To explore the different capabilities of the program for bringing in data, let's look at the text and graphics features.

Bringing Text into Ventura

Ventura can read files from many popular word processors, including all the products covered in the last chapter (if you convert DisplayWrite 4 files to DCA format). It also supports XyWrite and straight ASCII files. Again, most of the formatting information is lost when the file is loaded into Ventura. What is not immediately apparent is that Ventura also saves the text back to its original file name when the total document is saved. Thus, any formatting in the original document is lost. As a result, if you are working with a formatted document that you want to keep in its original format, make and use a copy of the file with Ventura.

Figure 8–3 shows the results of clicking on the Load Text/Picture option of the main File Menu. The Text file type is highlighted, and the different text formats show as solid text.

You can embed a lot of Ventura information in a word-processing file before you bring it into the desktop-publishing program. The easiest information to add are paragraph tags. Ventura assigns text attributes by paragraph, and you can label each paragraph with tag information where it starts. Any

FIGURE 8–3
Ventura Load Text/Picture: Text Options

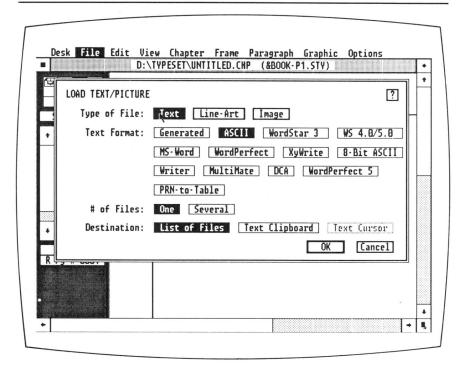

paragraph that is not tagged is treated as if it was tagged with the default format called *Body Text*.

The format for tagging paragraphs is as follows:

```
@TAGNAME = paragraph text
```

where "TAGNAME" is the name of a defined tag in the stylesheet used with the document, and "paragraph text" is the document text. Also, put a space on either side of the equal-sign character.

To understand how this works, take a file tagged within Ventura and examine the inserted tags. For some short documents, it may be easier to do the tagging with Ventura, but long documents that use lots of different tags are often easier to tag within the word processor.

There are two ways to tag the original file while working with a word processor. Try both ways to see which one works best.

The first way is to put in a short code, like "#1" or "*B**" at the start of each paragraph as you write it. After editing the document (using spell check and so on), you can then do a few global search-and-replace operations to transform the codes into their full tag names.

The other method is to create keyboard macros (either with a word processor or a separate memory-resident program like Keyworks from Alpha Software), and insert the full tag names along the way.

The advantage of the first approach is that there are fewer characters in the way when you edit the file. The advantage of the second approach is not having to use the search-and-replace process, and the macros will ensure that you enter the tag names consistently, which eliminates typos.

You can also insert various text attributes directly through a word processor. For all word processors supported by Ventura, you can use their own commands for bold and underline. You cannot insert the word processor commands that select fonts and other attributes, however. These commands are entered by inserting a letter bracketed by < and > characters. For example, <I> selects an italic font, and <D> selects the default setting. Here is a line of text that uses these embedded codes:

```
This line switches <I> to Italic type <D> and back again.
```

All font attributes, including bold and underline, can be accessed this way. These codes are listed in a reference table in Appendix E of the Ventura documentation. You can also select typeface, font size, color, and baseline adjustments.

You can also insert special characters. Ventura has a feature called *line break,* which forces a new line without starting a new paragraph. This is a handy feature to use for maintaining the line spacing used within a paragraph while starting a new line. You can embed a <R> to trigger a line break. You can also insert nonkeyboard characters by putting the ASCII decimal value within the > and < characters. For example, you can insert a Copyright symbol (the little circle with a *c* in it) when using a standard Ventura International Symbol Set font by including *<189>* in your document.

There is one more type of text file listed on the Load Text/Picture screen: Generated. This is a special type of file with a *.GEN* extension, and it is an ASCII file created by Ventura. The program can automatically generate a Table of Contents and/or an Index based on tagged text in the document. This information goes into a file that can be called up and loaded through the Load Text/Picture menu.

Bringing Graphics into Ventura

Ventura separates graphics into two categories: line art and images. They correspond to the defined lines and bit-image types described in the opening sections of this chapter.

Line-art files can be resized and will still print at maximum resolution without a loss of detail. An image on the other hand is created with a specific resolution by definition, and enlarging or reducing the picture size on the final page affects the resolution. As demonstrated earlier, changing sizes can also affect the appearance of the picture—especially when the image contains shades of gray.

As a result, try to create document illustrations as line-art files. This is impossible in most cases if you need to include shades of gray in the picture. Graphs, charts, and simple illustrations can be represented as line art.

Ventura Publisher recognizes 10 different line-art formats as shown in Figure 8–4. They include GEM Draw *.GEM,* AutoCAD *.SLD* slide format, Lotus 1–2–3 *.PIC,* Mentor Graphics, Video Show, Macintosh PICT format, Encapsulated Post-Script EPS format, CGM, Microsoft Windows, and HPGL.

Ventura works with these formats by converting a copy of the files to the GEM format before including them in the document. Unlike the text files, the graphics files are not modified by incorporating them in the document.

FIGURE 8–4
Ventura Line-Art Formats

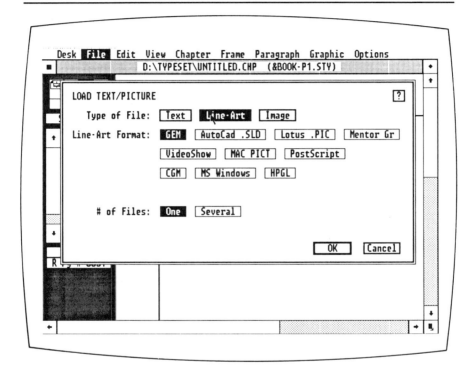

The AutoCAD *.SLD* files are produced by using the AutoCAD MSLIDE command, which is an option for the package. According to the Ventura documentation, you get better results using the HPGL method, so you may not need the slide option for AutoCAD.

The HPGL option takes a sequence of commands for a Hewlett Packard pen plotter and interprets them for Ventura. HPGL stands for Hewlett Packard Graphics Language, and many graphics programs on the market can "plot to disk" to create such a file. Set up your program to plot to an HP plotter, and then route the output to a disk file instead of a plotter. Note that fill areas may not work properly if you enlarge the image, so you will want to create the original image as close to the correct size as possible.

There is a third way to get images in from AutoCAD—using the Drawing Interchange Format or .*DXF* format. Ventura Publisher comes with a utility, DXFTOGEM, which can be used outside of Ventura to convert .*DXF* files to the GEM format.

The EPS format works differently than other line-art conversions. These files are not converted to a GEM file, and they do not display when loaded into a frame. Instead, the frame is filled with a large *X*. These images will not print on any printer but a PostScript compatible, since the file is not altered but fed to the printer when the document is printed.

Ventura also supports four image formats as listed in Figure 8–5: GEM Paint .*IMG* (also used by Dr. HALO), PC-Paintbrush .*PCX,* MAC Paint, and TIFF. These are bit-

FIGURE 8–5
Ventura Bit Image Formats

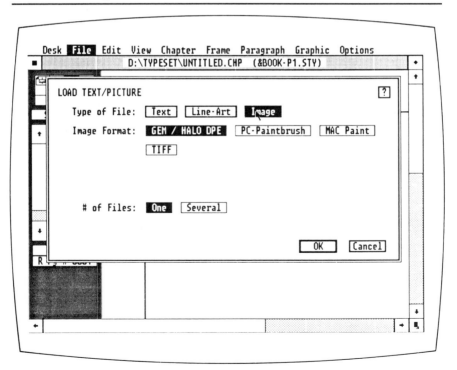

mapped pictures, and they are susceptible to unanticipated changes when enlarged or reduced. They are also the most common file format for clip-art collections, many of which were created on Macintosh computers. Scanners also produce one or more of these formats.

As with the line art, Ventura converts a copy of the image file to the GEM Draw format before bringing them into the document. The main complication with this process is that the MAC Paint images are always brought in as a full 8 × 10 page, no matter what the size of the original image. If you work with a clip-art collection (there are many useful images on Software Publishing's "First Publisher" disks), you will receive a full page of images from each file.

The temptation is to use the entire file—relying on cropping and scaling to put the desired image in the right place. This works, but there is a price to pay. First, you lose time in creating the document since you must drag the whole page around in your graphic frame to find a certain portion. Also, you must load in the entire graphic each time you bring up the document, which is a time-consuming process since the file is bigger than the needed portion. If you lack disk space, the extra space from unused portions of the file is significant.

The solution is simple. Find a graphics conversion program as discussed in Part 4, and convert the MAC Paint files into another format, such as PC Paintbrush, which you can edit with a graphics "paint" program. Cut the desired image and then save it in a separate file formatted so that Ventura can read it. It takes a little time, but you will be ahead before you finish working with your document. While you are at it, convert and edit a bunch of clip-art images for later projects.

ALDUS PAGEMAKER

PageMaker on the Macintosh was instrumental in starting the microcomputer desktop-publishing market. The current release for MS-DOS machines is version 3.0, which goes beyond the original Mac version.

PageMaker was initially better at crafting an individual page than Ventura, but it was not as good at long documents since there was so much more done by hand. The new version adds many features that relieve some of these problems; features such as style sheets that previously were associated with Ventura.

Since PageMaker runs under the Windows operating environment, you can use the Windows "Clipboard" feature to cut text and graphics from other Windows applications and then paste them down within the PageMaker document. You can also use the Place File option within PageMaker to import separate text and graphics files.

PageMaker comes with 16 different built-in file-conversion filters, which cover an assortment of text and graphics file formats. Also, you can install up to 10 additional import filters and 20 export filters. These may be specified when you first install the program, or they can be added later by modifying a Windows configuration file.

Unlike Ventura, PageMaker does not force you to choose between different source applications when you select the file to import. Instead, the program looks at the file extension of the selected file to determine its format. If the file does not match the expected format because it was a different extension, then you will see a box that asks you to indicate its source format.

This leads to a complication. The import file must have the correct extension to work automatically, which is a small problem. A bigger hitch is that if your file does not have an extension recognized by PageMaker as valid, its name will not appear on the list of available files.

This is not a problem for programs that automatically name all files with the same extension. For example, all MultiMate files have a .doc extension. Other programs are not so picky, such as WordStar or XyWrite, which let you create files with any extension or none at all. This will not do for PageMaker, however. You must use an extension on the "approved list" for it to recognize your file. Some of the supported extensions are listed in Table 8–1. Note in the table that to have PageMaker correctly identify WordStar and XyWrite files

TABLE 8–1
Sample File Import Extensions Supported by PageMaker

Application	Extension
AutoCAD and HPGL plot files	*.PLT*
DCA RFT	*.DCA* or *.RFT*
Encapsulated PostScript	*.EPS*
Lotus 1–2–3 graphs	*.PIC*
MacPaint	*.PNT*
Microsoft Word	*.DOC*
MultiMate	*.DOC*
PC Paint	*.PIX*
PC Paintbrush	*.PCX*
ASCII text	*.TXT*
TIFF	*.TIF*
Windows Paint	*.MSP*
WordPerfect	*.WP*
WordStar 3.3	*.WS*
XyWrite III	*.XYW*

from their names, you have to use extensions of .ws and .xyw respectively.

As with Ventura, there are significant differences in how text and graphic files are brought into PageMaker. We will look first at text files.

Bringing Text into PageMaker

Figure 8–6 shows the main File Menu within PageMaker. To bring in a file, select the PLACE option. The shortcut keystroke command is Ctrl-D.

After you select this option, the Place File Menu appears as in Figure 8–7. Note that no distinction is made at this point between text and graphics files. Click on the file name you want to select.

As mentioned earlier, PageMaker tries to determine the source-file format from its extension. If it determines that the selected file's format does not match its extension, then you see the screen in Figure 8–8 offering the chance to correctly identify its source.

PageMaker gives three options for flowing text into spaces on the page: automatic, semiautomatic, and manual. Automatic

FIGURE 8–6
PageMaker File Menu with Place Highlighted

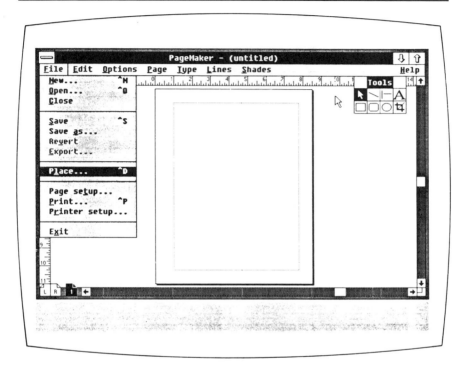

will flow from column to column and from page to page until the entire text file is loaded. Semiautomatic will fill the current column then wait for you to click on another space before filling it with any remaining text. Under the manual approach, you must select the space and the file each time until all file text is loaded.

PageMaker makes it easy to tell if there is more text to be loaded in the current text file. A frame that contains text has a special handle at the top and the bottom called *window-shade handles*. If there is a pound sign(#), the file is complete. (The pound sign and -30- are traditional typesetting symbols that mark the end of a story.) On the other hand, if there is a plus symbol (+), then there is more text to be loaded.

FIGURE 8–7
PageMaker Place File Screen

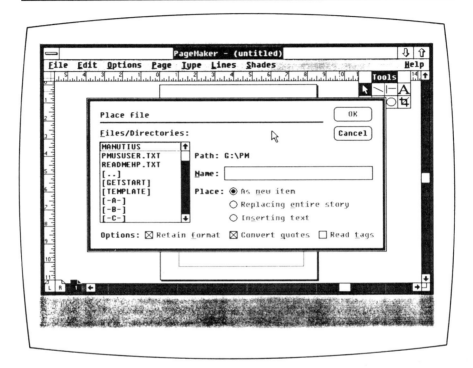

PageMaker treats file formats in different ways. Some formats, such as Windows Write and Microsoft Word, retain the majority of their formatting information. This includes print attributes such as bold and underlining, but it can include font selection and style-sheet definition. Other text formats such as DCA RFT and WordStar retain little of the original formatting detail. If you are not set on your choice of word processor and do lots of work with PageMaker, it may be worthwhile to tailor your choice of editor to match PageMaker's translation capabilities. This same consideration, from the other end, makes PageMaker the most logical choice for people upgrading from Microsoft Word or Windows Write to a more powerful desktop-publishing environment.

FIGURE 8–8
PageMaker Format Selection Screen

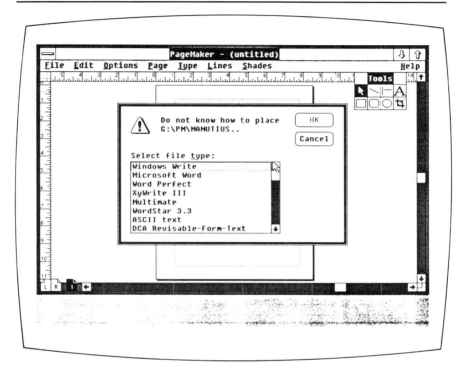

The one major import "gotcha" is the matter of ASCII text files and Carriage Returns. PageMaker relies on the Carriage Return to mark the end of a paragraph, so you must strip the extra ones appearing at the end of lines within paragraphs before bringing the text into PageMaker. You can edit them after you bring in the file, but it is faster and easier to use an editor's search-and-replace capabilities than to do it character by character within PageMaker.

You can pretag text for PageMaker. Enter the name of the paragraph style surrounded by < and > characters. For example, to tag a paragraph with the tag LIST, type the following:

```
<LIST>Here is an item in the list of this document. . . .
```

Note that PageMaker will assign an untagged paragraph the same format as the preceding paragraph.

Bringing Graphics into PageMaker

PageMaker supports various graphics formats, which it breaks into four categories: paint-type, scanned, draw-type, and Encapsulated PostScript. They are selected from the same Place File Menu as the text files mentioned in the last section.

In reality, the paint-type and scanned graphics are essentially the same; they are bit-mapped images. The main difference is that scanned images typically involve halftones or shades of gray, which do not scale accurately without distorting or developing checkerboard patterns.

PageMaker counters this scaling problem with a clever feature. If you hold down the Ctrl Key while dragging the corner of a graphic you wish to resize, it will only change to sizes that print properly using your printer's resolution. If you hold down the Shift Key and the Ctrl Key, the image's proportions are maintained.

Under draw-type graphics, you have some choices. The most useful is the HPGL *.PLT* format. This is a command file that drives a Hewlett Packard plotter, and it can be produced by most popular graphics programs.

All draw-type images are converted into a Windows metafile format by PageMaker, which can be dragged, stretched, and manipulated in various ways. There is a 64K limit to the size of a metafile, however, and file size is a function of the image's complexity. If your file will not load properly, then you will probably have to break it into smaller parts in separate files or eliminate some detail to simplify the total image.

The paint-type and draw-type images will be displayed as part of your document on the screen, but this is not the case with EPS images. EPS files are a collection of PostScript commands, and they are stored until it is time to send them directly to the printer as part of the printing process. On the screen, you will see a shaded box and the image name. EPS files can only be printed on PostScript printers.

SUMMARY

Desktop-publishing programs such as Ventura and PageMaker are the most complex data-exchange environments in the PC world since they depend so much on the output of other applications for the content of their documents. In general, these two programs have great flexibility and power in interpreting files from other programs.

This sharply contrasts with the products discussed in the next chapter: accounting software. For many good reasons, these programs care less about the input and output needs of other programs, yet there are ways to move data advantageously.

CHAPTER 9

MOVING DATA OUT OF ACCOUNTING PROGRAMS

Accounting: the term conjures an image of green visors, ink-stained fingers, and dusty ledgers. Some people love the challenge of balancing accounts and producing the esoteric financial reports required for compliance with the law and with modern management procedures. These people are probably in the minority, however, and thankfully desktop computers have taken out the drudgery of bean-counting tasks such as maintaining the company books.

Still, there is a significant limitation for nearly every accounting package on the market; you must look at the financial data in the format produced by the program. There is a selection of canned report formats from which to choose, and while in most cases the options are legion, sometimes you must settle for a report that isn't ideal.

In some cases, it's worse. If you need the data to create forecasts or a complex analysis, you take a printed report and type it into a spreadsheet or other program. This is risky business; one typo at this stage may mean the difference between a profit and a loss.

This chapter explores the best use of data with accounting programs, and it then examines specifics for two popular accounting programs: DAC Easy and Peachtree Complete II.

ONE-WAY STREET

The crucial point is this: expect to only move data in one direction—from the accounting system out to other applications. Don't expect to move data into your accounting program.

The reason is simple; accounting programs are complex. Even a straightforward application such as a General Ledger program can have untold levels of complexity. An accounting program involves multiple tables of interrelated information, and there are no standards for storing this information.

For example, a General Ledger program includes a Chart of Accounts, which lists all the accounts to which money can be credited or debited. Some programs support division or departmental accounts. Some programs offer a budget or last year's figures on each period for each account. Some keep every transaction in a file for the entire year (a useful but disk-hungry approach), while others merely bring a balance forward at the end of each period.

All of these options can be handled differently. The name of the accounts can be stored in a separate file and linked by means of the account code, or the Chart of Accounts can be stored as part of a larger file. Period totals and year-to-date figures can be stored with each account's description, or they can be in a separate file. Departmental information can be stored as part of a large file or split into different files.

In short, it can be difficult to know what you're looking for or how to know when you have found it. Even if you knew and thoroughly understood how the program stored your information, there are other problems associated with trying to add data directly to your accounting files.

One fact is that programs don't always try to maintain the data in a physically sorted file. This is impractical in many cases, since the information is often reported in a variety of sequences. For example, a Chart of Accounts listing might be requested in alphabetical order by name or in numerical order by account code.

As a result, most programs keep the data in large files with separate index files used to locate specific records more rapidly. Even if you could add information directly to the data file, you probably wouldn't maintain the index files in the process; these critical files would be useless. At best, the program would refuse to run with corrupted index files. At worst, it will appear to run correctly but give wrong information.

Another similar problem is summary data. Some programs produce current-period totals and so forth by recalculating each time based on current transactions. This is a waste of time, however, since the same effect can be achieved with faster results by keeping a running total. These totals are updated and stored with each set of transactions. The results can land in a separate file or as part of a larger file. The problem with adding data directly to your accounting system is that it is difficult to ensure that these running totals are maintained correctly in the process.

The bottom line is that you must go through normal channels if you want to ensure that your data lands in the correct place.

Cook Your Own Data

Some publishers offer the facilities to add batches of data. Typically, you are limited to reference-list data such as customers, employees, and products.

One example is Great Plains Software, which offers a product called Import Manager. This module can bring data into most master files and work files of the Great Plains Accounting Series modules. It can read both DIF and fixed-length record formats.

If you insist on accessing your accounting data directly, choose a system that uses dBASE .DBF format files. There are a number of public domain, shareware, and commercial accounting programs available that use dBASE or a similar product. SBT is a commercial package based on dBASE code and files.

With these programs, the same problems apply. You must be a competent dBASE programmer to unwind the source code and see exactly what information is maintained in which files. Only after you understand it completely can you experiment with adding data without the accounting program. Make a back-up disk of all files **before** you start to experiment—you may not have found everything on a first try.

If you have the technical expertise, there are other options. Most of the major accounting packages offer programmers some facility for direct access to data files. Some programs are written in COBOL, so a COBOL programmer will often purchase the program code to write custom modifications. Great Plains uses a file-management system called *Btrieve* and offers information on the file structures so programmers can create custom procedures. Still, this is heavy-duty programming, and it is beyond the reach of a typical business PC user.

Bringing It out

Extracting data from an accounting program is a different matter, however. You can't harm the data by looking at it.

Unless your program uses the dBASE .DBF or other standard format, however, you will probably have difficulty unraveling the native data files. Accounting programs typically go to great lengths to make data files smaller or faster to process. Numeric values often are packed into binary formats that are not immediately apparent. Pointers, tokens, and other unintelligible codes are buried in the records. Miscellaneous headers and blocking data break up the patterns of what otherwise appears as standard fixed-length records.

In short, the most reliable way to interpret the program's data files is through the accounting program. "All well and good," you might say, "but the whole problem is that I need the information in a form not offered by the accounting program." Simply use the accounting program to extract the needed data.

Recall from earlier chapters that a fixed-length record file looks like a columnar printout. In fact, in Chapter 4, I showed how to extract a fixed-length record file straight from Lotus 1–2–3 using the print-to-disk function.

Most accounting reports are columnar, and they fall into a fixed-length record format naturally. The problem is getting the information to disk.

A few accounting packages offer the option to send a report to a disk file, but they are in the minority. You can still capture most any report to disk, however, with a simple technique. There are some public-domain programs that take the printer output and store it in a disk file. I have encountered two: LPTX400 and RPRN. They can be quirky to use, especially if your program "plays tricks" in sending the data to the printer port. They work with straightforward programs, however, which covers most accounting programs. You can capture printed reports with either LPTX400 or RPRN.

If you have a Local Area Network at your disposal, you won't need one of these programs. If you spool the report to a disabled network printer, the server will store the printout in a disk file—waiting for the printer to be brought back on line. Instead, you can make a copy of this temporary file and edit it with a text editor.

All this is fine as long as the reports resemble what you need in the final product. Too much editing is as frustrating and time-consuming as retyping the information—and nearly as risky.

Fortunately, many publishers give additional choices. Some provide great flexibility within the reports they offer with the accounting programs. For example, you can select a range of accounts or client codes, you can suppress empty accounts, and you can select information based on the department or type of transaction.

Publishers also offer separate utilities. Great Plains, for example, offers Report Maker Plus, which allows you to create custom reports and to export your accounting data in various formats.

You can also receive these capabilities with low-cost accounting packages. In the next sections, we will look at two of the largest-selling accounting programs and their custom-report and export options.

DACEASY ACCOUNTING
AND GRAPH+MATE

General Ledger, Accounts Receivable, Accounts Payable, Billing, and Inventory for under a $100 list price? Impossible!

Or, at least that's how it was before DacEasy Accounting. Recently upgraded to version 3.0, this landmark product brings full-featured accounting within the reach of even the smallest kitchen-table venture. More than 400,000 copies have been sold according to DAC Software promotional materials, and it remains one of the best-selling accounting programs.

DacEasy also offers a Payroll module, disk-based tutorials, and a video tape. The product that we are most concerned with is Graph+Mate.

FIGURE 9–1
DAC Graph+Mate Calculator Screen

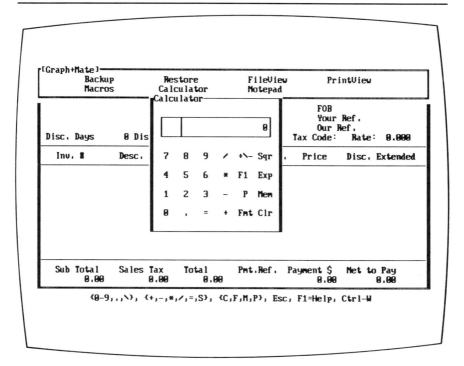

FIGURE 9–2
Graph+Mate Main Menu: Applications

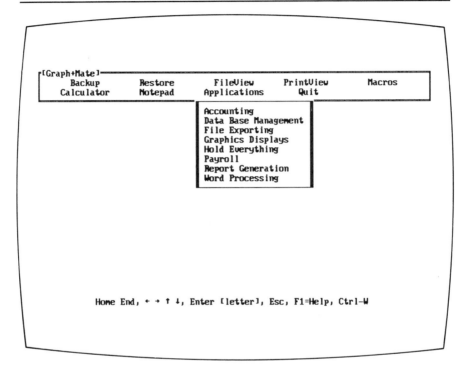

Graph+Mate lists for $99.95, and more than doubles the usefulness of DacEasy Accounting programs. It adds three sets of major features: desktop utilities, report capture, and data export.

Desktop Utilities

The desktop utilities can be accessed both outside and within the DacEasy Accounting. You can back up and restore the accounting program data files. You can also record, edit, and play back keyboard macros that can automate certain accounting procedures. You can call up a notepad, and its contents can be saved in a straight text file for use in other programs such as a word processor.

FIGURE 9–3
Graph+Mate PrintView Menu

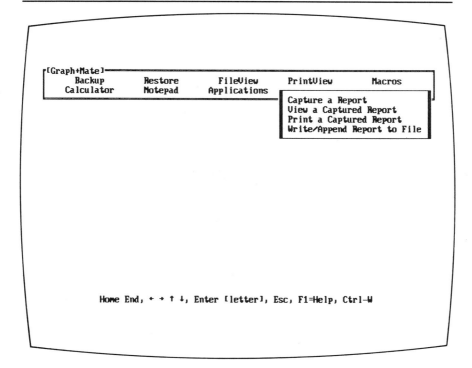

There is even a calculator that has a memory register, and the results of a calculation can be "pasted" into an accounting data-entry field with a single keystroke. Figure 9–1 shows a DacEasy screen with the calculator "popped up" on top.

Graph+Mate with Applications

You can also use Graph+Mate to call DAC applications. As shown in Figure 9–2, the Applications option on the main Graph+Mate menu lists different functions including the DacEasy Accounting and Payroll programs.

These options load and run these accounting programs automatically. When called from Graph+Mate in this way, the standard programs take on new features thanks to the

FIGURE 9-4
Graph+Mate Report Generation, Data-File Selection

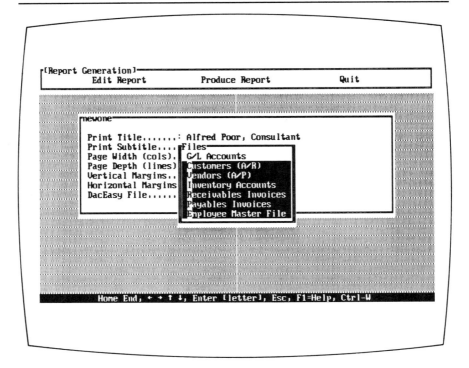

Graph+Mate program. Just press a "hot key" combination (Alt-F10) to bring up the Graph+Mate menu. For example, you can access the calculator and notepad. You can also look at the contents of almost any DacEasy Accounting data file using the FileView option.

Perhaps most useful, however, is the PrintView option shown in Figure 9-3. Here, you can choose to intercept a DacEasy Accounting report and save it directly to disk. This allows you to bring it to an editor for clean-up or to add it to a report. You can also view and print captured reports from this menu.

FIGURE 9–5
Graph+Mate Report Generation, Field Selection

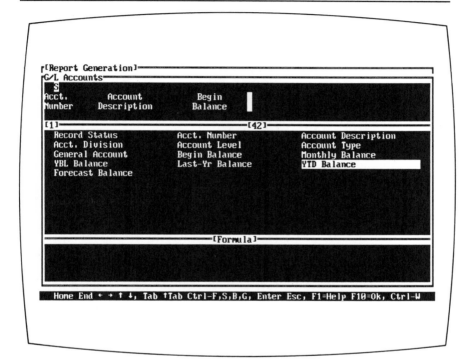

Data Export and Manipulation

These features alone would make the Graph+Mate program a worthwhile value, but DAC added more. It can export data in three flexible, useful ways.

The first way is a custom-report writer. You create custom report definitions that can be stored, run, and edited at will. Figure 9–4 shows the first step in creating a new report format, in which you specify the title, margins, and other details. You also select the desired accounting data file as shown in the pop-up window on the screen.

FIGURE 9–6
Graph+Mate Report Generation, Report Options

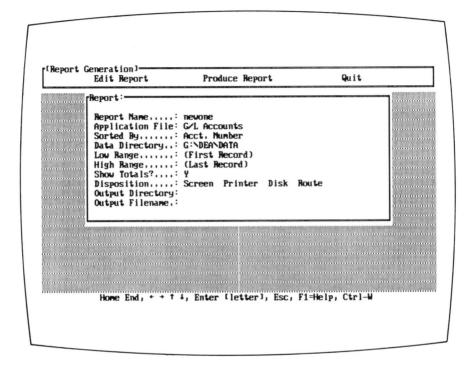

After selecting this information, you can choose fields for inclusion in the report, as illustrated in Figure 9–5. You can specify subtotal and grand-total breakpoints, as well as define formulas to be calculated. You are limited to 132 columns of data.

When using a report definition like this, you see a screen like the one in Figure 9–6. Here, you can specify the range of values to be used in selecting records to print, and you can route the output to the screen, printer, or a disk file. You can also send the results through any available parallel or serial port at this point.

Custom-report generation is useful, but you can move data into other programs more easily if you can have more control

FIGURE 9–7
Graph+Mate File Exporting, Data-File Selection

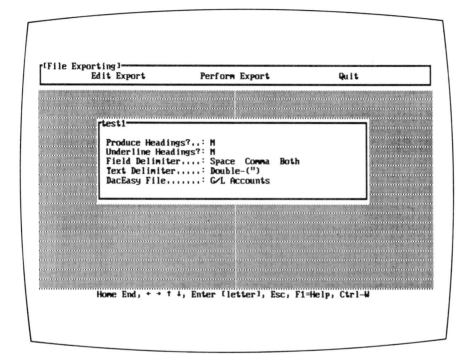

over the format of the data written directly to disk. File Exporting fills this bill, and it works almost identically to the Report Generator Application.

Figure 9–7 shows the initial specifications for an export-file format. You can specify field and text delimiters. They are commonly set to a comma and double quotes respectively, so as to produce a standard comma-delimited, quoted-string format file. Note that you also select the data file in the same manner as with the Report Generator.

Field selection is the same as with the Report Generator, including the 132-column limitation as shown in Figure 9–8. You do not specify sub-totals or other breaks, but you can define custom formulas.

FIGURE 9–8
Graph+Mate File Exporting, Field Selection

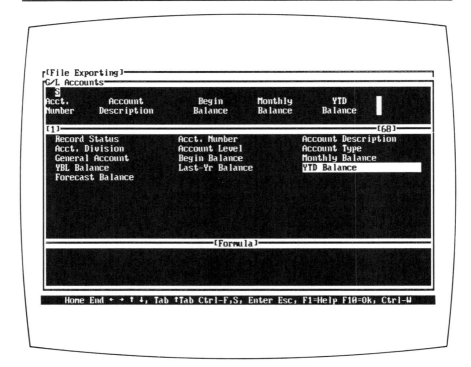

When you run an export format, you have the same choices in range of records as with reports. If you create the export with a quoted-string, comma-delimited format, you can bring the data directly into most spreadsheets and data base programs without further manipulation.

While the custom report and file export features are useful, the Graphics Displays is the flashy one. As shown in Figure 9–9, you have a choice of seven different graph formats. You also can select ranges or individual data elements to graph.

After creating a graph definition, you can run it and display the results on the screen, as shown in Figure 9–10. You can also print the graph if you have a supported dot-matrix

FIGURE 9–9
Graph+Mate Graphics Displays, Chart Types

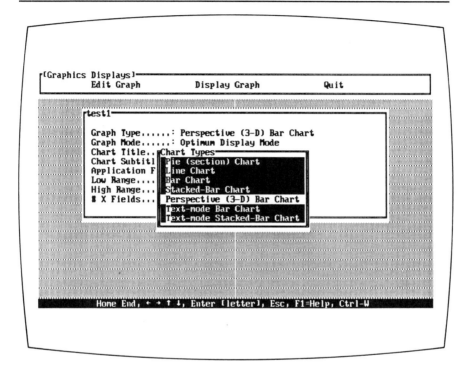

printer. You can also format ASCII files for use by Graph+Mate if you want to use it to graph data from other programs; the manual explains the required data-file format.

The end result is a pictorial display of your numeric data that is a more accessible method to view and analyze financial data.

When viewed in sum, the features added by Graph+Mate make the DacEasy Accounting information far more powerful and useful since it gives you an easy way to manipulate, view, and move the data around both within the DAC system and out to other programs that are used regularly.

FIGURE 9–10
Graph+Mate Graphics Display, Sample Graph

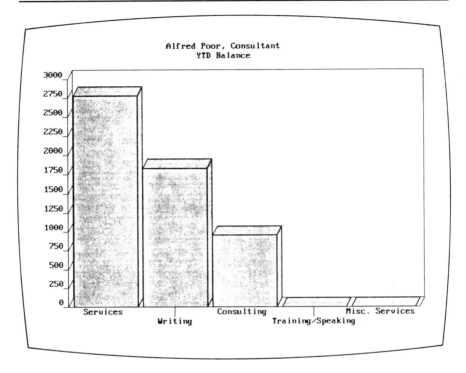

PEACHTREE COMPLETE II ACCOUNTING

Another accounting package on the best-seller charts is Peach-tree Complete II accounting. The history of this program is different than DAC's, however.

Instead of being built from the ground up as a new, low-cost package, Peachtree Complete started off years ago as a full-priced, full-featured accounting system. One version was even sold by IBM. Each of the separate accounting modules sold for hundreds of dollars with a total list price of $4,800.

After a while, accounting packages became more sophisticated. Multi-user, faster performance, more efficient programming code, and other features made the top end of the accounting market more competitive.

By this point, Peachtree had recovered its development costs on their accounting system and a profit, so they could have simply and quietly retired the whole system. This seemed silly, though, since the package was still adequate for many small business bookkeeping needs.

Instead of scrapping the programs, they scrapped the price. Instead of hundreds of dollars for the seven modules, they decided to charge $199 for the whole set: General Ledger, Accounts Receivable with Invoicing, Accounts Payable, Inventory, Fixed Assets, Job Cost, and Payroll. The experiment was so successful that they added features like windows, pop-up menus, and powerful improvements. The result is a large and powerful accounting system for a bargain price.

Peachtree Data Query II

Like DAC, there are plenty of reports built into the system. Also like DAC, Peachtree recognized that users may have some unique needs and requests that might not be included in the system, and as a result, Peachtree developed Peachtree Data Query II or PDQ for short.

PDQ is a stand-alone module (list price $199) that works with the Peachtree Complete accounting data files. PDQ offers the user access to different groups of fields organized into views. The views automatically pull sets of fields from related files. PDQ offers 35 different views that cover all the different modules. The views and the fields they include are listed in an appendix at the back of the manual.

Figure 9–11 shows the opening screen after the title screen. The data in the top window has been scrolled until the General Ledger Accounts option appeared, and the cursor highlights that selection.

The next screen asks you to choose a company's data files for use with this view. Once you have made a choice, you see a

FIGURE 9–11
PDQ—Select General Ledger Accounts View

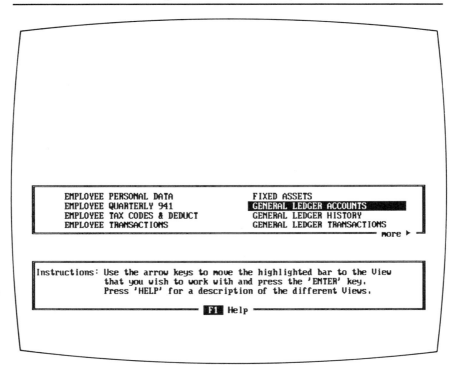

screen like the one in Figure 9–12. This screen shows the main choices available within PDQ.

Notice at the bottom of the lower window that there is a prompt stating F2 To Keyboard Input. This is a clue about the basic concept behind PDQ. The program is really a structured query programming language in which you assemble short-procedure files that you execute. PDQ stores, recalls, edits, and runs these procedures much like a data base program such as dBASE III.

You can press the F2 Function key and enter the commands directly on the screen, but most users find the prompted

FIGURE 9–12
PDQ—Select a Function

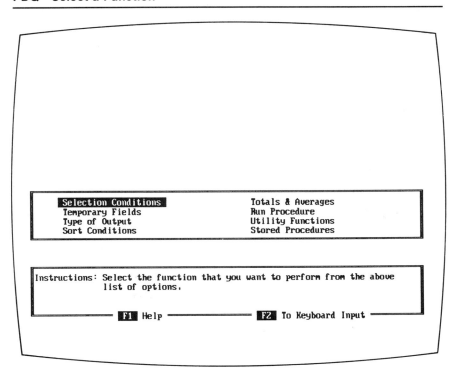

approach easier to use; it is capable of using about 90 percent of PDQ's features.

In Figure 9–13, we have started to create the query. First, we selected "Type of Output" as shown in the prior illustration, and the box in the upper left appeared. We chose "DISPLAY" to put the results on the screen, but instead we could have created a graph, a list on the printer, a custom report, or an export file with the other choices.

We then selected field names from the center window, which appeared in the "Command;" line as they were chosen. When we press the End key, the command will be entered as part of the current procedure.

FIGURE 9–13
PDQ—DISPLAY Example Screen

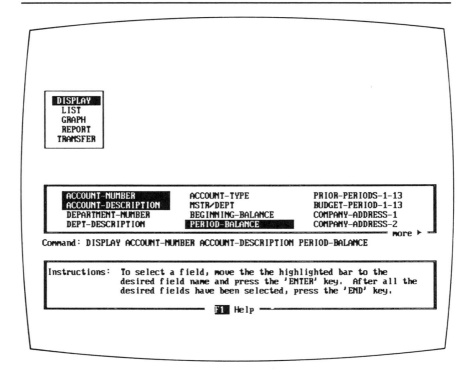

Figure 9–14 shows another option from the main menu of functions: Selection Conditions. We have made selections from the pop-up windows to select all records where the account type is equal to a constant value, "2." We have also selected an "AND" connective in preparing to add another selection criteria.

These two statements complete the procedure, so we can now select the "Run Procedure" as shown in Figure 9–15. Note that we have completed the selection statement by asking for records where the beginning balance is not equal to 0.

Press the Enter key, and PDQ adds the word "EXECUTE"

FIGURE 9–14
PDQ—Selection Conditions Example

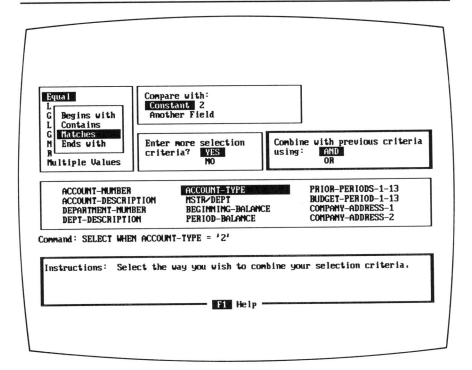

to the procedure; it assembles the answer to your request. It selects and sorts the requested records and then displays them on the screen.

If you choose to "SPOOL" the output of a procedure, you send the results to a disk file. As seen in the previous screen, the output is in a row-and-column format that results in a fixed-length ASCII text file when sent to disk.

It is almost as easy to create other export formats. Figure 9–16 shows a screen created using the "TRANSFER" option under the "Type of Output" choice on the main menu.

Note that PDQ supports Lotus .wks, MultiPlan, and DIF

FIGURE 9–15
PDQ—Query on Screen, Ready to Run Procedure

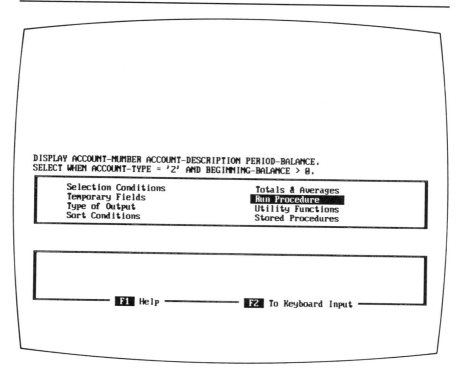

```
DISPLAY ACCOUNT-NUMBER ACCOUNT-DESCRIPTION PERIOD-BALANCE.
SELECT WHEN ACCOUNT-TYPE = '2' AND BEGINNING-BALANCE > 0.
```

Selection Conditions	Totals & Averages
Temporary Fields	**Run Procedure**
Type of Output	Utility Functions
Sort Conditions	Stored Procedures

F1 Help ──────────── **F2** To Keyboard Input

export formats in addition to the selected ASCII option. In fact, the ASCII format is a standard quoted-string, comma-delimited, text-file format. If you answer "yes" to the question about the data dictionary, PDQ will make an ASCII version of the Peachtree Complete data files, which takes time but can hasten subsequent queries.

As with the DISPLAY command, you select the fields to be included. You can also apply a selection command. Execute the procedure and the file will be written to disk.

PDQ has other useful features. You can produce bar charts and histograms and create complex custom-report formats

FIGURE 9–16
PDQ—Transfer Screen

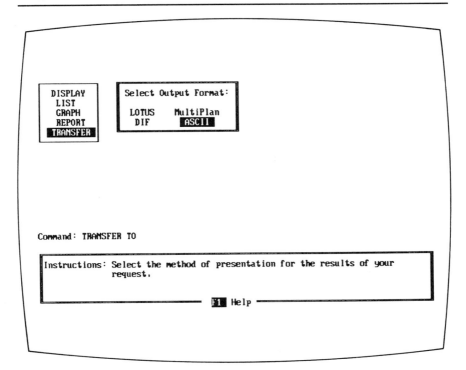

with subtotals and fancy formatting. You can specify calculated fields based on combinations of other fields and produce calculated fields. If necessary, you can use some advanced procedural commands for complex processing. For example, there is full logic-flow control in procedures through the use of IF/THEN/ELSE statements.

Peachtree Data Query gives powerful and flexible access to the wealth of accounting data contained in the Peachtree Complete II accounting system, and it provides a simple method to extract desired data for use in spreadsheets, word-processing documents, or data base programs.

SUMMARY

You must be careful when trying to directly manipulate accounting data, but depending on the package selected, you will find ways to safely extract data for use with other programs. A good utility designed by the accounting system's publisher can make this task faster, safer, and much easier to perform.

This completes the section on using built-in capabilities of specific programs. While most of the programs covered have some data-exchange facilities, there may be a time when you want to roll up your sleeves and get directly involved with your data. The next section is designed for do-it-yourself types; it explains some tools and tricks that you can use directly.

PART 3

DO-IT-YOURSELF SKILLS

As shown in the last chapters, many of the popular programs in use today offer a wide range of data-translation features. Although they cover many situations that might be encountered, they won't do it all.

There may be times when the data file is in one format and you need it in another format before the program accepts it. Or, perhaps the import file has information you want to remove before bringing in the data. Or, maybe you need to change all the part numbers in a file of inventory data to a new format before you feed it to your data base. Sometimes the pieces don't fit without a little whittling.

Part 4 introduces valuable third-party programs and utilities that ease this sort of data-file transformation. You don't need to spend more money to gain the power of making these changes.

If you have some sort of text editor (even if only the dreaded EDLIN that comes with DOS), Chapter 10 discusses handy tips on using it.

Chapter 11 gives some BASIC utilities that can perform simple transformations. Key them in and you can convert back and forth between comma-delimited and fixed-length files, remove any character from a text file, or turn a WordStar file into a text file.

In short, the next two chapters demonstrate the tools that can start you toward self-sufficiency in working with various text-based, data-file formats.

CHAPTER 10

TIPS AND TRICKS WITH TEXT FILES

As the first two sections of this book demonstrate, you will most likely encounter a text file when you begin to explore actual data-exchange situations. The text files you encounter will rarely be how you want them. Perhaps, there will be extra characters or fields that need to be eliminated or inserted, or perhaps you will need to change how the information elements are separated from each other.

There are many different solutions to these problems, but one good way to manipulate text files is through a text editor. This chapter describes some of available editors and shows handy ways to use them.

TEXT EDITORS

Before the advent of the word-processing program, the task of putting words into a computer and out on paper was divided into two steps.

The first step was the editor step, which permitted the user to enter characters and to change them. Early editors only worked one line at a time. To see this sort of editor in action, fire up the dreaded EDLIN on your MS-DOS disk. Try to write a one-page letter with EDLIN and you will discover why full-screen editors rapidly become popular.

Second, after entering the text and making corrections, you used a runoff program to format the text and send it to the printer or other output device.

The separation between the editor and runoff steps is increasingly blurred in many of the modern, high-powered, word-processing programs, yet they all follow the same design. In a few programs, the distinction is more apparent. For example, the Lotus Manuscript program has a runoff program that can be run directly from the DOS prompt. WordStar's printing module is so separate that you exit the editor to print a file.

Another step that happened in developing the word processor is that users' needs became more sophisticated. As a result, programs had to store much more information in a file than just characters to be printed. The runoff program then interpreted this extra information and made the necessary adjustments of changing margins, line spacing, text, fonts, headers and footers, footnotes, table of contents, and index entries. In short, the editor and runoff programs had to handle extremely complex formatting information along with the document's text.

Most word processors responded to this challenge by relying on a special file format to carry the extra information. As a result, few high-end word processors use straight text files as their basic format. XyWrite III is a notable exception to this statement. And, as shown in Chapter 7, the resulting Tower of Babel has created all sorts of problems for moving information between these applications. But what about the problem of editing a simple text file?

Fortunately, there are a few options. Some word processors, like XyWrite, can create and edit straight ASCII files without a problem. Others, like WordStar and WordPerfect, have facilities that let you perform such a task without too much difficulty. These are expensive and large programs, however, which lead to two drawbacks. They take a significant investment of money and time to learn, and they take a significant time to load when you want to use them.

You can still find some leaner and less expensive programs that work well with straight-text files. The following three programs each fit a slightly different niche; one of them will likely be a useful addition.

PC-Write Version 3.0

PC-Write is one of the biggest shareware success stories. Written by Bob Wallace, it is available for $16 from Quicksoft and for even less from many user groups, electronic bulletin boards, and shareware libraries. If you like it and use it, become a registered owner, which costs $89. This price gives benefits including a free future update, a handsome hardcover manual, and your own serial number.

The neat fact about your serial number is that Quicksoft pays a bounty to the registered owner every time someone registers based on a copy of that system. If you convince enough friends to register, you can receive the money you paid

FIGURE 10–1
Simple Batch File in DOS

```
prompt $P$G
set comspec=c:\command.com
PATH=C:\DOS;C:\XY;C:\ARC
mark
echo off
cls
cd \
metro
cd \mailsys
mlinit
comdrv
xpcdrv
mlmain
cd \
echo
echo  ┌─────────────────────────────────────────────────┐
echo  │                  Lotus Express                  │
echo  │   Copyright (C) 1985,1986,1987 Lotus Development Corp.  │
echo  │   Hold down [ALT][SHIFT] to view accessories menu.  │
echo  └─────────────────────────────────────────────────┘
if not exist \lehelp\*.* goto exist
echo  ┌─────────────────────────────────────────────────┐
echo  │                    WARNING                      │
echo  │ On non-hard-disk systems, you must leave the Startup  │
```

FIGURE 10–2
PC-Write Editor with Simple Batch File

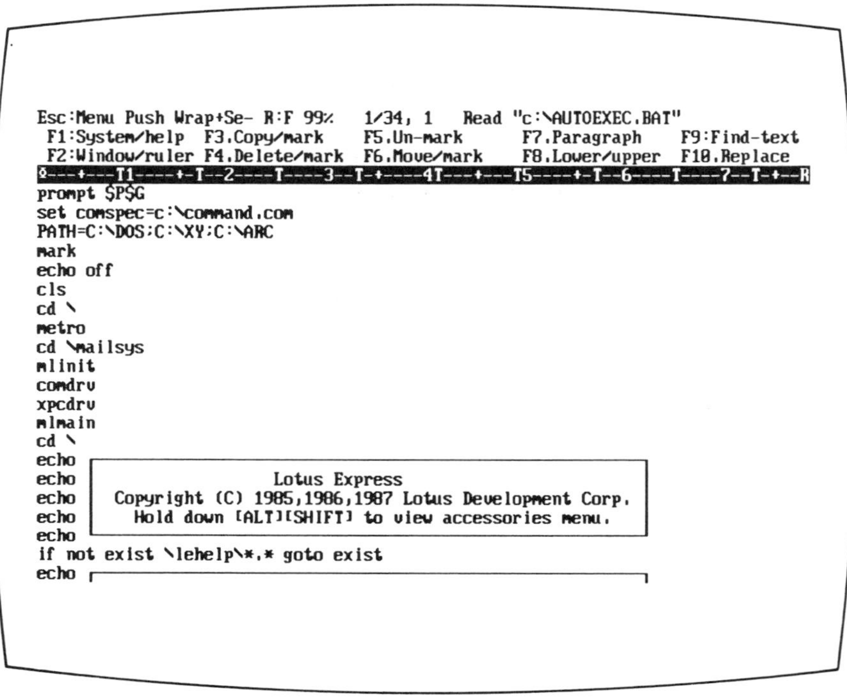

```
Esc:Menu Push Wrap+Se- R:F 99%   1/34, 1   Read "c:\AUTOEXEC.BAT"
 F1:System/help  F3.Copy/mark     F5.Un-mark      F7.Paragraph     F9:Find-text
 F2:Window/ruler F4.Delete/mark   F6.Move/mark    F8.Lower/upper   F10.Replace
----+---T1----+-T--2----T----3--T-+----4T---+---T5----+-T--6----T----7--T-+--R
prompt $P$G
set comspec=c:\command.com
PATH=C:\DOS;C:\XY;C:\ARC
mark
echo off
cls
cd \
metro
cd \mailsys
mlinit
comdrv
xpcdrv
mlmain
cd \
echo
echo                         Lotus Express
echo       Copyright (C) 1985,1986,1987 Lotus Development Corp.
echo         Hold down [ALT][SHIFT] to view accessories menu.
echo
if not exist \lehelp\*.* goto exist
echo
```

to register your copy! Quicksoft's annual sales run in the millions of dollars; the shareware marketing approach has not hurt them.

PC-Write is worth owning even if you have another word processor, and it is so good that you should consider it for your first word processor if you don't have one. It can create and edit pure text files, and it is also a full-blown professional word processor.

The program is complete with a spell-check, a full complement of commands and features, and it even provides excellent support of proportional fonts on laser printers. To see how good it is, look at the printed manual that was produced using PC-

FIGURE 10–3
PC-Write Misc-Stuff Menu

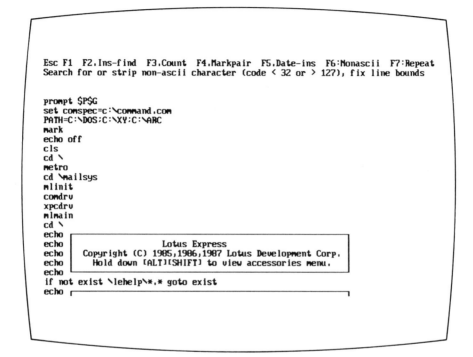

Write. Too many programs are weighed down by their own mass of features, but not PC-Write. Even when running huge files, it is generally as fast as the fastest programs on the market.

For people who want to customize their work environment, PC-Write is compliant. You can totally redefine the keyboard and the commands to match almost whatever layout or custom functions you want to create. And, as mentioned above, it works with straight-text files. Figure 10–1 shows a simple batch file as viewed from DOS.

Figure 10–2 shows the same file as viewed in the PC-Write editing screen. Since no print formatting codes are used, the file contains only the straight ASCII text characters.

FIGURE 10–4
PC-Write FIND Carriage Return/Line Feed Combination (F8 Wildcard)

```
Esc  F9:Find "♪♫"  F10:Replace ","
F1.Help          F3.Copy-Marked  F5.Alpha/digit  F7.Any-char     Esc.Cancel
F2.Copy-Find     F4.Next-notwild F6.Non-alpha     F8.Line-bound   Enter.Resume
Grey±.Search forward/backward  sGrey±.Search from start/end     cF10.Swap-F9/F10
prompt $P$G
set comspec=c:\command.com
PATH=C:\DOS;C:\XY;C:\ARC
mark
echo off
cls
cd \
metro
cd \mailsys
mlinit
comdrv
xpcdrv
mlmain
cd \
echo
echo                    Lotus Express
echo    Copyright (C) 1985,1986,1987 Lotus Development Corp.
echo      Hold down [ALT][SHIFT] to view accessories menu.
echo
if not exist \lehelp\*.* goto exist
echo
```

PC-Write has another useful feature. It automatically offers to create a back-up version of a file before editing it. This helps ensure that you keep an untouched version of the file before making changes.

PC-Write uses nontext characters for various formatting and print-attribute purposes. As a result, it is inflexible about locating these characters.

Figure 10–3 shows the PC-Write "Misc-Stuff Menu." The F6 Function key will move the cursor to the next nonprintable character or extended character (one with a decimal value between 128 and 255.) This will work to find Line Feed characters that are not paired with Carriage Returns.

You can also search for Carriage Return/Line Feed character combinations. For this operation, use the regular FIND command. Press the F9 Function key then press the F8 Function key. Figure 10–4 shows how the screen should appear at this point.

Although it is not documented, you can use the FIND option to search for many unprintable characters. Press the F9 Function key to call up the FIND menu, then hold down the Alt key and the Shift key. Then, enter the three-digit ASCII code for the character. Some characters will produce unexpected results, such as the Line Feed character (ASCII 010), but others work fine. You cannot enter Null Character (ASCII 000), but you can enter many other unprintable characters with this method.

Personal Editor II

Personal Editor II, or PE2, is one of the IBM Personally Developed Software series; they are programs developed and tested by IBM employees. IBM subsequently set up a mechanism to market them. Typically priced under $100, they have little or no printed documentation and are not developed by IBM directly.

PE2 is an excellent text-file editor. It is not a word processor because it is limited in its formatting and other printout features. It is a favorite among programmers, however, for both its speed and flexibility.

To begin with, you can have up to four windows open on a screen at once. You can have up to 20 files open at once. If you have the same file open in two or more windows, changes in one window automatically occur in the other windows. This means that you can view different portions of the same file and not worry about which view is updated.

The keyboard and commands can be redefined, and you can create custom commands including a macro language that is almost its own programming language that allows for automation of some sophisticated tasks and assignments to keystroke combinations.

SideKick

SideKick was a landmark product in many ways. It was the first product from Borland International that was an end-user's tool but not a programming language. It was also the first TSR (Terminate and Stay Resident) utility to gain broad acceptance and start the danger-laden trail of memory-resident programs. It was also a huge success because of the useful features available with just a keystroke.

In addition to its calculator, calendar, address book, and ASCII reference table, SideKick included a Notepad feature that is a miniature text editor. It uses commands similar to WordStar, so it was instantly familiar to thousands of users. It creates and edits pure text files, so it was immediately useful for thousands of programmers. (In fact, it was an in-house tool developed by Borland programmers for their own use, and it was only later that it was discovered that end users might also be interested in it.)

As a programming aid, the SideKick Notepad is tough to beat. For example, say you are creating a procedure file in dBASE III Plus. You can use the dBASE editor, but this means loading the editor and the command file, editing it, saving it, and then testing the procedure again. With SideKick, you leave the procedure loaded in the Notepad, make your edits, save the file, and then close SideKick. You are immediately at the dBASE prompt, ready to run the procedure. If you need to make further changes, one keystroke instantly reopens Side-Kick with the file already loaded and the cursor still at the same location as left at the end of the last editing.

You can use SideKick to edit any text file. Some people have problems because the program has a limit to the size of the file that it will load in the Notepad. This is not a permanent situation, however. The version of SideKick I have permits files up to 50,000 characters—enough for 25 pages of double-spaced text. This increased capacity comes at the cost of more memory lost when SideKick is loaded, so it pays to limit the Notepad capacity to only what is needed.

For most short-text files, the default setting of 4,000 characters should be sufficient. Figure 10–5 shows the sample batch file as viewed in a SideKick Notepad window.

FIGURE 10–5
SideKick Notepad with Sample Batch File

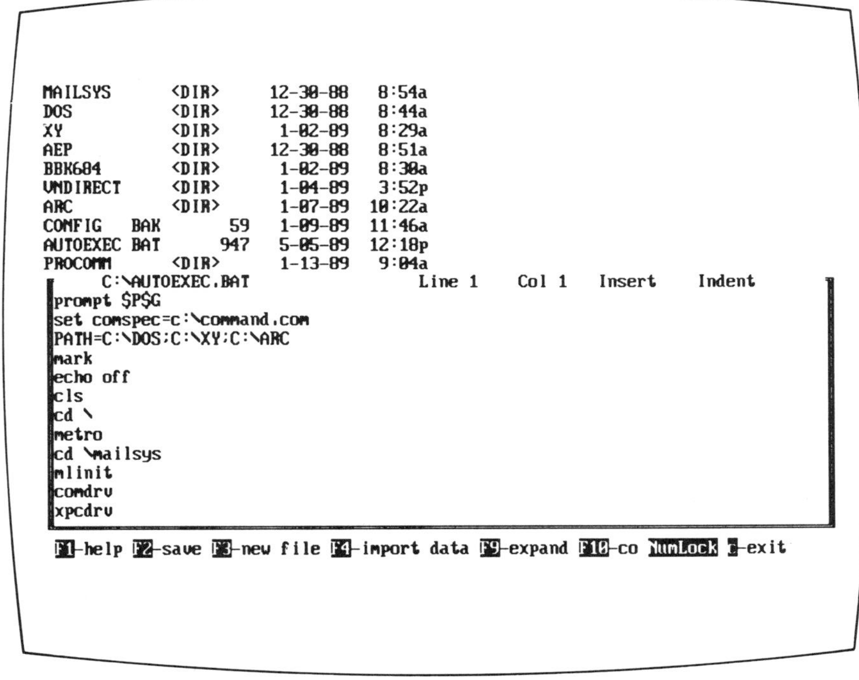

```
MAILSYS       <DIR>        12-30-88    8:54a
DOS           <DIR>        12-30-88    8:44a
XY            <DIR>         1-02-89    8:29a
AEP           <DIR>        12-30-88    8:51a
BBK684        <DIR>         1-02-89    8:30a
VMDIRECT      <DIR>         1-04-89    3:52p
ARC           <DIR>         1-07-89   10:22a
CONFIG   BAK        59      1-09-89   11:46a
AUTOEXEC BAT       947      5-05-89   12:18p
PROCOMM       <DIR>         1-13-89    9:04a
        C:\AUTOEXEC.BAT              Line 1     Col 1     Insert      Indent
prompt $P$G
set comspec=c:\command.com
PATH=C:\DOS;C:\XY;C:\ARC
mark
echo off
cls
cd \
metro
cd \mailsys
mlinit
comdrv
xpcdrv
```
F1-help F2-save F3-new file F4-import data F9-expand F10-co NumLock -exit

SideKick can cut and paste text to and from regular applications. This is a handy feature when you want to include a
calendar with a document; cut it from the Calendar in Side-
Kick, and then paste it into your word processor on its editing
screen.

SideKick also has a powerful search-and-replace facility. It
cannot search for an ASCII decimal 001, which is a Ctrl-A,
because it uses this as a wild-card character for its searches. It
searches for almost any other character, however, including
Carriage Returns and Line Feeds.

Figure 10–6 shows the start of a SEARCH command within
SideKick. The "^[" on the top line of the Notepad window represents a Ctrl-[, which produces an ASCII decimal 027, which

FIGURE 10–6
SideKick FIND Command

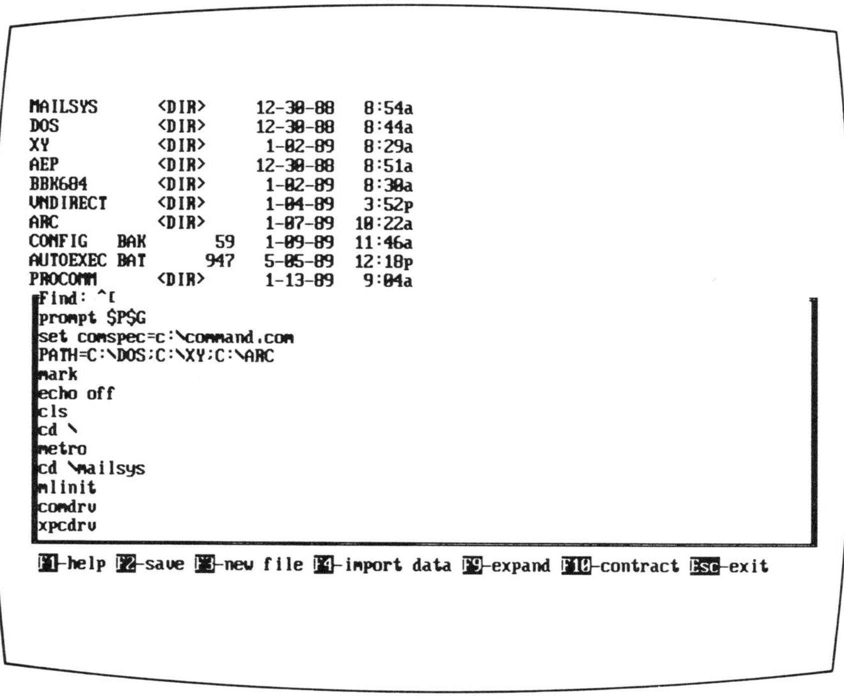

```
MAILSYS       <DIR>    12-30-88    8:54a
DOS           <DIR>    12-30-88    8:44a
XY            <DIR>     1-02-89    8:29a
AEP           <DIR>    12-30-88    8:51a
BBK684        <DIR>     1-02-89    8:30a
UNDIRECT      <DIR>     1-04-89    3:52p
ARC           <DIR>     1-07-89   10:22a
CONFIG   BAK        59   1-09-89   11:46a
AUTOEXEC BAT       947   5-05-89   12:18p
PROCOMM       <DIR>     1-13-89    9:04a
Find: ^[
prompt $P$G
set comspec=c:\command.com
PATH=C:\DOS;C:\XY;C:\ARC
mark
echo off
cls
cd \
metro
cd \mailsys
mlinit
comdrv
xpcdrv
```

F1-help F2-save F3-new file F4-import data F9-expand F10-contract Esc-exit

is better known as the Escape Character. This is handy for printer commands. You can also enter this character in a Notepad file. You produce nonprintable characters within the Notepad by pressing Ctrl-P, then Ctrl and the corresponding character for the ASCII code you want to produce (see Appendix B for an ASCII table). A Carriage Return is Ctrl-M and a Line Feed is Ctrl-J; SideKick can search and replace with both characters.

SEARCH AND REPLACE FOR SUCCESS

No matter which text editor you select, there are basic procedures for editing text files. You can work quickly by using the editor's search-and-replace facility.

The following examples describe some basic operations. Follow them and apply their concepts.

Remove Extra Carriage Returns

This example is similar to examples for word-processing programs from Chapter 7. If you use one of the programs described in that chapter, you might prefer to turn to those sections now rather than read about the generic approach described here.

Assume that you have a document file with Carriage Returns at the end of every line but no Line Feeds. This is a common circumstance, and it can be hard to identify because your program may behave as if there are Line Feeds with each Carriage Return. Assume further that you want to create a version of the file that has Carriage Return and Line Feed characters between each paragraph.

The first step is to make a copy of the original file and keep the original in a safe location.

Next, find a way to uniquely identity the paragraph breaks. You may find that each paragraph is separated by a pair of Carriage Returns, or perhaps the first line of each paragraph starts with a Tab character or a set of spaces. For this example, let's assume there is a Tab at the start of each new paragraph.

So, start at the top of the file and replace the paragraph breaks. Search for a Carriage Return and a Tab pair of characters. The keyboard equivalents are Ctrl-M and Ctrl-I, and the decimal values are 013 and 009. Replace them with a character (or characters) not used elsewhere in the document. I typically use an asterisk, but to be safe, you might use "$%" or an equally improbable pair of characters.

Next, examine the ends of each line. Is there a space before the Carriage Return character? If there is, fine. If there isn't, be careful so that the last word of one line does not become joined to the first word on the next line. Assume that there is no space.

Next, return to the top of the file and search for the single Carriage Return characters (Ctrl-M or decimal 013). Replace them with a single space.

Once this is complete, go back to the top of the file and replace the characters you used to reestablish the breaks between paragraphs. Put it back as it was with the Tab at the start of the first line, but also put in the Line Feed. As a result, you replace three characters: Carriage Return, Line Feed, and Tab (or Ctrl-M, Ctrl-J, and Ctrl-I, or ASCII decimal 013, 010, and 009).

When the dust settles, the file should be reformatted correctly, and it is ready for import into the final application. Save the file and continue.

Change a Fixed-Length File to Delimited

Assume that you have a fixed-length record file containing names and addresses (no numeric fields) that you need to put in quoted comma-delimited format for import.

The first step is making a copy of the original file and keeping the original in a safe location.

Now, we need to eventually put quotes around each field, and put a comma between each field in the line. Assume that scanning the data shows that there are padding spaces after almost every field except the state field, which is filled and runs right into the zip-code field, which ends at the Carriage Return character at the end of each record.

Start by replacing all occurrences of Carriage Return characters with a Double Quote, a Carriage Return, and a Double Quote. Also, add a single Double Quote at the start of the first record, and erase an extra one that this procedure leaves stranded after the last record.

Now, get rid of some extra spaces. Start at the top of the file, and replace all occurrences of three spaces with two spaces. Repeat this operation until you get a message that there are no more sets of three spaces left. Now, replace the two spaces with a Double Quote, Comma, Double Quote set of characters. We didn't shrink the extra spaces down to a single space because then we couldn't tell the difference between a space within a street address and the space between the first and last names.

That takes care of all the fields except between the state and zip fields and where there were either one or no spaces between fields in some records.

Let's tackle the state and zip problem first. If your editor can create programmed macros, you can handle it quickly. Make a procedure that searches for the Carriage Return, and then moves the cursor back seven characters—the Carriage Return, the Double Quote at the end of the line, and the five zip-code digits. This will place the cursor at the start of the zip-code data. Then, have the procedure insert the Double Quote, Comma, Double Quote characters.

Assume that you don't have this capability, however. Instead, let's assume that the majority of your records come from a few states. Search on the state values, and add the trailing quotes and comma. For example, search for "MA" and replace with "MA," Double Quote, Comma, Double Quote. Repeat the pattern until you have covered most states.

The last step must be done by hand. Scan the records one by one, and make sure that they all have the quotes and commas between all fields. You might want to set up a macro that contains the Double Quote, Comma, Double Quote combination so you can insert it into a record with a single keystroke. Watch for fields that have either one or no spaces between it and the next data field.

When you are finished, save the file. It's easy to double-check your work if your editor has an option to repeat a command. For example if you had five data fields, you could have the editor search for every 10th Double Quote character. Each time the search occurs, the cursor should stop at the end of the line since there should be two Double Quote characters for each data field. If the cursor falls short or overshoots, you know there are missing or extra quotes.

PROBLEMS TO AVOID

These search-and-replace techniques can save lots of time, and even if you have to perform final edits by hand, it can save lots of time over rekeying. There are some problems to watch out for, however.

First and foremost, copy the data file and put the original away. If you are unsure about whether your original is safe, then make a good copy (use the /V for verify option with the DOS COPY command to be sure) onto a floppy and take the floppy out of the computer and lock it in a drawer. That protects you from most errors; you can always at least return to the starting point.

The other important point is being comfortable and confident with the tools. Don't make changes on a file and then use it without experimenting on relatively harmless examples first.

For example, I once had a frantic call from a client who was unable to make the company PC start up properly. It would boot fine, but none of the special printer configuration files or user menus would load and run. It was late Friday afternoon and the payroll had to be run right away, but they couldn't get started. The problem was that the AUTOEXEC batch file was corrupted. The cause was an innocent mistake.

The day before, the operator had a few extra minutes on her hands, and so she decided to poke around a little and learn more about her machine. She had been working in Word-Perfect, and she used it to call up a directory of the hard-disk root directory, which contains the files used at boot up, including the AUTOEXEC.BAT file. She saw AUTOEXEC.BAT and called it up on the screen.

The file appeared double-spaced on the screen, but as she scrolled down through the lines, it collapsed to single space. She then went to exit WordPerfect, and she was asked if she wanted to save the file. Knowing it was an important file, she didn't want to take any chances with losing it, and so she answered "yes." The computer ran normally the rest of the day, and she turned it off before going home. The next morning, it failed to boot.

What happened? The file looked fine on the WordPerfect screen, but it wasn't. The WordPerfect file format doesn't use Carriage Returns, but batch files and other standard text file formats use them. WordPerfect was confused by these extra characters, which led to the double spacing on the screen. The reason that the extra spaces closed up as the cursor scrolled down the file was that WordPerfect was busy throwing away the extraneous Carriage Returns. When it was saved, DOS looked at the file and only saw one long line.

Had the operator copied the file and looked at it, there would have been no problem. Had she not saved the file before leaving the program, there would have been no problem. Had she used the WordPerfect TEXT IN and TEXT OUT commands to load and save it, there would have been no problem. Any one of these changes in the story would have resulted in no story. So, the moral is to work with a copy, keep the original safe, and know your tools.

One more point about copies. Most editors automatically create a backup of your file when you edit it. Do not have a false sense of security with this feature. The first time you edit the file, your original is safely tucked away in a back-up file. But, if you stop editing and start again, what happens to your files? Your first edited version becomes the backup and your supposedly safe original goes to the big bit bucket in the sky— gone forever. So, don't rely on automatic backups to keep your originals safe.

SUMMARY

A good text editor is an essential tool for modifying data files in text-file formats on the way from one application to another. While many word processors can be used in a pinch, there are others on the market that are leaner, faster, and more flexible when working with unprintable characters like Escape and Carriage Return.

You can go further and build your own tools. Currently, almost every MS-DOS computer comes with some version of the BASIC programming language, and in the next chapter you will learn how to use it for some data-transformation tasks.

CHAPTER 11

TRANSFORMATIONS ON YOUR OWN—A BASIC APPROACH

There are dozens of products on the market that help move information from one application to another, but not everyone needs their sophisticated features. Some people take a self-reliant approach to their work; they would rather build tools for their projects than buy them already made.

This chapter meets the needs of both groups of people. It contains four BASIC programs for entering into your computer to perform simple data-file transformations. The intent is not a tutorial on programming in BASIC but an offering of straightforward techniques on data handling.

HOW TO USE THESE PROGRAMS

Each program is listed fully. They were written for interpreted Microsoft BASIC used for the IBM PC, and they run with all MS-DOS versions including BASIC.COM, BASICA.COM, and GWBASIC.COM.

To use one of these programs, start by loading BASIC, which is often found on one of the two MS-DOS disks that accompany the computer. Note that many clone manufacturers do not license DOS or BASIC from Microsoft, and they often leave you to find copies of the programs. It is also common for clone manufacturers to sell DOS without BASIC, which can be purchased separately.

The BASIC prompt is a simple "Ok," as opposed to a typical DOS prompt that states the current disk drive. At this point, you can start typing in the program as listed here. It doesn't matter if you type the lines into the computer in the same sequence as long as the lines are numbered correctly. For example, if you entered line 140 after line 120, go ahead and enter line 130 and the program will still work properly.

The LIST command displays the program as the computer has it stored in memory, and you can use this command to check your work. Use the SAVE command to store the program before trying to run it. You can give the programs any names; the ones offered here are suggestions.

Once you have entered the programs, tested them, and made corrections, save the edited version before you leave BASIC. You can return to the DOS prompt with the SYSTEM command. If you later want to run the program again, you can do so from the DOS prompt by typing "BASIC program," where "program" is the name of the BASIC program. For this to work, however, you must either have BASIC in the current drive and directory or have the appropriate directory in your PATH statement.

Use these programs as general tools and as a jumping off point for additional projects. The programs are minimal in length for ease in entry, yet they maintain a usable interface and appropriate safeguards. You may find ways to further streamline them or to add more bells and whistles.

Also, remember that they are demonstrations. If you need more power, speed, ease of use, or flexibility, consider using one of the commercial products listed later in Part 4. Many of them are excellent values and worth evaluating if you have lots of conversions to perform or if you are faced with complex requirements.

When using these BASIC programs, however, follow the same procedures as recommended in the last chapter. Never work with your only copy of the original data file. I have tested these programs but cannot guarantee that one won't eat your data file under some circumstances. Keep an original copy safe from changes before you start to shove it through one of the programs or any other data-manipulation program.

FIX2DEL.BAS: Fixed-Length to Comma-Delimited Conversion

This program takes a fixed-length ASCII text file and converts it to a quoted-string, comma-delimited format. It will work for files where the records are separated by a Carriage Return and Line Feed combination, and where the maximum record length is 255 characters and there are no more than 255 fields.

The program starts by asking for input and output file names. Figure 11–1 shows the main screen as the program displays the first record from the input file and asks for the type and length of the first field. The program cannot tell where one field stops and the next field starts by looking at the record; you must enter this information. By the same token, it cannot

FIGURE 11–1
Sample Screen from FIX2DEL.BAS

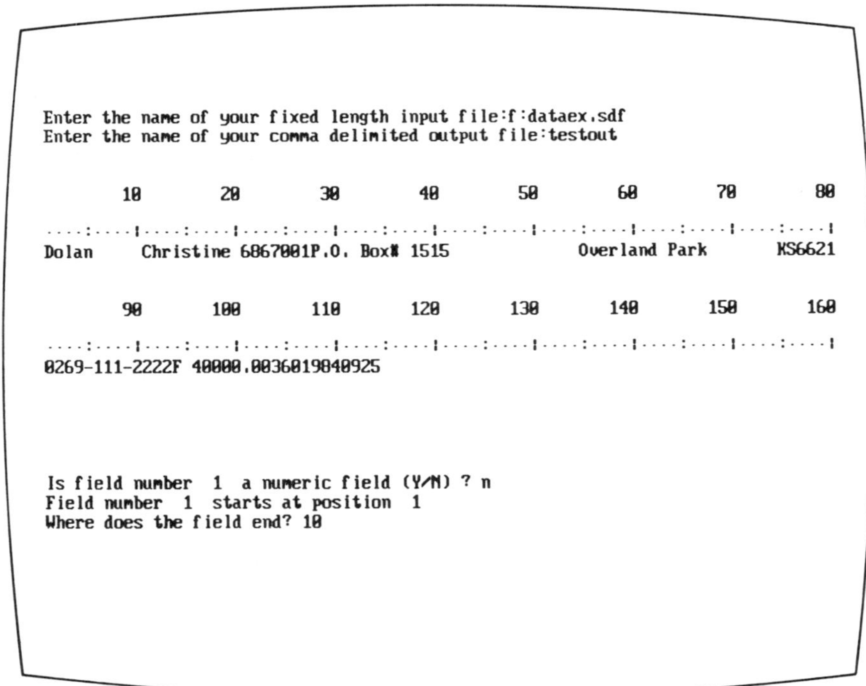

```
Enter the name of your fixed length input file:f:dataex.sdf
Enter the name of your comma delimited output file:testout


      10       20       30       40       50       60       70       80

....:....!....:....!....:....!....:....!....:....!....:....!....:....!....:....!
Dolan      Christine 6867001P.O. Box# 1515          Overland Park        KS6621


      90      100      110      120      130      140      150      160

....:....!....:....!....:....!....:....!....:....!....:....!....:....!....:....!
0269-111-2222F 40000.0036019040925




Is field number  1 a numeric field (Y/N) ? n
Field number  1 starts at position  1
Where does the field end? 10
```

tell what fields will be quoted strings, and which will be left as numeric values.

The program displays a running total of the number of characters left in the record length, and when all the field types and lengths have been specified, the conversion proceeds.

LISTING 11–1
FIX2DEL.BAS

```
1 REM Program: FIX2DEL.BAS A program to convert fixed-length
to comma-delimited data files
2 REM Written by D. Shepard Poor, 1988
10 SCREEN 0,0,0: WIDTH 80: KEY OFF: CLS
20 REM Input names of files and open files
30 INPUT "Enter the name of your fixed length input
file:",FILEIN$
40 OPEN FILEIN$ FOR INPUT AS #1
50 INPUT "Enter the name of your comma delimited output
file:",FILEOUT$
60 OPEN FILEOUT$ FOR OUTPUT AS #2
70 REM Read in and then write out the first record under a
ruler
80 LINE INPUT#1,INITIALLINE$
90 FOR LOOP = 1 to INT( (LEN(INITIALLINE$)-1) /80 +1)
100 PRINT:PRINT
110   FOR LOOP2 = 10 to 80 STEP 10
120       PRINT USING "       ###";(LOOP-1)*80+LOOP2;
130   NEXT
140   PRINT
150   FOR LOOP2 = 1 TO 8
160       PRINT "••••:••••|";
170   NEXT
180   PRINT MID$(INITIALLINE$,(LOOP-1)*80+1,80);
190 NEXT
200 REM Ask user for lengths and types of fields
210 DIM FIELDLENGTH(255)
220 DIM FIELDTYPE(255)          '0 for string, 1 for numeric
230 LENGTHUSED = 0
240 INDEX = 0
250 WHILE LEN(INITIALLINE$)-LENGTHUSED > 0
260   LOCATE 20,1
270   INDEX = INDEX + 1
280   PRINT "Is field number ";INDEX;" a numeric field
(Y/N)    "
```

LISTING 11–1 *(concluded)*

```
290    LOCATE 20,43
300    INPUT FIELDTYPE$
310    IF FIELDTYPE$="y" OR FIELDTYPE$="Y" THEN FIELDTYPE(INDEX)
= 1 ELSE FIELDTYPE(INDEX) = 0
320    PRINT "Field number ":INDEX;" starts at position
";LENGTHUSED+1
330    PRINT "Where does the field end?    "
340    LOCATE 22,25
350    INPUT FIELDEND
360 FIELDLENGTH(INDEX) = FIELDEND-LENGTHUSED
370    LENGTHUSED = FIELDEND
380 WEND
410 OPEN FILEIN$ FOR INPUT AS #1
420 WHILE NOT EOF(1)
430    LINE INPUT#1,NEXTLINE$
440    TOTALLENGTH = 1
450    FOR LOOP = 1 TO INDEX
460       STRSEGMENT$ =
MID$(NEXTLINE$,TOTALLENGTH,FIELDLENGTH(LOOP))
470       IF LEN(STRSEGMENT$) <>0 THEN IF
RIGHT$(STRSEGMENT$,1) = " " THEN
STRSEGMENT$=LEFT$(STRSEGMENT$,LEN(STRSEGMENT$)-1):GOTO  470
480       IF FIELDTYPE(LOOP) = 0 THEN GOTO 520
490          IF LEN(STRSEGMENT$) <>0 THEN IF
LEFT$(STRSEGMENT$,1) = " " THEN
STRSEGMENT$=RIGHT$(STRSEGMENT$,LEN(STRSEGMENT$)-1):GOTO  490
500          PRINT#2,STRSEGMENT$;
510          GOTO 530
520          PRINT#2,CHR$(34)+STRSEGMENT$+CHR$(34);
530       IF LOOP <> INDEX THEN PRINT#2,",";
540       TOTALLENGTH = FIELDLENGTH(LOOP)+TOTALLENGTH
550    NEXT LOOP
560    PRINT#2,""
570 WEND
580 CLOSE #1
590 CLOSE #2
600 END
```

DEL2FIX.BAS: Comma-Delimited to Fixed-Length Conversion

A companion piece to the first program, this one reverses the process. It takes a quoted-string, comma-delimited file and transforms it into a fixed-length record file. It will work with a file that has records no longer than 255 characters and no more than 255 fields.

Here, the program knows whether a field is a string or numeric because it checks whether a field starts with a double quote or not. Numeric fields will be padded with leading spaces, and strings will be padded with trailing spaces.

The problem is that the program cannot tell how long a field should be, and this is the information you must supply as

FIGURE 11–2
Sample Screen From DEL2FIX.BAS

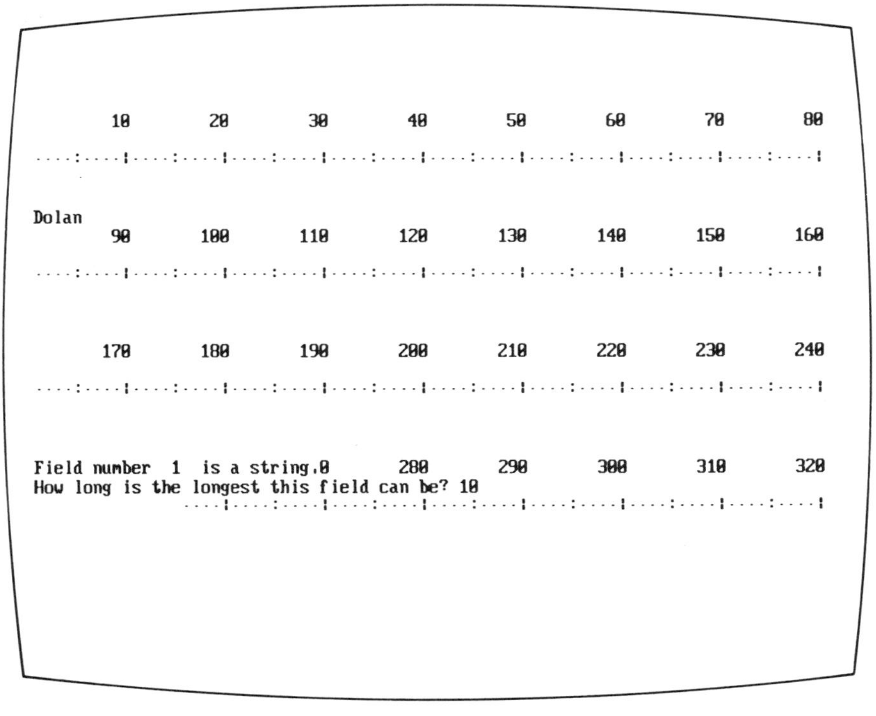

shown in Figure 11–2. Once the program knows the input and output file names, it displays the fields one at a time on the screen and asks for the maximum field length.

After the lengths of all fields are specified, the conversion occurs. If the program encounters a field that has more characters than permitted in its maximum length, it will truncate it and you will lose some data.

LISTING 11–2
DEL2FIX.BAS

```
1 REM Program: DEL2FIX.BAS   A program to convert
comma-delimited to fixed-length data files
2 REM Written by D. Shepard Poor, 1988
10 SCREEN 0,0,0: WIDTH 80: KEY OFF: CLS
20 REM Input names of files and open files
30 INPUT "Enter the name of your comma delimited input
file:",FILEIN$
40 OPEN FILEIN$ FOR INPUT AS #1
50 INPUT "Enter the name of your output file:",FILEOUT$
60 OPEN FILEOUT$ FOR OUTPUT AS #2
70 REM Write out the first record under a ruler
80 LINE INPUT#1,INITIALLINE$
90 FOR LOOP = 1 TO 4
100 PRINT:PRINT
110   FOR LOOP2 = 10 TO 80 STEP 10
120       PRINT USING "        ###";(LOOP-1)*80+LOOP2;
130   NEXT
140   PRINT
150   FOR LOOP2 = 1 TO 8
160       PRINT "••••:••••|";
170   NEXT
180 PRINT
190 NEXT
200 REM Ask user for lengths and types of fields
210 DIM FIELDLENGTH(255)
220 DIM FIELDTYPE(255)           ' 0 for string, 1 for
numeric
230 INDEX = 0
240 WHILE LEN(INITIALLINE$) > 0
250   INDEX = INDEX + 1
260   IF LEFT$(INITIALLINE$,1) <> CHR$(34) THEN 330
270   REM This field is a string
```

LISTING 11–2   *(continued)*

```
280     FIELDTYPE(INDEX) = 0
290     POSITION = 2
300     IF MID$(INITIALLINE$,POSITION,1) <> CHR$(34) THEN
POSITION = POSITON +1: GOTO 300
310     NEWLINE$ = MID$(INITIALLINE$,2,POSITION-2):
POSITION = POSITION +1
320     GOTO 390
330   REM This field is a numeric
340   FIELDTYPE(INDEX) = 1
350     POSITION = 1
360     IF LEN(INITIALLINE$) > POSITION THEN IF
MID$(INITIALLINE$,POSITION+1,1) <> "," THEN POSITION =
POSITION +1: GOTO 360
370     NEWLINE$ = MID$(INITIALLINE$,1, POSITION)
380   IF LEN(INITIALLINE$) > POSITION THEN POSITION =
POSITION +1
390   IF LEN(INITIALLINE$)-POSITION > 0 THEN INITIALLINE$=
RIGHT$(INITIALLINE$,LEN(INITIALLINE$)-POSITION) ELSE
INITIALLINE# = ""
400   LOCATE 4,1
410   NEWLINE$ = NEWLINE$ + SPACE$(255-LEN(NEWLINE$))
420   FOR LOOP = 1 TO 4
430     PRINT:PRINT:PRINT:PRINT
MID$(NEWLINE$,(LOOP-1)*80+1,80)
440   NEXT LOOP
450   LOCATE 20,1
460   PRINT "Field number "; INDEX; " is a ";
470   IF FIELDTYPE(INDEX) = 0 THEN PRINT"string." ELSE
PRINT"number."
480   PRINT"How long is the longest this field can be?      "
485   LOCATE 21,42
487   INPUT FIELDLENGTH(INDEX)
490 WEND
500 CLOSE # 1
510 OPEN FILEIN$ FOR INPUT AS #1
520 REM load data, convert, and write to new file
530 WHILE NOT EOF(1)
540   LINE INPUT#1,NEXTLINE$
550   FOR LOOP =  1 TO INDEX
560     IF FIELDTYPE(LOOP) = 0 THEN 620
570     LENGTH = 0
580       IF LEN(NEXTLINE$) > LENGTH    THEN IF
MID$(NEXTLINE$,LENGTH +1,1) <> "," THEN LENGTH = LENGTH
+1: GOTO 580
590         NEXTSTR$ = LEFT$(NEXTLINE$,LENGTH)
```

LISTING 11–2 *(concluded)*

```
600        NEXTSTR$ = SPACE$(FIELDLENGTH(LOOP)-
LEN(NEXTSTR$)) + NEXTSTR$
610        GOTO 660
620        LENGTH = 2
630        IF MID$(NEXTLINE$,LENGTH,1) <> CHR$(34) THEN
LENGTH = LENGTH +1:GOTO 630
640        NEXTSTR$ = MID$(NEXTLINE$,2,LENGTH-2)
650        IF FIELDLENGTH(LOOP)-LEN(NEXTSTR$) > 0 THEN
NEXTSTR$ = NEXTSTR$ + SPACE$(FIELDLENGTH(LOOP)-
LEN(NEXTSTR$))
660        PRINT#2,NEXTSTR$;
670        LENGTH = LENGTH + 1
680        IF LEN(NEXTLINE$) > LENGTH THEN NEXTLINE$ =
RIGHT$(NEXTLINE$,LEN(NEXTLINE$)-LENGTH)
ELSE NEXTLINE$ =        ""
690     NEXT LOOP
700     PRINT#2,""
710  WEND
720  CLOSE #1
730  CLOSE #2
740  END
```

FILTER.BAS: An ASCII Character Filter

Perhaps you have an editor that can search and replace nearly any ASCII character. Chances are that there is at least one character it will have trouble handling, no matter how good it is.

For example, a favorite editor is XyWrite III Plus from XyQuest, but it has a miserable time with the tilde character (ASCII 126), which it won't display under normal conditions. There have been many times when I have had data base procedures fail to run correctly because an "invisible" tilde was mistakenly typed into the file.

FILTER.BAS reads in a file character by character, and it will remove all occurrences of any ASCII character that is specified. The program prompts you for the decimal value of

FIGURE 11–3
Sample-Screen From FILTER.BAS

```
Enter the ASCII decimal value for the character to be stripped
(or press Return to strip the Carriage Return Characters)  ==>27
Enter the name of your input file:test
Enter the name of your output file:testout
```

the character to remove, and for the input and output file names, as shown in Figure 11–3. It then reads the file character by character until it is finished. If you press Return at the first prompt, the program will remove all Carriage Returns.

There are two characters that give this program trouble. First, it can't work with ASCII 0, the Null Character, since there is no way to enter a 0 value. Secondly, it can't work with ASCII 26, which is Ctrl-Z, because this is the character used by DOS to mark the end of a file. Aside from these two exceptions, you can find and remove any character. It is simple to

LISTING 11–3
FILTER.BAS

```
1 REM Program: FILTER.BAS A program to strip all
occurrences of a specified ASCII character
2 REM Written by D. Shepard Poor, 1988
10 SCREEN 0:WIDTH 80:KEY OFF:CLS
20 PRINT "Enter the ASCII decimal value for the character
to be stripped "
30 INPUT "(or press Return to strip the Carriage Return
Characters) ==>",STRIP$
40 IF LEN(STRIP$) = 0 THEN STRIP$ = CHR$(13) ELSE STRIP$ =
CHR$(VAL(STRIP$)
50 INPUT "Enter the name of your input file:",FILEIN$
60 OPEN FILEIN$ FOR INPUT AS #1
70 INPUT "Enter the name of your output file:",FILEOUT$
80 OPEN FILEOUT$ FOR OUTPUT AS #2
90 WHILE NOT EOF(1)
100   NEXTCHAR$ = INPUT$(1,#1)
110   IF STRIP$ <> NEXTCHAR$ THEN PRINT#2,NEXTCHAR$;
120 WEND
130 CLOSE #1
140 CLOSE #2
150 END
```

modify this program to replace the removed character with another character.

WS-STRIP.BAS: WordStar to ASCII Conversion

The fourth program converts the standard WordStar file to a pure ASCII text file that can be brought in and edited with almost any word processor.

The program passes through unchanged almost all characters. It only strips the high-bit setting off the first character of each word and removes the soft line editing within paragraphs. Each paragraph becomes a single line of text—although it is simple to modify the program to put a hard ending with a Carriage Return and Line Feed combination at the end of each line.

All print attribute characters and embedded dot commands stay intact. Search and replace them with the appropriate characters or commands for your word processor after importing the text for editing.

The program is simple to run, as shown in Figure 11–4. You are prompted for input and output file names, and then the program begins the conversion and returns you to the BASIC or DOS prompt when finished.

FIGURE 11–4
Sample Screen From WS-STRIP.BAS

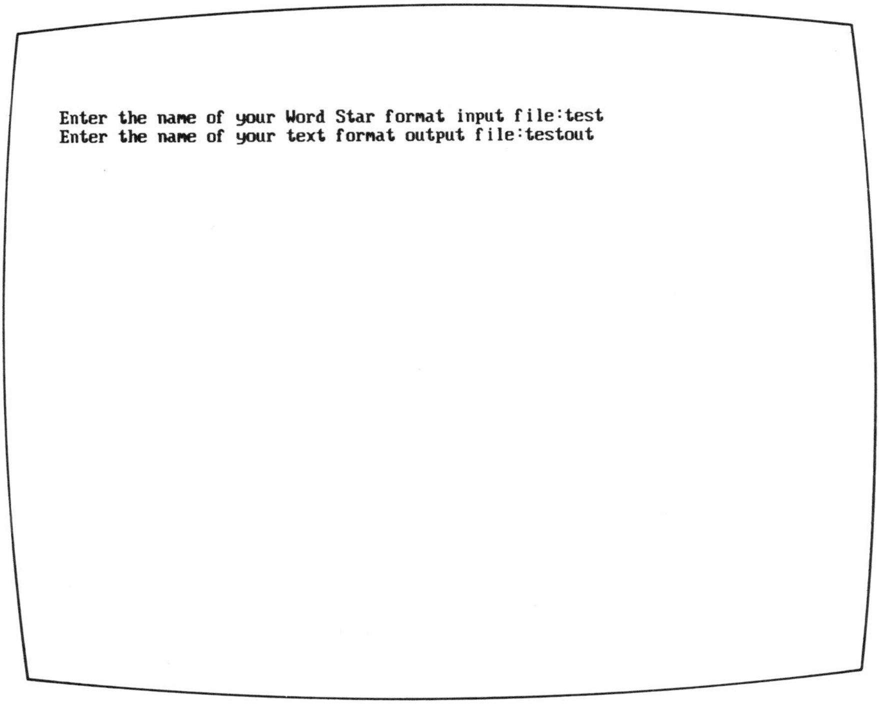

```
Enter the name of your Word Star format input file:test
Enter the name of your text format output file:testout
```

LISTING 11–4
WS-STRIP.BAS

```
1 REM Program: WS-STRIP.BAS   A program to convert WordStar
to text files
2 REM Written by D. Shepard Poor, 1988
10 SCREEN 0: KEY OFF: WIDTH 80:CLS
20 INPUT "Enter the name of your Word Star format input
file:",FILEIN$
30 OPEN FILEIN$ FOR INPUT AS #1
40 INPUT "Enter the name of your text format output
file:",FILEOUT$
50 OPEN FIELOUT$ FOR OUTPUT AS #2
60 WHILE NOT EOF(1)
70      NEXTCHAR$ = INPUT$(1,#1)
80      REM Remove any soft returns
90      IF ASC(NEXTCHAR$) = 141 THEN NEXTCHAR$ =
INPUT$(1,#1) : IF NEXTCHAR$ = CHR$(10) THEN NEXTCHAR$ =
INPUT$(1,#1) ELSE NEXTCHAR$ = CHR$(13)
100      REM Remove all high order bits
110      If ASC(NEXTCHAR$)>127 THEN NEXTCHAR$ =
CHR$(ASC(NEXTCHAR$)-128)
120      PRINT#2,NEXTCHAR$;
130 WEND
140 CLOSE #1
150 CLOSE #2
160 END
```

SUMMARY

These four programs are extremely useful. You may need a fancier, more sophisticated program, but in a pinch, one of the four may do the job while you're waiting for the cavalry to arrive.

The commercial programs also have a lot to offer, as shown in Part 4. You will find short evaluations of products that can do wonders for data conversion.

PART 4

HELP FROM OTHER SOURCES

Much can be done with the stand-alone programs described in Part 2 and the self-help solutions offered in Part 3, but at times these choices may be more work than you desire.

This section looks at various off-the-shelf solutions to a range of data-exchange problems. These programs are tailored to certain tasks, and they offer more depth and flexibility than the corresponding features found in general programs. The programs listed in these chapters are a recommended few from the market.

Each of these programs makes at least one sort of data exchange faster, easier, and safer. None of these packages are the best at everything. Look carefully at what the program can and can't do. Also, understand that there are some good options among the programs not included in these pages. A few were eliminated because they did not work or made the task harder, but most were passed over because they were not as good at a task as another program. And, despite efforts to be comprehensive, there are some worthy programs on the market that were not considered.

View these recommendations as descriptions of excellent programs that make at least one type of conversion better. If you find one here that does what you need to do, you can put it at the top of your evaluation list with confidence. If you do not find what you need, do not despair, because it is possible that the product you want does exist but just failed to make the cut for inclusion in this section.

Chapter 12 covers programs designed to handle data files such as spreadsheet, data base, or mail-merge files. Chapter 13 looks at products that handle document conversions between word-processing programs, and Chapter 14 covers some ways to convert graphics files from one format to another.

CHAPTER 12

DATA-FILE CONVERSION PROGRAMS

In this context, a *data file* refers to a collection of information that is generally viewed in a row-and-column format: lists of names and addresses, financial tables, and similar details. This contrasts with a *free-form file,* which is not easily organized in this manner, such as a letter or report.

As shown in Part 2, expect a certain amount of help from dBASE and 1–2–3 when moving data from one format to another. The same is true for most other spreadsheet and database management programs, although some offer more help than others. No matter the program used, you will still find circumstances where the conversion support makes it either too difficult or impossible to move data over in the desired format.

Enter, stage left, the off-the-shelf solutions. These programs exist (in most cases) solely to help move data from one point to another. Depending on your needs, you can find one or more programs that are useful additions to your data-exchange bag of tricks.

Remember that sometimes the best solution may not be a utility. For example, ALPHA/three® from Alpha Software Corporation is designed as a stand-alone data base management system that can read and write dBASE .DBF files. However, it also offers a host of import and export features including the ability to read and write 1–2–3 and Symphony worksheets, MultiPlan SYLK files, DIF, PFS, dBASE II, and both comma-delimited and fixed-length text files. So as you read about the following programs, keep in mind that you may already have similar capabilities sitting on your shelf.

GOOD NUMBERS

The Facts:

Product Name:	Good Numbers
Publisher:	Creative Synergy Corporation 2839 Paces Ferry Road, Suite 320 Atlanta, GA 30339
Phone:	(800) 255-3926 Ext. 260 (404) 438-0033
Price:	$189
Requirements:	IBM PC, PS/2, or compatible, PC-DOS or MS-DOS, 256K memory, 2 floppy drives or one floppy drive and a hard disk. Color monitor not required but recommended.
In a Nutshell:	A lean and intelligent program that turns print files of tabular data into Lotus worksheet and DIF files.

Let's say you have a text file on a disk with some information you want to use in a 1–2–3 or Symphony worksheet. Perhaps it is a company's annual report, which includes some financial data. Perhaps it is an employee directory printed from a data base program. Perhaps it is a collection of historical stock prices downloaded from an on-line data base service.

If the data were perfectly clean and in row/column format, you could use the 1–2–3 DATA PARSE command sequence. But, the chances are excellent that the data is not clean. There will be extraneous lines of text sprinkled throughout, titles and subtitles needing deletion, and columns of unwanted data. You could bring it all into a worksheet and then clean it up, but there is a better way.

Good Numbers is the better way. Simply load a text file into this program and create a translation "mask." If desired, the program will look at your file and attempt to automatically assign columns to your data, but this often results in some definition errors. A better approach is the option that lets you pick a sample row; it creates the column definitions based on the sample row.

Once you let Good Numbers create the initial mask, you can edit the definition to refine it. For example, you can delete the definition of some columns and eliminate that data from the translation process. You can also change the defined column width to make it larger or smaller as required.

Good Numbers also lets you alter your mask on a row-by-row basis. This permits you to bring in some rows as data—with the cells defined by the columns you have defined. You can also define other rows as titles that will be brought into your worksheet intact. Figure 12–1 shows a typical text file after you have defined a translation mask with Good Numbers.

FIGURE 12–1
Good Numbers Translation Mask

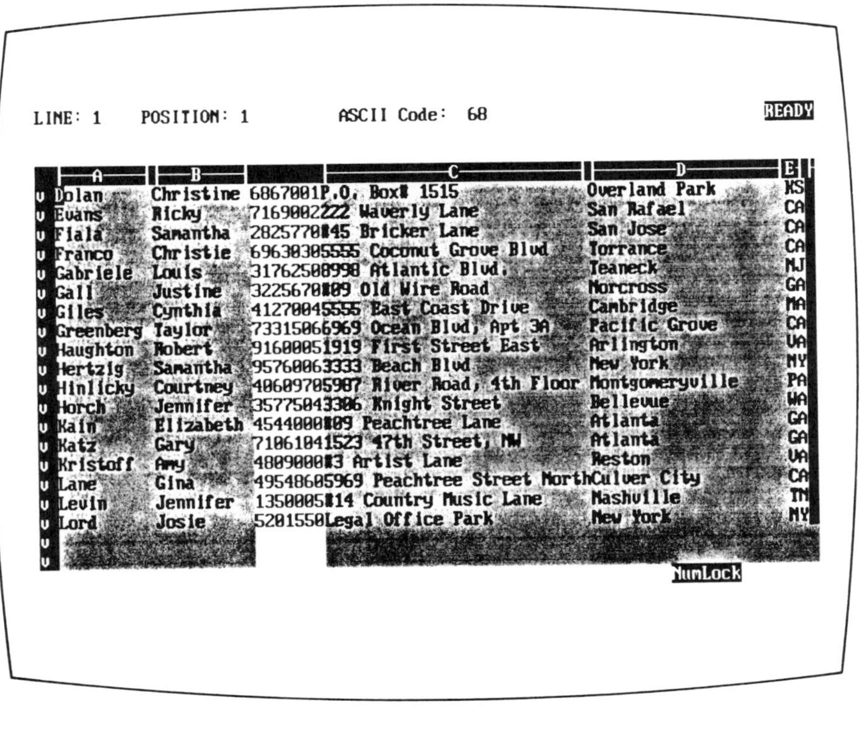

FIGURE 12–2
Good Numbers Sample Worksheet

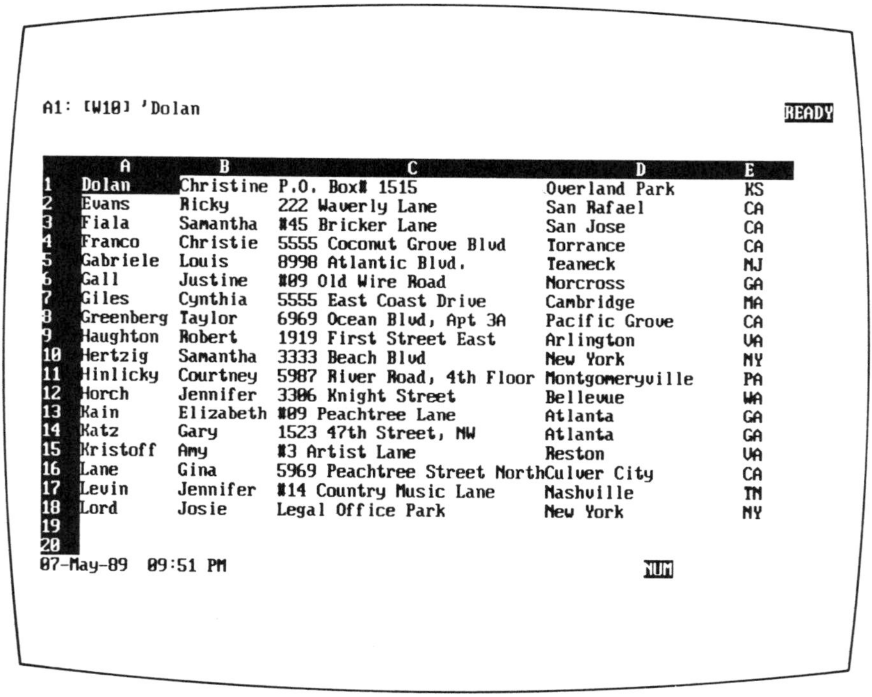

```
A1: [W10] 'Dolan                                              READY

        A          B         C                    D          E
1   Dolan      Christine  P.O. Box# 1515       Overland Park  KS
2   Evans      Ricky      222 Waverly Lane     San Rafael     CA
3   Fiala      Samantha   #45 Bricker Lane     San Jose       CA
4   Franco     Christie   5555 Coconut Grove Blvd  Torrance   CA
5   Gabriele   Louis      8998 Atlantic Blvd.  Teaneck        NJ
6   Gall       Justine    #89 Old Wire Road    Norcross       GA
7   Giles      Cynthia    5555 East Coast Drive  Cambridge    MA
8   Greenberg  Taylor     6969 Ocean Blvd, Apt 3A  Pacific Grove  CA
9   Haughton   Robert     1919 First Street East  Arlington   VA
10  Hertzig    Samantha   3333 Beach Blvd      New York       NY
11  Hinlicky   Courtney   5987 River Road, 4th Floor  Montgomeryville  PA
12  Horch      Jennifer   3306 Knight Street   Bellevue       WA
13  Kain       Elizabeth  #89 Peachtree Lane   Atlanta        GA
14  Katz       Gary       1523 47th Street, NW  Atlanta       GA
15  Kristoff   Amy        #3 Artist Lane       Reston         VA
16  Lane       Gina       5969 Peachtree Street North Culver City  CA
17  Levin      Jennifer   #14 Country Music Lane  Nashville    TN
18  Lord       Josie      Legal Office Park    New York       NY
19
20
07-May-89  09:51 PM                              NUM
```

Figure 12–2 shows the same data after it has been converted into a Lotus 1–2–3 Release 2.01 worksheet using the defined translation mask. Note that the data that was not marked in the mask does not appear in the worksheet.

As mentioned at the start, Good Numbers can produce worksheet files for either 1–2–3 or Symphony, including the .WKS, .WK1, .WRK, and .WR1 formats. It does not stop there, however.

It can also produce a text file of the results, which can then be imported into almost any word-processing program. This is a useful tool when you need to edit large tabular reports for inclusion in a document.

The program can also translate the data into a comma-delimited text file, which makes it easier to move data from a text file into a program that does not handle fixed-length record or worksheet formats.

Finally, Good Numbers can produce DIF files. It is almost unique in that it can produce both types of DIF files. As described in Part 1, the DIF standard was originally defined as able to be organized by either row or column. Most programs that support DIF today do so in only one direction, and some support only row-wise, and others support only column-wise orientations. Good Numbers, on the other hand, can produce DIF files organized in either direction. If you try to move data into specialized applications such as presentation graphics or business charting programs, the ability to produce both types of DIF files saves hours of rekeying.

Once you have defined your translation mask, save it before performing the translation. This enables use of a mask without redefining it every time. As a result, you can create a library of standard masks and automate the translation process for files with similar formats. For example, you might receive monthly sales reports by department from a mainframe accounting package, and the only thing that changes from month to month are the specific numbers. You can use Good Numbers to define a translation mask for that report format and then quickly translate each report file when it arrives each month. You can even run a Good Numbers translation from a DOS prompt, so you can automate the entire process in a batch file.

Good Numbers has a few shortcomings. For example, it doesn't automatically define a mask well with fixed-length record files, although you might be tempted to try it. The program works best when there is at least one space between fields, which is not the case when a fixed-length record field is filled. You also can have problems with numeric-string data such as zip codes being defined as numeric. On the other hand, Good Numbers is still faster, more flexible, and easier than the 1–2–3 DATA PARSE command sequence. Good Numbers is an excellent tool for taking text files and making the data contained within available in a Lotus worksheet format.

DATA JUNCTION

The Facts:	
Product Name:	Data Junction
Publisher:	Tools & Techniques, Inc. 1620 West 12th Street Austin, TX 78703
Phone:	(800) 444-1945 (512) 482-0824
Price:	$195
Requirements:	IBM PC, PS/2, or compatible, PC-DOS or MS-DOS 2.0 or later, 512K memory, two floppy drives or one floppy drive and a hard disk.
In a Nutshell:	Offering power and flexibility, Data Junction not only can import and export between dozens of programs, it also can serve as a stand-alone data-entry program with sophisticated entry-edit features.

Good Numbers is designed for a narrow range of source and target formats, but can handle great variety in source-file content. Data Junction is the opposite; it can handle a wide range of input and output formats, but it works only with data files of straightforward row-and-column information.

As with any complex program, you may find it difficult to wrap your mind around all the features and capabilities offered by Data Junction. Perhaps the most useful concept is thinking of the program as the center hub of a wheel with spokes connecting it to other applications.

The central hub represents the Data Junction native data file format, and the spokes connect it with many different file formats supported by the program. They include comma-delimited and fixed-length text files, dBASE .DBF, Lotus 1–2–3 worksheets, and DIF files.

There are two choices in how to use Data Junction. You can start with a format from another program, which is converted to the Data Junction format and then converted to your target format. The other choice is to enter data directly into the Data Junction format and then convert it to the desired format.

Data Junction offers incredible intelligence and sophistication. It can perform automatic pattern-matching, which permits it to identify standard types of fields such as two-letter postal abbreviations for state names or social security numbers. You can create numerous data-entry details that can make data entry faster and more accurate—such as look-up tables and default-entry values.

The central-data format can be connected with a host of useful formats including text file, dBASE, Paradox, 1–2–3, Symphony, Supercalc 4, DIF, and R:BASE. In each case, you have the ability to exclude specific fields, to include only certain records based on selection criteria, to sort the records as they are processed, and to change the sequence of fields.

Some of the connections have extra features. For example, when you create a worksheet from a Data Junction file, you can choose a spread format, which separates items into different columns. For example, you may have a long list of total sales figures for each division by month. This option can create a worksheet where the divisions are listed in a left-hand column, and the months are listed across the top with the respective values creating a rectangular table within the headings. This cross-tabulation feature can save hours of effort for some applications.

As with Good Numbers, you can save the translation specifications so that they can be reused on similarly structured files. Also like Good Numbers, Data Junction translations can be run entirely from the DOS prompt, so that you can automate translation procedures in a batch file.

VP/BASE AND VP/TABS

If you don't use Ventura Publisher and do not intend to in the future, turn to Chapter 13. If you use Ventura, then this information may be a welcome surprise.

Why talk about a desktop publishing program in a chapter on data-file translation products? The answer lies in a fundamental problem with desktop publishing. Most data base and spreadsheet programs only know how to print reports using

---

The Facts:

Product Name:	VP/BASE and VP/TABS
Publisher:	The Laser Edge 360 17th Street, Suite 203 Oakland, CA 94612
Phone:	(415) 835-1581
Price:	$89 each
Requirements:	A computer system capable of running Ventura Publisher.
In a Nutshell:	These two utilities are each designed to handle a single task: to format data files for use in Ventura Publisher. One works with dBASE files, and the other works with Lotus worksheets. If you don't use Ventura, you don't need them, but if you do, these programs can save hours of effort and hundreds of dollars.

---

monospaced fonts, which means each character in the alphabet takes the same amount of space as any other, as is the case with most typewriters. People love laser printers like the Hewlett Packard LaserJet because they can produce proportional fonts, in which some letters take more space than others. (For example, compare the space required for 10 *M*s and 10 *i*s: MMMMMMMMMM versus iiiiiiiiii.) Proportional fonts look great until you try to use one to print a dBASE or 1–2–3 report, and then all the columns undulate down the page instead of giving straight, vertical columns.

Many people want to print database or spreadsheet material as a part of desktop-publishing documents. The undulating column problems are solved manually by inserting tabs between each field, but this can take a long time. The task approaches impossibility if you want one field to appear in bold type, another field in a larger font, and another field in italic characters. It takes forever to insert all the appropriate paragraph tags.

Until the release of Ventura 2.0, the only way to perform these tasks was to by hand or to rely on third-party utilities. The latest version of Ventura can create tables from dBASE and 1–2–3 files, but only with limitations and purchase of the Professional Extension module, which adds $595 to the program's list price.

There is a cheaper alternative. VP/BASE handles these problems for dBASE files and VP/TABS does the same for 1–2–3 worksheets. Both have limitations, but hasten bringing tabular data into a Ventura document.

VP/TABS is easier to use and more limited than its stablemate. It requires that your source spreadsheet conforms to strict formatting constraints. It is possible to name a range within your worksheet rather than use the entire file, which can make the requirements easier to accommodate. Restrictions include details such as all data in a column must be formatted in the same way, and there must be at least two spaces between each column.

When you process a worksheet with VP/TABS, you receive a text file that has all the data tagged with Ventura paragraph tags, and the data elements are separated by tab characters. Just adjust the tab settings for those paragraph tags, and the data appears in your document in even columns. VP/TABS also recognizes title rows and rows that are empty or appear before rows of hyphens or equal signs. These rows get their own tag, so you can define them as using a different font, different spacing, or with rules below as needed. The program does not include a method to automatically change fonts or text attributes within a row; that is performed manually.

VP/BASE takes a few more steps, but offers more flexibility. Start by creating a sample page in a Ventura document that shows the field names you want to use, their positions, and the fonts to be used. It takes work, but you can define multiple tags for a single line to use different fonts for different fields.

Then, use VP/BASE to create a dBASE program based on the sample page. Since you use the dBASE file-field names, you can specify that only certain fields should be included, and you can change their sequence from the original dBASE file-structure order.

Then, process the dBASE table using the program generated by VP/BASE. It produces a text file with all the data appropriately tagged with Ventura tags and separated with tab characters. Bring the file into a Ventura document, and you are ready to print.

VP/BASE offers some sophisticated options as well. You can force empty records to print or not print as you choose. You can automatically build index entries, create two types of headings, and cause items to print or not print based on a field's contents. VP/BASE even handles dBASE memo fields.

Both of these products represent an excellent value if you are faced with creating formatted tables of information with Ventura. In spite of their limitations, they save hours of effort.

SUMMARY

There are many conversion products on the market that make the job of converting data files faster, easier, and safer. The four products listed here handle various situations, and they cover most tasks encountered by the majority of users.

Data-file conversions are simple compared to word-processing conversions, since documents are less structured and can contain more formatting information. Chapter 13 describes some programs designed to handle these conversions. One of the programs is perhaps the most sophisticated translation program, and while it does an excellent job on word-processing files, it also does magical transformations on data files.

CHAPTER 13

WORD-PROCESSING FILE-CONVERSION PROGRAMS

First there was the Tower of Babel, but then someone invented word-processing programs, and then we really started to have problems!

Perhaps more than any application, a person develops a special bond with a favorite word-processing program. More than one heated discussion has arisen from casual remarks praising one package or razzing another. Otherwise cooperative coworkers come apart at the seams whenever someone raises the subject of selecting an office standard for word processing so that everyone will use that program.

With word-processing programs, there are more differences than similarities. Files are stored and organized in unique ways. Cryptic codes and unprintable hieroglyphics hide the crucial details of what letters will be printed in bold type, and which letters will be underlined. Page breaks, soft hyphens, floating footnotes, and running headers on alternate pages are examples of the complex formatting information that must be embedded in the file along with the author's deathless prose or memos about paper clips.

So, this is a field where everyone wants to continue using their favorite program and are driven bonkers because colleagues won't use the same program so that the files can be shared easily. Also, translating word-processing formats is particularly sticky given the variety of formats and the complexity of data. This chapter presents a pair of powerful alternatives for document conversions, but it starts with a caveat.

BEFORE YOU LEAP

Expect some snags in the conversion process. This is a fact of life because there are no two programs with the same set of features and capabilities.

For example, there are few word processors that support all the different font cartridges for the HP LaserJet. So, if you have a document needing a specific font from a specific cartridge, you cannot realistically expect the conversion program to accurately move that information across to the new file.

Similarly, some word processors support hanging indents; some support embedded index and table of contents entries; and some support multiple-line headers and footers.

One response is resigning yourself to the problem, and creating a method of editing text so that everyone can access it quickly and easily—saving the final formatting for a time when the text has stabilized sufficiently.

Consider using straight-text files as the exchange format, and develop a pseudocode to mark formatting features. You can later use search-and-replace techniques to swap the fakes for true formatting commands. If you haven't already done so, read a discussion of this approach in the first part of Chapter 7. The text-file system is simple and can be handled quickly and easily by nearly every popular word processor.

THE SOFTWARE BRIDGE

If you need to translate word-processing documents from one program to another and retain as much of the formatting information as possible, your best bet is The Software Bridge from Systems Compatibility Corporation.

One of the strongest features is its broad range. Here is a list of word-processing formats that it supports:

WordPerfect	MultiMate	CEOwrite
WordStar	Volkswriter 3	WordMarc
WordStar 2000	Samna	Sprint
Microsoft Word	DCA/RFT	Navy DIF
DisplayWrite 3	DCA/FFT	DEC/DX
DisplayWrite 4	Wang PC	

The Facts:

Product Name:	The Software Bridge
Publisher:	Systems Compatibility Corporation 401 North Wabash, Suite 600 Chicago, IL 60611
Phone:	(312) 329-0700
Price:	$149
Requirements:	IBM PC/XT/AT or compatible, 384K memory, two floppy disk drives
In a Nutshell:	For ease of use and reliable performance, you can't do better than The Software Bridge. Its price makes it an attractive value, which is even better if you can use it with one of the low-priced versions dedicated to Word Perfect or Microsoft Word.

If your favorite program isn't on the list, then there is a good chance that your program can at least put out a file in a format that this package can handle. The biggest exception to this observation is XyWrite.

Another strong feature is that the program is easy to use. Almost every selection is prompted clearly on the screen. For example, when you are asked to select a file (or many files) to convert, you can request a list of files in a given directory. Then, all you do is highlight what you want.

Start by choosing the source and target formats. There is a list in the center of the screen; select what you want. Once a format is selected, it is removed from the list of available choices so that you cannot choose the same format for source and target at the same time.

Each format can have its own set of parameters so that you can choose how to handle the conversion of certain details such as tab settings. Another powerful feature allows you to construct a font-translation table for the conversion so that you can remap the fonts from the source program to the supported fonts in the target program. This is an excellent solution to a sticky problem. There is a similar character filter that allows you to translate certain characters during the conversion process.

No translation program does a perfect job of converting every document, but Software Bridge comes close. The manual is clear, concise, and includes thorough documentation of all its constraints and limitations depending on the format used as source and target.

At $149, it is an excellent value, especially when compared to the time spent rekeying and proofreading many documents. Systems Compatibility Corporation also makes stripped versions that will only convert to or from a specific program such as WordPerfect or Microsoft Word. The single format can be converted to or from all the other formats on the list; all you give up is the ability to convert between the other formats directly. Depending on your needs, these limited versions can represent a better value.

XCHANGE

The Facts:	
Product Name:	Xchange
Publisher:	Emulation Technologies, Inc.
	1501 Euclid Avenue
	Cleveland, OH 44115
Phone:	(216) 241-1140
Price:	$495 (plus options)
Requirements:	IBM PC or compatible, 320K memory
In a Nutshell:	This product is sophisticated and industrial strength— not to be taken lightly. It is more like a programming language than a utility, but as a result of this difference, it performs amazing feats on word-processor files and a host of other data-file formats.

If the Software Bridge is easy, then Xchange is hard. This program is powerful and flexible, but it can be a conceptual stretch to get it working as desired the first few times.

This product was developed for the professional typesetting industry as a means of quickly translating formatting codes from machine-readable files into typesetting codes. Rather than building a single program to perform specific conversions, Emulation Technologies chose to create a translation engine that can be adapted to various tasks.

The concept is simple. Xchange is a programming language of sorts that can help define complex pattern-matching procedures and that can replace selected portions of the matched data. In other words, you can tell it to look for "cat," replace it with "dog," and it will do it.

Xchange is more powerful, however, than the search-and-replace options in your favorite word processor. For example, it accepts nonprintable ASCII codes with ease. It also offers a wide range of powerful wildcard matches including choices like relative position and memory variables.

You define individual search-and-replace tasks, but it can have dozens of tasks defined for a single translation procedure. The program reads in the data from the file and compares it to all the available tasks. As soon as one of the matches is made, the program performs that replacement and then starts over with the next data from the source file.

This is a powerful and flexible process, but the logic of sequencing your search-and-replace definitions can get complex to ensure that the procedures will make the expected changes. The manual is filled with excellent examples, but expect to take time before you are comfortable with building your own procedures. While you can use some tricks to make the replacements efficient, you may still have a translation that takes two separate collections of replacement tasks to make all needed changes.

Once you have a procedure created, it is simple to select a file for translation. Then, Xchange really shows its stuff; this program is fast!

You can store translation procedures to be used again on other files. Emulation Technologies also supplies useful example procedures with the program, and it offers more as extra-cost options. Use them to perform some translations directly, but since many of them are designed to put typesetting codes in text files, you may find them more useful as examples to copy.

The important item here is that Xchange doesn't just work on documents. It is excellent at modifying data files, such as reversing the sequence of fields, replacing state names with postal abbreviations, concatenating or splitting fields, or reformatting a file as a mail-merge file with a word-processing program.

In short, Xchange is the high-priced spread, but if you need its skills, it's worth its weight in memory chips. Be prepared to spend more than money on it; it takes time to be comfortable with its logic and features. For serious conversion problems, however, it has no equal.

SUMMARY

Word-processing files present some special problems in terms of converting them from one program to another while preserving as much formatting information as possible. If you need to do this often, one of the two programs described here will make the process more bearable.

There is a small consolation in that word processing and data files are typically made up of somewhat coherent bits of information. You can often at least find a few legible words or characters in such a file, but that is not so with graphics.

Graphics programs are collections of data about dots that should be turned on or off, and they are typically undecipherable by simply looking at their contents. There are nearly as many graphics formats as word processors, however, and you may often be stuck with a needed image in an unusable format. Chapter 14 addresses some solutions to this problem.

CHAPTER 14

GRAPHICS FILE-CONVERSION PROGRAMS

Computer graphics was a rarely-used feature in most businesses for a long time. The initial PC often came with a text-only monochrome display, and few people felt the added expense of a graphics display was worth the cost to print low-quality 1–2–3 graphs.

All of that has changed. The field of business-charting programs has boomed. People now think nothing of including a few bar charts or line graphs in reports and proposals, and we are becoming jaded about details like high-resolution fonts and three-dimensional diagrams.

Desktop publishing and presentation applications are increasing the demand for quality graphics. The new higher resolution offered by EGA and VGA displays and laser printers are coupled with fast processing speeds offered by the latest 286 and 386 computers to produce sharp images that don't require an afternoon to compute and print.

There are numerous utilities that make it possible to include graphic images in word-processing documents. Some programs, including Lotus Manuscript and Word Perfect 5.0, give this capability without any extra programs.

The problem is where you find your images. You might produce a chart in a business-graphics program, or scan an illustration with a desktop scanner, or find a collection of line art produced on a Macintosh. How will you put these images into your application?

HIJAAK

The Facts:	
Product Name:	Hijaak
Publisher:	Inset Systems Inc. 71 Commerce Drive Brookfield, CT 06804
Phone:	(800) 828-8088 (203) 775-5866
Price:	$149
Requirements:	IBM PC or compatible, 640K memory, DOS 2.0 or later
In a Nutshell:	This program is versatile and easy to use. It has a screen-capture utility, and it can convert to and from 15 different formats including Macintosh and Amiga.

Hijaak comes from Inset Systems, Inc., the makers of Inset which allows the inclusion of graphics in almost any word-processing program. Hijaak is designed and executed with the same straightforward style that offers ease of use and powerful flexibility.

You run Hijaak from the DOS prompt, and a title screen gives way to the Conversion screen. Here, you fill out the various choices for file conversion. You can select the "to" and "from" formats, the file names, and the extensions. There also are switches and settings to specify, but the default values often do the trick.

There are plenty of features with the program. For example, whenever you have a choice to make, Hijaak lists them. If you want a list of available formats, press the space bar and they appear. The space bar will also bring up a directory of available files when you search for a file name.

You can convert a group of files at one time by using wildcards in the file name. Inset will then convert all files with the matching name. The program keeps you posted on the conversion process for each file so that you can see how long each conversion takes.

Hijaak also includes a screen-capture program. It isn't as extensive as Inset; it can't print or edit images. It can capture the print stream intended for a LaserJet printer, however, to be used as a source for a graphics conversion. Note that not all LaserJet print streams are in the correct format for this technique, but it works in many circumstances.

In fact, the only problem encountered with the program wasn't a problem with Hijaak. If you bring a converted file into PC Paintbrush, sometimes the image has been split into multiple layers with each layer appearing in a different color. This creates a modern, almost spacey image, but it is a far cry from the crisp and legible image you might have hoped to find.

A little experimentation shows that the fault lies at the PC Paintbrush end of the connection. If you bring in an image that expects to be in a two-color application, and it lands in a copy of Paintbrush installed for many colors, you have a mishmash effect. To solve it, reinstall your copy of Paintbrush for a two-color palette, and the converted image will arrive safely in one black-and-white piece.

Many graphics and desktop-publishing programs come with large collections of clip art and other useful graphics. Hijaak is one of the best utilities on the market to help use these files or to create your own.

SLEd: THE SIGNATURE/LOGO EDITOR

If you are more interested in manipulating, creating, and converting graphics, then you may also want a copy of SLEd from VS Software. This programming tour de force is a sneaky little program purchased for one reason that has multiple other uses.

Its main claim to fame is that it can take a graphic and convert it to an HP LaserJet soft-font format. Thus, to print a logo or a signature in a word-processing document, just send the correct escape sequence to switch to that font, and then send a string of letters that result in your image printed right on the page. Unlike other approaches, this requires no memory-resident programs or complex graphics-handling techniques, since the graphic is stored as a font in your printer.

SLEd can read in PC Paintbrush .PCX, GEM Paint .IMG, or TIFF files. Since it also can save these formats, you can use it to convert between all three.

The Facts:

Product Name:	SLEd
Publisher:	VS Software P. O. Box 6158 Little Rock, AR 72216
Phone:	(510) 376-2083
Price:	$149.95
Requirements:	IBM PC/XT/AT or compatible; PC-DOS or MS-DOS 2.0 or higher; 512K memory; CGA, EGA, VGA, or Hercules adapter and display; two floppy-disk drives or one floppy disk and a hard disk (recommended). Mouse, scanner, and laser printer not required but recommended.
In a Nutshell:	SLEd makes it easier to incorporate graphics in a standard-text document when printed with a laser printer. It is a valuable and useful tool that can be used for much more.

The benefits do not stop there. You can use SLEd to drive a scanner and capture images. You can edit soft fonts and images, and manipulate them in various ways including slanting, bolding, and turning into outline fonts. You can even edit at the pixel level: drawing lines, filling and erasing, and performing block copies and moves. If you have a laser printer, you probably need SLEd.

SUMMARY

In the last three chapters, you have seen how several stand-alone programs make moving data between programs faster, safer, and easier. There is one more aspect to data transfer that must be explored; what to do when the files are on different computers. The answer is addressed in Part 5.

PART 5

MOVING DATA FROM HERE TO THERE

To this point, I have assumed the data you work with already exists on your computer, and that you also want the results of your data exchange to be on your computer when finished. This is a fundamental assumption that can cause trouble.

A colleague may have some data that you need. Or, perhaps you have some information that your colleague needs. A corollary of Murphy's law is that the more important the sharing of information, the more likely that you and your colleague use different programs and the greater the distance between the two of you.

The different programs part of the problem is what the rest of this book has covered. For the final section, the distance problem is covered. Chapter 15 gives an introduction to the physical side of data exchange: how to move data from where it is to where it needs to be.

CHAPTER 15

COMPUTER TO COMPUTER: MOVING DATA OVER DISTANCE

This chapter covers the rudiments of data communications and physically moving data from place to place. There are ways to deal with different disk formats, how to move data on and off laptop computers, and how to cope with the mysteries of sending files over telephone lines.

This is not, however, a comprehensive treatise on the topic. Let's face it—this information can take a whole book; a single chapter is limited to basic information. If you need more information on the topic, however, find a book with a more in-depth and comprehensive treatment of communications topics.

FLOPPY DISKS

Perhaps the easiest way to move data over short distances (or longer ones) is to record the data on a floppy disk and move it to the other computer. This is often referred to in networking circles as the *SneakerNet* approach.

SneakerNet is a fast and safe method; your original data remains behind unchanged, and you don't have to tie up both machines at the same time, and the data-transfer rate is acceptably fast for a floppy disk. The only feature missing from the list of SneakerNet attributes is simple.

What is so hard about storing data on a floppy disk and moving it to another computer? In most cases, there is no problem. The difficulties arise from common circumstances, however, and the two problems are disk formats and file sizes.

Different PC-Disk Formats

There was a time, albeit fleeting, where PC and PC Sneaker-Net transfers were simple. Those were the early days, however, before hard disks and when everyone had single-sided, double-density floppy-disk drives. The biggest problem was fitting enough usable information on the disk before we filled its 180K capacity. Of course, we also had the different problem of how to read and write disks from computers other than PCs, like Osbornes, but that is another matter.

The foundation of the Disk Format Tower of Babel was laid early in the PC's development, and soon all new machines were shipped with double-sided floppy drives that could hold 360K of data. These new disk drives could read the single-sided disks, but the old drives couldn't read a double-sided disk. The problem was only beginning as users scrambled to pull their old floppy drives and replace them with the new 360K drives.

We were distracted for a while by hard-disk drives, but that problem went away when the XT appeared, except for the fact that it took a big deck of 360K floppies to back up a 10 Meg hard disk. So, there was little surprise when the new IBM AT arrived on the scene, and it sported new floppy-disk drives capable of storing 1.2 Megs of data. This solved the back-up problem (until 10 Meg drives gave way to 40 Meg and larger hard disks.) But, it created a new set of problems—would the disk written on your machine be readable on another machine?

Then, the situation worsened. The Macintosh (and to a lesser degree, the HP PC compatibles) opened a new area of yearning among PC users. The cute little 3.5-inch floppy disks that these machines used were more durable and easier to handle than the traditional 5.25-inch floppy disks. Perhaps the smaller disks wouldn't have caught on if not for our peripatetic nature, but the portable computer manufacturers decided that these little disks were perfect for the new breed of PC-compatible laptops.

At first, the 3.5-inch floppies only had a capacity of 720K, but the demands for more online data in light packages led to the doubling of a full 1.44 Megs per disk.

So where does that leave us today? We now have two 5.25 floppy formats (360K and 1.2 Meg) and two 3.5 floppy formats (720K and 1.44 Meg). New high-power machines are routinely delivered with two floppy drives: a 1.2 Meg 5.25-inch drive and either a 360K 5.25 drive or a drive of the 3.5-inch variety. How do you cope?

First, you will never get a 5.25 drive to read a 3.5 disk or vice versa. The physical pieces are too different.

Next, you will almost always read a lower-capacity disk on a high-capacity drive. In other words, you should have little trouble reading a 360K disk on a 1.2 Meg drive or a 720K disk on a 1.44 Meg drive. The exception to this is when the source has a problem such as being off in speed or alignment. In such a case, the source drive may read and write to the disk without a problem but other drives of either capacity will probably have difficulty.

Also, you will never read a 1.2 Meg floppy on a 360K drive, or a 1.44 Meg floppy on a 720K drive. The lower capacity drives don't know how to read such densely packed data, which is why they have a lower capacity.

The biggest problems occur when you try to go from the high-capacity drives to the low-capacity drives. The new drives are carefully designed to be compatible with prior versions. As a result, the additional capacity is typically achieved by storing more tracks on each disk. This requires some technical tricks, including a much finer read/write head so that the computer can record the tracks closer together.

An analogy might be the difference between a 78 rpm and a 33 ⅓ rpm record. They both have about the same diameter, but the second holds 10 times as much music. Part of this extra sound is gained by turning the disk slower, but the rest comes from putting the grooves of the record closer together. To play the smaller grooves, you need a finer needle. Ever compare the point of an old Victrola needle with a modern elliptical diamond stylus? Well, the same technological shrinking occurs between the regular and high-density disk formats.

Floppy-disk designers wanted to ensure that the new drives were compatible with old drives so they made them able to read, write, and format the earlier versions.

The place for trouble is when you format a disk on a high-density drive with a lower-density format. This often leads to reading errors on 360K drives when you try to read a disk that has been written by a 1.2 Meg drive. Some people solve this problem by putting a 360K drive in their AT or 386 machine, but it's better to use the space for a 3.5-inch drive instead.

Ensure that you format 360K disks on a 360K disk drive in a PC or XT. Then, write to that disk with a 1.2 Meg drive, and read the data on the 360K drive. The same is true for 3.5-inch disks. Using this approach, less than 1 percent of my SneakerNet exchanges between different drive formats have ever had problems.

File Sizes

There is a related topic that many people fail to consider with SneakerNet—file size. It isn't a problem unless you deal with large data bases or graphics, but it can become a problem quickly. What do you do when your file is too big for the disk? If you work with a 360K drive, it is common.

If you are a familiar DOS user, you know that Microsoft wisely created a pair of utilities that handles this problem: BACKUP and RESTORE. The first of these, BACKUP, will take a file and split across two or more floppy disks. RESTORE naturally reverses the process and puts the file back in place on the hard disk. It sounds simple, but there are two distinct problems.

The first problem is that the file must be restored to a directory on the same disk drive and with the same name as the original. For example, if you use BACKUP to get a large scanned image called PICTURE.PCX from the C:\GRAPHICS\SCANNER directory, then the RESTORE program will only put that file back on Drive C: in a directory called \GRAPHICS\SCANNER. Once you have RESTORED the file, you can then copy it to the directory you want.

What if you don't have the directory? Then, you must either create it first or let RESTORE create it by using the "\S" parameter.

That's not too big a deal, but what if you don't have the same drive? In these days of large hard disks, it is common for someone to have a system with drives labeled "E:," or "F:," or further down the alphabet. In this case, you must use the DOS SUBST (for substitute) command. This permits referral to a path on your disk as if it were its own drive. So, for example, if someone sends you a file that was backed up from E:\LETTERS, you can create a \LETTERS directory on your C: drive, and then issue the following command:

```
SUBST E: C:\
```

This will make your computer think it has an E: drive, but the contents will be the same as your C: drive. You can then use the RESTORE command.

If you ever need to find out what drive and directory a back-up file came from, use the DOS TYPE command to look at the first line of the file. It will show you the original drive and path so that you know where the RESTORE command will want to put the file.

There are times when you can't use the RESTORE command, however. This is a sneaky and frustrating circumstance, and it occurs when you and the other user have different versions of DOS. If you get a file with BACKUP files on it, and you try to RESTORE them, you can get an error message—that you have the wrong version of DOS.

The reason for frustration is that it can be difficult to solve. The safest solution is to reboot your computer with the same version of DOS as used to BACKUP the files initially, and then use that version's RESTORE command. You are in for a difficult time, however, if you can't find out what version of DOS was used first. Since it is a copyright violation to give the other person a copy of your DOS and its utility programs to use to either BACKUP or RESTORE your files, you will want another way to coordinate the versions used on each end to ensure compatibility.

Other Disk Formats

There is another area in which data transfer with floppy disks gets sticky, and that is when you move data between a PC compatible computer and a PC incompatible. The incompatible might be a dedicated word processor, a piece of typesetting equipment, an older CP/M computer, or a Macintosh. For the Macintosh, there are several quality products to choose from that will let you read and write PC disks on a Macintosh.

For other cases, there are numerous disk-conversion programs on the market that can work well, but unless you have a permanent situation where you will regularly convert many disks, stay away from software solutions. There are many professional services that will convert disks at a reasonable charge. Many firms advertise in the back of the *PC Week* advertising section. If you need your own equipment for converting 9-track tapes or 8-inch floppy disks, you could start by contacting Flagstaff Engineering in Flagstaff, Arizona.

The only other special case to consider is the Apple II family. There are still thousands of these machines in use in homes and schools across the country, and they are slowly being pushed out by more powerful, low-cost PC compatibles. You cannot read an Apple II DOS disk on a PC disk drive without adding special hardware. Cordata of Compton, California, has addressed the problem in a big way with their Bridge computer that reads and writes both PC and Apple formats and runs programs written for either machine. It also includes a utility to translate data files between formats.

BEYOND SNEAKERNET: DIRECT CONNECTIONS

There are times when you may want to move data regularly between two or more computers and don't want to use floppies every time.

One solution is a local-area network, but at $200 to $500 per computer and up, this is often more expensive than many installations can afford. Also, most local-area networks are difficult to set up and cantankerous to maintain. There are endless tradeoff games between cost and speed, security and ease of use, and capacity and data security. Don't enter into a local-area network solution lightly, especially when there are better alternatives.

Tailored Products

The Facts:

Product Name:	LapLink
Publisher:	Traveling Software, Inc. North Creek Corporate Center 19310 North Creek Parkway Bothell, WA 98011
Phone:	(800) 343-8080 (206) 483-8088
Price:	$129.95
Requirements:	IBM PC or compatible, 192K memory
In a Nutshell:	A program and a cable that make it easy to move files back and forth between two PC-compatible machines. Traveling Software also makes a version that works between a PC and a Mac, and another version allows one PC to use another PC's printer and disks.

There are some products on the market designed to make data transfer between two computers fast and easy. A favorite in this category is LapLink (and its stablemate, DeskLink) from Traveling Software. It consists of a thin little manual, a pair of disks, and a funny-looking cable with a pair of connectors on each end.

All you do is hook up the computers via their serial ports, and run the program on each machine. You then drive from either machine; you see directories for both computers on one screen and can change directories, tag files for transfer, and then send them across at high speed. Figure 15–1 shows what a screen looks like when you run LapLink.

The product makes it easy to move files between a laptop and a desktop PC, but it works equally well between two desktop units. Traveling software now has versions that let two PCs share a printer and a hard disk, and another version that hooks a PC to a Mac for a file transfer. Fast, safe, and easy to use, LapLink is a wonderful program.

FIGURE 15–1
LapLink Screen

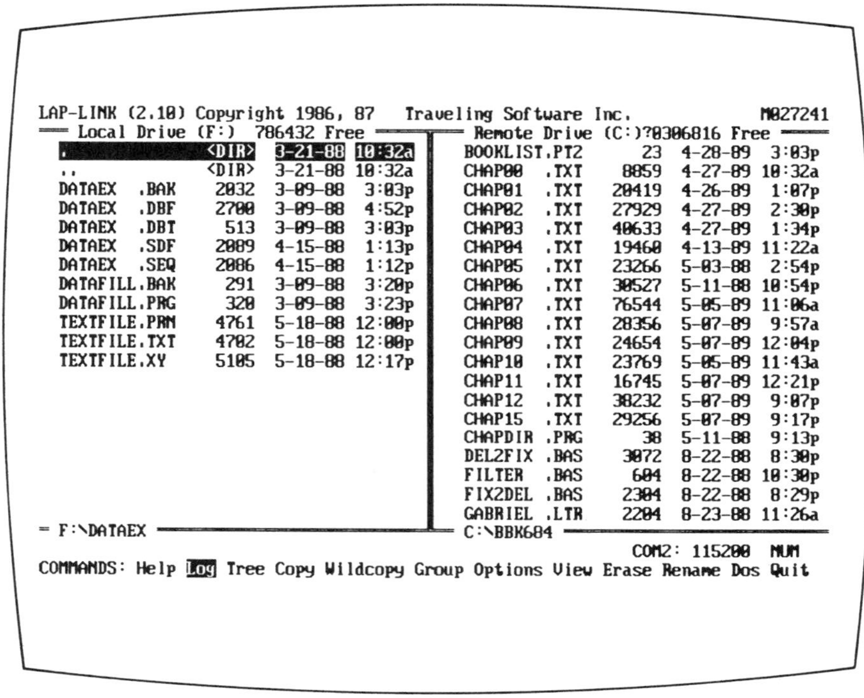

```
LAP-LINK (2.10) Copyright 1986, 87   Traveling Software Inc.            M827241
== Local Drive (F:)  786432 Free ==           == Remote Drive (C:)?83ٍ06816 Free ==
   .            <DIR>  3-21-88 10:32a       BOOKLIST.PT2        23  4-28-89  3:03p
   ..           <DIR>  3-21-88 10:32a       CHAP00  .TXT      8859  4-27-89 10:32a
   DATAEX   .BAK  2032  3-09-88  3:03p       CHAP01  .TXT     20419  4-26-89  1:07p
   DATAEX   .DBF  2700  3-09-88  4:52p       CHAP02  .TXT     27929  4-27-89  2:30p
   DATAEX   .DBT   513  3-09-88  3:03p       CHAP03  .TXT     40633  4-27-89  1:34p
   DATAEX   .SDF  2009  4-15-88  1:13p       CHAP04  .TXT     19460  4-13-89 11:22a
   DATAEX   .SEQ  2006  4-15-88  1:12p       CHAP05  .TXT     23266  5-03-88  2:54p
   DATAFILL .BAK   291  3-09-88  3:20p       CHAP06  .TXT     30527  5-11-88 10:54p
   DATAFILL .PRG   320  3-09-88  3:23p       CHAP07  .TXT     76544  5-05-89 11:06a
   TEXTFILE .PRM  4761  5-18-88 12:00p       CHAP08  .TXT     28356  5-07-89  9:57a
   TEXTFILE .TXT  4702  5-18-88 12:00p       CHAP09  .TXT     24654  5-07-89 12:04p
   TEXTFILE .XY   5105  5-18-88 12:17p       CHAP10  .TXT     23769  5-05-89 11:43a
                                             CHAP11  .TXT     16745  5-07-89 12:21p
                                             CHAP12  .TXT     38232  5-07-89  9:07p
                                             CHAP15  .TXT     29256  5-07-89  9:17p
                                             CHAPDIR .PRG        38  5-11-88  9:13p
                                             DEL2FIX .BAS      3072  8-22-88  8:30p
                                             FILTER  .BAS       604  8-22-88 10:30p
                                             FIX2DEL .BAS      2304  8-22-88  8:29p
                                             GABRIEL .LTR      2204  8-23-88 11:26a
 = F:\DATAEX ==                            == C:\BBK604 ==
                                                      COM2: 115200  NUM
COMMANDS: Help Log Tree Copy Wildcopy Group Options View Erase Rename Dos Quit
```

Other Direct Connections

You can achieve similar results with a bit more work by hooking the two computers together with a serial cable and using a communications program at each end. Since you will do a bit more work in this way, however, let's cover the basics of serial communications.

Most users are familiar with the fact that a typical PC has two kinds of ports: a parallel port and a serial port. Their names come from how they send their data.

A parallel port sends its information in parallel—down eight wires at once. It signals the individual bits with patterns of off-and-on signals, and eight of these signals are sent at a time so that the full 8-bit character is received at the other end at the same time. The parallel ports on almost every microcomputer use the Centronics parallel interface, which is why it is easy to hook up a parallel printer.

On the other hand, a serial port sends its information one bit at a time down a single wire. It lines up the bits needed to make up a character, pads them with some other information so that the other computer knows when they start and stop, and then sends it. There is no single set of rules about how these bits should be sent, which is why we have so much trouble connecting two serial devices at times.

For example, both machines need to agree on how fast the bits will be sent. This translates into how much time the sending computer should allow for an on-or-off signal before sending the next signal. There also is the question of how many signals make up a single character: 7-bits or 8-bits? How many signals come at the end—one or two? Should a signal be sent as a check sum to verify whether the other bits were received correctly?

All these questions turn into the arcane settings known as baud rate, word length, stop bits, and parity. Without great detail, here are some rules of thumb for direct connections. First try 9600 baud, 8-bit words, one-stop bit, and no parity on both machines. If that doesn't work, try 9600, 7-bit, one-stop bit, and even parity. If that fails, try it at 2400 baud, first with 8-bit settings and then with 7-bit settings.

Of course, the settings are premature without a connection between computers. Here, you need a special type of cable known as *null-modem cable*. You can also use a standard serial cable with a null-modem adapter on the end. It is misleading to talk about standard serial cables and null-modem adapters since there are many different ways of wiring them, and none works in every situation.

Basically, your computer talks out of the second pin on a 25-pin serial connector, and it listens to pin three. Most programs need some or all of another eight pins to be connected in certain ways, but these two are the most important. If you use a cable with the pins connected straight through, both computers will talk on one wire (attached to pin 2) and listen on another wire (pin 3); with both listening on the same line, they won't hear anything. But, by crossing pins 2 and 3, one computer talks to the other's listening wire, and vice versa.

The crossing of pins 2 and 3 is what the null modem cable accomplishes. Now, you will also need a gender changer in most cases, since most serial cables come with one male connector and one female connector. PCs use 25-pin male connectors for their serial ports, so you need a cable with female connectors on both ends. You can get a gender changer that will convert a male end to a female end.

If you use an AT or a 386 computer, you may also need a pigtail converter. These newer machines typically use a 9-pin connector for serial ports instead of a 25-pin connector. The pigtail converts a 25-pin connector to a 9-pin connector. Or, you can use a 9-pin serial cable from the start if you have one.

Once you have the correct cable hooked up, all you need is a program to make the transfer possible. Use a good communications program such as Procomm from Datastorm Technologies. Procomm is a shareware product available through many public domain/shareware distributors, bulletin boards, and user groups, or, purchase the commercial version Procomm Plus from a retailer or mail-order firm.

Set both computers for the same baud rate and serial transmission parameters starting with 9600, 8-bits, 1-stop bit, and no parity. You should be able to type on the screen of one computer and have the letters appear on the other computer. If not, try the other parameters, double-check your cable and that you are connected to the serial port your program is using, and try again. If it still doesn't work, get help from a professional. You can spend a lifetime chasing down serial communications problems, and unless you want to make a career of it, this is the time to call in the cavalry.

Assuming that it all works, now send your files from one machine to the other. There are two ways to do this.

The first works only if you have pure text files. The first machine can list the file on the screen, and the second computer can capture the information in a file. In Procomm, this is done using the log feature. This is a slightly risky approach, however, since you can't be certain that all characters sent are the same as the characters received.

The answer is to use an error-checking protocol to govern the transfer. This is also your only option if you send a file with nonprintable characters, as might be found in a word processing file, a data-base file, or a Lotus worksheet.

The most common protocol is XMODEM, which allows you to send a single file at a time. There are faster ones, such as YMODEM Batch, which allow you to use DOS wildcards to specify files that are then sent one at a time with a single command.

The problem with this approach is that it ties up both computers and operators while the transfer occurs. But, it is inexpensive compared with a network, and it opens up an interesting opportunity if you have more than two computers, or if you have a peripheral to share such as a laser printer or a modem.

The Logical Connection for Direct Connections

The Logical Connection is the name for a device made by Fifth Generation Systems, Inc. of Baton Rouge, Louisiana. It is a long, flat box with eight 25-pin connectors in it. It has four serial ports that can transmit data in either direction and four parallel ports that are essentially one-way streets. Two of the parallel ports are outbound, and they are hook-ups for printers, and the other two are inbound, which connect to the parallel port of a computer.

The box serves valuable purposes. It is an intelligent switching device, so that you can send commands that will connect any one port on the box to almost any other. For example, a computer might be attached to one of the serial ports. By sending a specific set of characters (in a DOS batch file or via a pop-up program that comes with the unit), you can tell that port to connect to a laser printer or a parallel port, or a modem on a serial port, or even another computer attached to another serial port on the box.

If the port wanted is busy (such as if the laser printer were already printing for another port), the Logical Connection has built-in memory that holds data until the requested port becomes available. Since the Logical Connection comes with either 256K or 512K memory, the buffer is large enough to hold most print jobs, making it a productivity boost when sharing a printer.

The Logical Connection also works well at managing direct connections for file transfers between computers using a program such as Procomm. The result is that you can hook a computer up with a single serial cable to this box, and then connect to any number of different computers or peripherals without having to change cables.

If you need more ports than the eight offered by the single unit, there is a way to daisy-chain the boxes to add more ports. The end result is a system that offers less capability than a local-area network, but the box does what many business settings need at a lower cost.

OVER THE PHONE

Finally, what do you do about your colleague who is across the street or across the state line? Your best bet is a modem, which allows you to send data over telephone wires. There are many makes and models to choose from, but in today's market, it's best to pick an external 2400-baud model from a trusted source. I recommend the 2400-baud because it is twice as fast as the common but aging 1200-baud models, yet only costs a bit more. It also is more reliable and more widely supported than the more costly 9600-baud models. I also recommend the external model despite its covering precious desk space because it is easier to move from one computer to another if a computer fails. Also, you can see the diagnostic lights on an external modem, which can be helpful if you run into trouble and entertaining when all works well.

The same comments about computer-to-computer transfers apply as in the last section. Procomm is a good communications program, and it makes it easy to perform error-checking protocol file transfers such as XMODEM and YMODEM Batch. It also gives access to many useful parameters and configuration options. If you call another computer, you will want to use one of the error-checking protocols because this protects against unwanted noise on the phone lines.

You can also send files to someone else without calling their machine directly. This involves electronic mail, which is offered by a number of services, including CompuServe, the Source, and others. MCI Mail is highly recommended.

In general, you can only send text via electronic mail services. Most of these services also cannot accept a line longer than 80 characters, so expect that long lines of data will be cut up and unusable if you try to send ASCII data files.

With MCI Mail, however, there is a way to send files with long lines or unprintable characters. You need to use the Express program from Lotus Development Corporation in Cambridge, Massachusetts, but this program has the ability to attach such a file to a regular text message and send it under an error-checking protocol. Express also does some other nifty things, including calling and getting your mail in "the background," leaving you free to use your computer for other uses at the same time. It also helps manage your mail, and it has a simple full-screen editor that you can use to write and edit your messages.

Between Express and MCI Mail, you can send nearly any type of data file at any time. Your recipient doesn't have to be at his or her computer at any specific time, and you do not have to struggle with complex communications parameters in the process. And, since most people can reach MCI Mail with a local call, you will have better telephone-line quality than you might get with a long-distance call.

SUMMARY

Moving your data from here to there is not without its pitfalls, but in many cases it can be accomplished quickly and safely with minimal hassle. Know your limitations in this area, and don't be afraid to experiment a little, but be ready to bring in help before it starts to take longer than you can afford. By now, you can move your data around with ease, and enjoy the benefits from receiving more value out of the same amount of effort and information. Making the most of your data is one of the most important keys to making the most out of your computer investment.

APPENDIX A

GLOSSARY

ASCII: Stands for "American Standard Code for Information Interchange," and describes a standard that assigns characters, digits, punctuation, and other items to the values 0 through 127.

BASIC format: A general term used to describe a delimited data-file format, in which a Carriage Return is used as a record delimiter, a comma is used as a field delimiter, and string data is enclosed in double quotes.

baud: The rate at which data is transferred between computers in bits per second; it translates roughly to 10 times the number of characters transmitted per second.

binary file: A file that is composed of codes that can be loaded directly into memory in binary format; its contents can't be interpreted using ASCII code.

bit: A binary information unit, either a 0 or a 1, which represents the smallest unit of information.

byte: A collection of eight bits (often referred to as a *word*), which represents a piece of information as interpreted by a computer; typically, a byte holds as ASCII code value and represents a single character.

Carriage Return: The ASCII character with a decimal value of 13, typically used with a Line Feed character to mark the end of a line.

comma-delimited format: A frequently used data-file format in which a Carriage Return is used as a record delimiter and a comma is used as a field delimiter; this doesn't work reliably when fields contain commas unless those fields are surrounded by quotes.

.DBF format: The extension and format used by dBASE data base files; these contain a file header of data base definition information followed by fixed-length records with no delimiters.

DCA format: "Document Content Architecture," which is an invention of IBM, designed to facilitate the exchange of word-processing files between different IBM computers and programs in such a way that the formatting codes are maintained; now on the way to becoming a standard word-processing data-interchange format with wide support from many product developers.

delimiter: A character used to mark the separation between fields or between records in a data base file.

DIF: "Data Interchange Format," invented by Software Arts, creators of VisiCalc; a text-file format that defines the contents of cells in a table, such as a spreadsheet, which is inefficient but one of the first attempts to find a common data structure for microcomputer application files and, as a result, is now widely supported.

.DOC format: An extension that generally refers to a document file stored in a word processor's format.

DOS: The "Disk Operating System," which controls the reading and writing of information from and to disk files (among other useful tasks).

embedded commands: Formatting commands to control special features, such as bold or underlined print, that are included in a file such as a word-processing file.

Escape character: A nonprinting character with an ASCII code value of 27 (decimal) that is often used for printer control.

Escape command or Escape sequence: Special character sequences, often starting with the ASCII Escape character, that trigger special print features such as bold or underlined print.

executable file: A file containing program code that can be loaded into a computer's memory and run simply by calling the program from the DOS prompt; they must have extensions of either .EXE or .COM.

extension: The characters of a file name that follow the period, and they may consist of zero to three characters; many programs use a specific extension as a naming convention for specific types of files.

file-transfer protocol: An error-checking process that ensures that data is exchanged between two computers without errors in transmission.

filename: A string of one to eight characters (spaces not allowed) followed by a period and zero to three additional characters (the extension).

fixed-length record format: A text file that contains data base records; each record's data ends in a Carriage Return, and each field's data begins in the same relative position.

formatting codes: Codes that control the way a file will appear when printed, such as centered lines or special print features like bold or underlined.

high-order characters: characters with ASCII values greater than 127. There is no single agreed-upon set of characters assigned to these values.

Line Feed: The ASCII character with a value of 10, typically paired with a Carriage Return character to mark the end of a line.

print files: Files that have been produced by an application program instead of being routed to a printer; these may or may not contain special printer Escape command sequences.

printer codes: Special character sequences, often starting with the ASCII Escape character, that trigger special print features such as bold or underlined print.

.PRN format: An extension that generally refers to a formatted print file produced by an application program, and often contains Escape commands to control special printer features.

RS-232 connection: A serial connection, typically based on a 25-pin or 9-pin connector, that permits the serial transmission of data between two devices (such as a computer and a modem, or two computers).

SDF: "System Data Format" is the term used by dBASE for a fixed-length record file.

SYLK format: The format used for data exchange with MultiPlan.

text file: A file that is composed of standard text characters, or in other terms, a straight ASCII file; in general, a text file will not contain any "unprintable" characters.

.TXT format: An extension that generally refers to a text-file format, but it is used by many word-processing programs to identify files in the word processor's format.

TYPE: A DOS command that allows you to display the contents of a file on the screen; this is handy when trying to identify the contents and format of a file.

.WKS and .WK1 format: The extensions and formats used to store worksheets for Lotus 1–2–3 versions 1A and 2 respectively.

.WRK and WR1 format: The extensions and formats used to store worksheets for Lotus Symphony versions 1.0 and 1.1 respectively.

XMODEM: A data-exchange protocol used to guard against errors in transmission between two computers; typically used for binary-file transfer, but it can be used for any file.

XON/XOFF: A hand-shaking protocol used between serial devices to control the data flow.

APPENDIX B

ASCII TABLE

Decimal	Control	Character/Name	Decimal	Character/Name
0		NULL	34	"
1	^A	SOH	35	#
2	^B	STX	36	$
3	^C	ETX	37	%
4	^D	EOT	38	&
5	^E	ENQ	39	'
6	^F	ACK	40	(
7	^G	BELL	41	)
8	^H	Backspace	42	*
9	^I	Tab	43	+
10	^J	Line Feed	44	'
11	^K	VT	45	−
12	^L	Form Feed	46	.
13	^M	Carriage Return	47	/
14	^N	Shift Out	48	0
15	^O	Shift In	49	1
16	^P	DLE	50	2
17	^Q	DC1/XON	51	3
18	^R	DC2	52	4
19	^S	DC3/XOFF	53	5
20	^T	DC4	54	6
21	^U	NAK	55	7
22	^V	SYN	56	8
23	^W	ETB	57	9
24	^X	CAN	58	:
25	^Y	EM	59	;
26	^Z	SUB (File End)	60	<
27	^[	Escape	61	=
28		FS	62	>
29		GS	63	?
30		RS	64	@
31		US	65	A
32		{space}	66	B
33		!	67	C

Decimal	Character/Name		Decimal	Character/Name
68	D		116	t
69	E		117	u
70	F		118	v
71	G		119	w
72	H		120	x
73	I		121	y
74	J		122	z
75	K		123	{
76	L		124	|
77	M		125	}
78	N		126	~
79	O		127	▓
80	P		128	Ç
81	Q		129	ü
82	R		130	é
83	S		131	â
84	T		132	ä
85	U		133	à
86	V		134	å
87	W		135	ç
88	X		136	ê
89	Y		137	ë
90	Z		138	è
91	[		139	ï
92	\		140	î
93	]		141	ì
94	^		142	Ä
95			143	Å
96	`		144	É
97	a		145	æ
98	b		146	Æ
99	c		147	ô
100	d		148	ö
101	e		149	ò
102	f		150	û
103	g		151	ù
104	h		152	ÿ
105	i		153	Ö
106	j		154	Ü
107	k		155	¢
108	l		156	£
109	m		157	¥
110	n		158	₧
111	o		159	ƒ
112	p		160	á
113	q		161	í
114	r		162	ó
115	s		163	ú

Decimal	Character/Name		Decimal	Character/Name
164	ñ		210	┰
165	Ñ		211	╨
166	ª		212	╘
167	º		213	╒
168	¿		214	╓
169	⌐		215	╫
170	¬		216	╪
171	½		217	┘
172	¼		218	┌
173	¡		219	█
174	«		220	▄
175	»		221	▌
176	░		222	▐
177	▒		223	▀
178	▓		224	α
179	│		225	β
180	┤		226	Γ
181	╡		227	π
182	╢		228	Σ
183	╖		229	σ
184	╕		230	μ
185	╣		231	τ
186	║		232	Φ
187	╗		233	Θ
188	╝		234	Ω
189	╜		235	δ
190	╛		236	∞
191	┐		237	ϕ
192	└		238	ϵ
193	┴		239	$\cap$
194	┬		240	$\equiv$
195	├		241	$\pm$
196	─		242	$\geq$
197	┼		243	$\leq$
198	╞		244	$\int$
199	╟		245	
200	╚		246	$\div$
201	╔		247	$\approx$
202	╩		248	$\circ$
203	╦		249	●
204	╠		250	·
205	═		251	$\sqrt{}$
206	╬		252	η
207	╧		253	²
208	╨		254	■
209	╤		255	

INDEX

Accounting programs, 238–42
  DacEasy, 243
  Peachtree Complete II, 238, 249–53
  Peachtree Data Query II, 253–58
  SBT and, 240
Alphabet monospaced fonts, 299–300
Alpha Software Corporation, 293
ALPHA/three, 293
American Standard Code for Information
    Interchange; *see* ASCII
APPEND command (dBASE)
  additional options, 112
  from DELIMITED, 110–12
  importing DIF files, 104–6
  importing files with, 100–104
  importing SDF formats, 107–10
  importing SYLK formats, 106–7
  and Lotus Translate utility, 100–101
ASCII, 17–20
  BASIC character filter, 286
  BASIC conversion to Wordstar, 288–90
  and dBASE files, 28–29
  exporting data from dBASE, 133
  File Import Text (Lotus), 57–58
  Null Character, 269, 287
  and word-processors, 150
  WordStar Print option, 171–72
ASCII data files
  DacEasy and, 250
  DisplayWrite 4 and, 209–11
  electronic mail and, 327
  fixed-length conversion, 280–82
  MicroSoft Word 4.0 and, 206
  PageMaker and, 235
  PDQ and, 255–56
  Ventura and, 224
Ashton-Tate, 97, 99, 176, 193
ASSIST mode (dBASE), 120
AutoCAD, 228–29
AUTOEXEC.BAT, 276

Back-up procedures, 9–10
Barber-pole effect, 28
BASIC programs, 278–82
  ASCII character filter, 286
  comma delimited to fixed length, 283–84
  DEL2FIX.BAS, 283
  FILTER.BAS, 284
  FIX2DEL.BAS, 280
  string variables, 25

BASIC programs—*Cont.*
  WS-STRIP.BAS, 288
  WordStar to ASCII, 288–90
Batch files, 18
Baud rate, 323
Bernoulli Box, 224
Binary code, 19
Binary format, 17
  in accounting programs, 241
Black holes, 11, 14
Body Text, 225
Borland International, 270
Btrieve, 241

CAD programs, 221
Carriage Return/Line Feed
  and ASCII, 19–20
  BASIC programs and, 280
  and comma-delimited files, 24
  in /File Import Numbers, 58
  in MicroSoft Word, 199–202, 202–4
  MultiMate Advantage II, 189–92
  in PageMaker, 235
  in WordPerfect, 34
  in WordStar, 33
Central shared-disk storage, 10
Chart of Accounts, 239
COBOL, 241
Comma-delimited files, 23–26
  APPEND command (dBASE), 110–12
  COPY to from dBASE, 128–33
  in DacEasy, 249
  and/File Import Numbers (Lotus), 58–59
  to fixed-length with BASIC, 283–84
  Good Numbers conversion, 297
  MicroSoft BASIC and, 26
  in MicroSoft Word 4.0 mail merge, 206–8
  WordPerfect 5.0 mail-merge, 159–61
  WordStar 5.5 mail merge, 175–76
CompuServe, 327
Computer rental firms, 10
Computers, transmitting between, 422–27
  Logical Connection and, 325–26
  tailored products, 321
Computer users group, 12
Control G character, 19
COPY command (dBASE), 121–22
  base syntax for, 122
  exporting DIF files, 127–28
  to file DELIMITED, 128–33
  TYPE WKS option, 122–27